Here's What They're Saying about
THE ART OF SPORTSCASTING...

Tom Hedrick is both a fine practitioner and a dedicated student of the craft of sportscasting. Here he has assembled a collection of observations, insights, and anecdotes that should be of interest to any aspiring broadcaster, or, for that matter, any sports fan.—Bob Costas, NBC Sports

Quite frankly, I wish this book had been around when I was in college. THE ART OF SPORTSCASTING *provides an accurate and applicable foundation for learning the intricacies of the sports broadcast field, based on the real-life experiences of the people who live in this business. It took me years to learn half the stuff that's packed between the covers of this book.*—Linda Cohn, ESPN Sports

This is the best "how-to" guide for our business I have ever seen! A must for anyone thinking about a career in sportscasting! Real life experiences and sage advice from those who have and continue to work in this unique business. A great read...—Wayne Larrivee, Voice of the Green Bay Packers

Tom Hedrick has established himself as one of sports broadcastings best teachers. Not only has he achieved the highest levels of success in this business himself, he has unselfishly shared with students the components of that success—hard work, dedication, and a love for his craft.—Kevin Harlan, CBS Sports

THE ART OF SPORTSCASTING *says it all. From Bob Costas to Vin Scully, sportscasting is art, not science; poetry, not prose. Tom Hedrick has written a primer on the radio/TV craft—with a little help from his friends—broadcasters we regard as extended members of the family. This terrific book shows how art imitates, and enhances, life.*—Curt Smith, author of THE STORYTELLERS and VOICES OF THE GAME, the definitive book on baseball broadcasting

Over the years I've had hundrends and hundreds of inquiries about how to build a career in sportscasting. Finally there is a first-rate book that has the answers. Fascinating and helpful, this book is a grandslam.—Ernie Harwell, Hall-of-Fame broadcaster

The Art of Sportscasting

The Art of Sportscasting:
How to Build a Successful Career

by Tom Hedrick
*Featuring a special chapter on baseball broadcasting
by Joe Castiglione, Voice of the Boston Red Sox*

DIAMOND COMMUNICATIONS
An Imprint of The Rowman & Littlefield Publishing Group

Lanham • South Bend • New York • Toronto • Oxford

The Art of Sportscasting:
How to Build a Successful Career
Copyright © 2000 by Tom Hedrick

Published by Diamond Communications
An imprint of The Rowman & Littlefield Publishing Group, Inc.
4501 Forbes Boulevard, Suite 200
Lanham, Maryland 20706

Distributed by National Book Network

Library of Congress Cataloging-in-Publication Data

Hedrick, Tom, 1934-
   The art of sportscasting : how to build a successful career / by Tom Hedrick.
      p. cm.
   ISBN 1-888698-24-1
   1. Radio broadcasting of sports--Vocational guidance--United States.
2. Television broadcasting of sports--Vocational guidance--United States.
I. Title.

GV742.3 .H43 1999
070.4'49796'02373--dc21

                                                                99-048275

Contents

AUTHOR'S NOTE

I am writing this as an inspiration from the two persons who inspired me the most, my mother and father. The book is dedicated to my mother, who was an elementary school reading and music teacher. My father always told me, "Thomas, we're not sure your mom knows what you do for a living."

I'd say, "Dad, all she knows is that I get paid to talk and I love it. Maybe that's all she needs to know."

I remember when I broadcast Super Bowl IV for CBS Radio and the only thing she heard was that I did not make a grammatical error. She also knew I was performing to the best of my ability and that I always did my homework. The day she died, I broadcast not one game, but two games, because my mother would have told me, "Tommy, do your work. Watch your grammar, and have fun."

I also dedicate this to my father, the Methodist preacher, who preached for 63 years and never had a canned sermon. Every word he ever delivered from the pulpit was from scratch. He would sit down on Thursday, put together a game plan, and then follow it on Sunday. People understood what he said. He would tape his sermon so he could critique it, just like I've always done.

After he read the first two chapters of this book one night, he laid down the manuscript laughing at the thought.

"You know, Thomas, it's amazing how similar what you do is to what I do."

"That's true, Dad, it is similar, isn't it?"

(I laughed, too, but partly, I'm sure, for a much different reason. I never wanted to tell him, but I had made up my mind as a sophomore in high school that, by God, I didn't ever want to do anything my dad did.)

"The difference is: I'm selling sports, and you're selling Jesus Christ and the good life. And you don't have to give the score."

"Oh, yeah, I have to give the score, too," responded Dad, "but it takes me a lot longer."

ACKNOWLEDGMENTS

First, to the professional announcers who gave of their time for this project—all of whom have very jammed schedules (they are busy preparing!)—I thank you, and each aspiring sportscaster or young professional who draws from your experience and wisdom thanks you.

I owe a special debt of gratitude to those among them who willingly gave extra time. Bob Costas gave all sorts of time. Jim Nantz sat through a couple of interviews. Several came through time after time—Bob Starr, Joe Castiglione, Kevin Harlan, Mitch Holthus, Wayne Larrivee, John Rooney, Ernie Harwell, Bob Carpenter, Jon Miller, Sean McDonough, Roger Twibell. These were particularly invaluable because they were available for a second, even a third shot to hit a point that might not appear to be all that important, but to a young, would-be broadcaster is vital.

PREFACE

The primary purpose of this book is to assist the aspiring student/sportscaster, or a young professional a few years into the broadcasting business, who wants to become a sportscaster by explaining what's the score within the industry. He or she hears or watches the big-name talents like Bob Costas, Jim Nantz, or Robin Roberts and says, "How do I get there?"

This is the first book written to that end. Sportscasters have written numerous good books about the profession—Marv Albert, Gary Bender, two by Curt Gowdy, two by Red Barber among them. They all recount how they got their start, and they regale you with enjoyable tales of the booth, but there's no book out there that takes you step-by-step through the process of preparing yourself, getting hired, staying hired, and moving on *and* up. No other book tells you the score.

The Art of Sportscasting will instruct you—from the basic fundamentals of finding voice and preparing a basic sportscast to the next level of performing play-by-play in football, basketball and baseball. You'll learn how to produce an audition tape, and ultimately—in a unique chapter that ruffles some feathers—how to play one of the most important facets of the business, the politics (Chapter 13). You'll also enjoy a special chapter on baseball play-by-play by one of the best in the business, Joe Castiglione of the Boston Red Sox, plus we have some useful appendices, such as the ways and means of the Internet and World Wide Web.

The combination of the author's 30 years in the college classroom and 41 years active in every size radio and television market, ranging from major league baseball and Super Bowl football to daily sportscasts on stations of 500 watts to major networks of 350 stations (such as CBS), will boost young broadcasters into the field, arming them with the know-how and savvy required for success.

In addition to the aspiring sportscaster or student, we have kept in mind the active sportscaster in Hutchinson, Kansas, in Kilgore, Texas, in Waltham, Massachusetts, in Zanesville, Ohio, who says, "I don't have a game plan for the next step. I'm in my 20s and want to move on. How do I get out of here?" When he or she reads this book, that game plan will be laid out as clear as day. It then is up to him or her to rise from the smaller market—a good place to be, by the way, for the learning experience—and reach for other goals.

I am telling you things that nobody in the industry is going to tell you. There is a dearth of communication within the communication business. The hardest thing for young announcers to get is feedback on their work—how did I do today? And nobody will tell you. Here, you will learn how to critique your own tape. For example, how are you sounding—talking too fast? repeating a phrase? giving the score enough? You can learn to critique yourself, and that is vital.

The final subject you will encounter is the politics of the business. When I entered this noble profession, 70-80 percent of success was driven by talent. I always knew there was politics. But nowadays, as Mitch Holthus, the voice of the Kansas City Chiefs, points out, your success trail moves on about 30 percent skill and 70 percent politics. That's true. I'm going to show you how to prevent some heartache, and stay employed by doing an effective job in the area of people skills and in the political arena.

Start with the fundamentals in Chapter 1. Every student who enters my class and says, "I want to be a sportscaster," I look right in the eye and say, "Do you?" Then I tell them what it takes. First, a voice; a voice somebody can listen to for three hours. Second, a strong work ethic. Many will tell you that's No. 1. The common thread woven through every stitch of material from our contributors is preparation, preparation, and more preparation. Third, writing and production skills. Pay attention in that required English Composition course. Journalism classes can help, too. The fundamentals include education—either liberal arts or journalism—internships and part-time work, wearing out a tape recorder, developing diction, pacing and style, listening and interviewing methodology, dressing and behaving in an appropriate professional manner, and acquiring people skills.

After a thorough breaking-in on the fundamentals, each chapter will take you through the component parts in detail. In Chapter 2 you will bury yourself in preparation. Remember the common thread?

The next two chapters will cover play-by-play techniques for radio and television, featuring the specific techniques employed by some of the greats of the business—(football) Wayne Larrivee of the Green Bay Packers and Mitch Holthus of the Kansas City Chiefs, (basketball) Kevin Harlan of the Minnesota Timberwolves and Bob Costas on network, (baseball) five Hall of Famers—Ernie Harwell of the Detroit Tigers, Vin Scully of the Los Angeles Dodgers, Herb Carneal of the Minnesota Twins, Jack Buck of the St. Louis Cardinals, and Milo Hamilton of the Houston Astros. Plus, Joe Castiglione has graced us with a guest chapter that covers his approach to baseball.

A special chapter deals with hockey and Olympic sports, which also touches on the non-mainstream sports that you will encounter in sportscasting. Good interviewing techniques are essential, and Chapter 7 runs the gamut of ways to conduct an interview and solicit material from various sources (when and how to go off the record, for example).

In exploring the shape of the industry, two chapters survey trends: former players and coaches in the booth, and the outlook for women and minorities in the industry. Another revolutionary trend in radio is the talk show, and Chapter 10 delves into this rampant phenomenon. The Sports Center—e.g., ESPN, CNN-SI—has created profound effects on the way sports fans feed their habit; so Chapter 11 delineates the workings of that medium, and the trickle-down to the traditional local, nightly news segments of sports.

Heading down the stretch, this book climaxes with its main purpose—putting you to the task in the field. Remember, every one of my former students has a job, and that includes a range from local news staffs such as Gordon Docking and Lief Lisec in the Kansas City markets, to Brian Sexton in a high-paying position in sales in Houston, to the high-profile voices like Kevin Harlan, Roger Twibell, and Gary Bender.

The concluding chapters take you step-by-step to your first professional experience (and includes some amazing tales of the way several proven talents started in the business), and, in the frank and politically incorrect finale, Chapter 13, the ways for you to play the politics game.

By the time you finish reading and working through this book, you'll know exactly what the score is. You'll have a game plan to make it to the top.

And then, it will be up to you to see if you're willing to pay the price to get there.

CHAPTER 1
THE FUNDAMENTALS

DATELINE: INDIANAPOLIS, INDIANA, MARCH 31, 1997
SCENE: NCAA MEN'S DIVISION I BASKETBALL FINAL FOUR
TIME: 7:59:30

Minutes away from tipoff between defending champion Kentucky and upstart Arizona, Bob Dekas, the producer of CBS-TV Sports, whispers into a headset hook-up, "Good luck, guys. Have a good one, in five, four, three, two, one...."

Pat O'Brien takes the cue: "On this Monday night in Indianapolis, the state of Indiana is the basketball capital of the world...It's time for Arizona and Kentucky. So let's send you down to Jim Nantz and Billy Packer, who have the best seats in the house. And now, so do you. Gentlemen."

Nantz: "Billy, great to be with you courtside again for the national championship. Where has Cinderella been in the '90s? We have not had a Cinderella champion since Kansas in 1988."

Packer: "The '80s, Jim, were the Cinderella century, I mean decade. The '90s, we haven't had one. This could be the first."

Nantz: "The officials, the three T's. Tim, Ted, and Tom. Hopefully, we won't have to call on a fourth 'T' before this game is over . . . ."

Nantz: "In the Minnesota-Kentucky semifinal . . . . Here we go, Arizona in the dark blue. Simon almost stole the tip, but Kentucky controls."

Packer: "Dickerson on Mercer, not Davis on Mercer. Nice switch by Simon."

(End of regulation)

Nantz: "Kentucky needs a three to tie. Epps fires it. Good! Game's tied at 74 . . . We are going to overtime."

(Overtime.)

Nantz: "The first overtime game in the final in the '90s. The last was Michigan over Seton Hall, 1989."

Packer: "Jim, Kentucky played their first game this year on this floor, in overtime, and lost to Clemson. They lost another overtime game to South Carolina. We had Arizona in an overtime loss to Michigan."

Nantz: "But then last week Arizona beat Providence to make it here of the Final Four, to the Final Four, with an overtime win against Providence."

Packer: "One of the key things now, think of it, Turner is on the (Kentucky) bench with five fouls, Prickett is on the bench with five fouls, so Arizona has a slight advantage."

(The clock winds down with Arizona in possession.)

Nantz: "Bibby retrieves."

Packer: "Pushes the ball up court."

Nantz: "Who else but Simon? They're not going to foul. Just about two seconds to go. It's only Miles, the ball is in his hands. A milestone victory for Arizona."

Packer: "Simon says championship."

Nantz: "Final score, Arizona 84, Kentucky 79."

▲ ▲ ▲

Is this what you want to do? The work of Nantz and Packer at the Final Four? Or become the voice of a professional team, a network, a TV station? Stay tuned. In the following pages, you're on your way through a success formula based on the insights of dozens of America's best in the booth.

They said the same thing in many different ways: find your voice, and work diligently with passion and enjoyment. You hear it in the opening Final Four passage. You also notice that it isn't just two guys shooting the breeze over nothingness; they had a well-planned, tightly-written script, born of countless hours of interviews, attending shoot-around practices, and late-night brainstorming and fact-finding. Then they talked. And you were informed, entertained, and primed for the action.

How did they get to that stage? You're about to find out. If you want to become a successful sports broadcaster, dive right in . . . .

Kansas City Chiefs football voice Mitch Holthus'
formula for success in sports broadcasting:
"Do whatever it takes."

One well-known sports broadcaster, the late Bob Starr, said that as he considered the profession after completing military duty. Somewhat doubtful, he wondered out loud how he would ever do it. To which his father responded, "All you have to do is talk. You can talk, can't you?"

Ah, were it but that simple. Certainly, an aspiring broadcaster of any sort must talk. But not just talk. The talk must have resonance and comfortable style *(voice)*. The talk must have credibility and be informative *(preparation)*. The talk must be entertaining and energetic *(style)*.

And how does the broadcaster move from "just talk" to a sound that gives a listener/viewer something to enjoy, to digest and savor, and to take to the bank as true and accurate information and insight?

By doing whatever it takes *(work ethic)*.

That might mean formal voice training. It certainly means advanced education in this high-tech era of Web-surfing and satellite coordinates by armchair coaches and quarterbacks everywhere.

It might mean internships and part-time bits on the outer fringe. It certainly means countless hours of tape recording, wearing out the playback button, practicing, practicing, and practicing some more.

To become good at it, to succeed at the highest level of your capability, it means—without question, and without exception—total dedication and endless fine tuning. Fred White, an esteemed long-time voice of the Kansas City Royals who also broadcasts college basketball in the off-season, says, "If you think you're working hard, work harder. If you think you're working the hardest you can and you're tired, reach for something extra and work even harder."

So, your starting point to becoming a supreme sports broadcaster is to develop your voice, then walk the talk with boundless preparation, which includes learning language and rhetoric, developing style . . . and, have we mentioned work ethic?

Oh, and while you are in the process of toiling and sweating your way to peak performance, if you discover that you are not loving it, every minute of it, then one word of advice: Quit.

Keith Jackson of ABC college football renown says, "You've got to be damned sure this is what you want to do. Because it's hard. And there are hundreds of others who want the job. You'd better be committed, ready to work 16-18 hours a day, 5-6 days a week, sometimes all seven, and wishing you had nine to get it all done. You might be screaming for mercy."

Your passion is tell-tale. This career must be a calling, not a job. And if you don't know the difference, be assured that listeners or viewers do. They can tell in a nanosecond either that you revel in what you're doing, or that you can't wait to get off the mike and take a hike.

FIRST, VOICE (OR IS IT PREPARATION?)

At the outset we have a chicken-or-egg situation. Remarkably, a similar strain ran through the thoughts of all 77 professional broadcasters who contributed to this learn-a-thon: Each said something (most said a lot) about preparation. Bob Costas points out, "All sportscasters share one thing in common if they're going to be any good—they are willing to prepare." [He is definitive on the subject, and you'll indulge in his entire say on the matter in Chapter 2.]

While each source agrees that style alone will not carry lack of substance, each also recognized that unless and until you develop a voice, all the preparation in the world will do nothing more than buy you a cup of coffee (if you have

50 cents to go with it). If you have a shrill screech, the listener will turn you off. IfYouTalk100MilesAnHourAndRunAllYourWordsTogether, nobody can listen, even if they want to. If your diction is poor, if your sentence is fragmented, if your tone is mono-, if your speech, uh, patterns are, uh, in major dis-, uh, ray . . . uh, forget it. Your "On Air" light will go dark forever.

Voice, then, is where we begin.

WHERE TO GO GET A VOICE

Keith Jackson, forever, it seems, the *voice of college football,*
on how he developed his voice:
"Good whiskey."

We don't recommend that! But it serves to illustrate the variety of resources available to you for developing your main meal ticket. You must arrive at a voice that holds appeal to a listener for hours at a time. That voice contains many facets.

Fret not if you do not naturally possess what has always been known as the "big" voice, or the "golden throat." That can be overcome through training, personality, and (that word again) preparation, which gives you credibility. Work with what you have.

Costas says, "I'm never going to have the set of pipes that Charlie Jones or Bob Trumpy has. But I was able to make the voice that God gave me a little bit better through voice lessons and practice. Don't take that too far, because then you sound effected and forced. Nothing is worse. It's great to have a distinctive or deep voice, but more important is whether the audience is comfortable listening to you. And if you try to sound like something that you are not, faking it will make them uncomfortable."

Odd as it might seem, the "big" voice could actually work against you. ESPN's Dan Patrick, who says his voice came from his grandmother, Bobo, said he finds that too much importance is placed on voice sometimes. "Dick Vitale doesn't have a good voice," he says. "Chris Berman doesn't have a great voice. I think if you communicate well, then people might notice you have a good voice and it will accentuate what you do. But I don't think [lacking big voice] detracts as much as we're led to believe. And, too many would-be broadcasters think that if they have a good voice, they can do this job. It's so far removed from that. Your success isn't predicated on having a great voice. It still comes down to, 'Can you communicate?' and 'Are you willing to work hard?'"

Brian Sexton made it to NFL football with the Jacksonville Jaguars without the big voice, staking his reputation on strong football knowledge. He is but one of many such examples, which exemplifies a change in the trend from 20-30 years ago. Now, persona, spirit, and knowledge (homework and writing) take precedence over the smooth, golden tones.

I found this differing viewpoint in one of my former students, Terry Shockley, the owner of television stations in four Wisconsin markets. Years after passing through the University of Kansas, Shockley told me, "You and I tend to disagree on the importance of voice. I believe it's more important to have a voice that shows personality, has entertainment value, and expresses clear diction, rather than the so-called big voice. We look for people with expressive voices."

> When Terry Shockley was a graduate student at the University of Kansas in 1962, rooming with Gary Bender, Shockley broadcast a freshman football game. He went to my office on Monday with his tape and asked what I thought about his work. I walked him to a water cooler and asked, "Do you want to feel good, or do you want the truth?" I told Shockley that he didn't have the voice to make good. In the '60s, that was vital. A few days later, Shockley, still feeling low, heard this from his professor: "You can still be a winner in this business. You'd be great in radio or television management." Today, Shockley owns KCOW-TV in Madison, Wisconsin, and three affiliates.

As Dan Patrick concludes, "The unique nature of the business is that you don't have to sound like some computerized chip that says, 'I am a play-by-play man and I have a great voice.' If someone has this overbearing, deep voice—a voice from God, or Ted Baxter with Mary Tyler Moore—it can be scary and spoil the listener's comfort level."

Regardless of your given qualities—your "voice print," if you will—you can pursue many different avenues for polishing and improving all the nuances of full voice. Take it from the pros:

The late Bob Starr, California Angels, the one whose father admonished, "You can talk, can't you," attributed his deep resonance to days in the military. "I developed my voice by barking out orders as an Army drill sergeant. I learned to speak clearly and to project. I also learned how to shout orders all day and still save my voice for the rest of the night."

Note: You never know from what source you might gain a lesson. Learn how military orders are delivered. If your father was in the military, interview him. Or a recruiting officer. Or monitor an ROTC class drill at your school.

• Jack Buck, renowned for his distinctive, gravelly calls of St. Louis Cardinals baseball for decades and formerly of National Football League radio with Hank Stram on CBS, is another example of a "lesson from life." He said, "Selling papers on the street corner all day long helped me project and strengthen my voice." Can't you just hear this kid, one day to become famous on the air waves—"Extra! Extra! Read all abouuuut it!"

• Others gained from more formal, structured, or planned activity, such as Costas hiring a voice coach not only to learn about voice, but to rid himself of a pronounced New York accent. "My voice was tinny sounding, at a high register," Costas revealed. "[From] voice lessons I learned to speak from the diaphragm, instead of from the chin up, to give more warmth and resonance to my voice. You can only work with what God gives you, but you can improve it through practice."

• Jim Nantz is one of the most versatile television commentators in the business—working golf, tennis, college basketball, and football. His work at the Final Four helps open this chapter. He, too, had specialized training, but for a far different reason—one that could have precluded him entering the broadcast profession. During fifth grade his school teachers determined that he didn't pronounce the letter L properly. "I worked for two years with a speech therapist. I'm still very cognizant of that. When I trip on a word, it's often when there's a double-L."

• Gary Bender, a Masters degree graduate from the University of Kansas William Allen White School of Mass Communications, brings unusual training to the microphone of the Phoenix Suns, Chicago Bears, and some network projects. He grew up on a farm in western Kansas desiring to play high school football. His mother relented only after he agreed to take singing lessons and appear in a school play. He said he learned pacing, proper breathing, and voice control from those experiences. "That, and preparation, have been the keys to my success."

• Marty Brennaman, Cincinnati Reds play-by-play announcer, took acting lessons for 10 years because he dreamed of Broadway. "My original desire in life was to become a professional actor on the stage in New York," he says. "I took drama lessons from age 7 until my sophomore year in high school and did a lot of theater work. That helped me with whatever voice I have, more than anything else." He transferred the skills he learned to the baseball booth.

Note: Several sportscasters (including the author) learned from thespian pursuits. Consider taking a course or two in the drama department, or enter forensics competition, as Mitch Holthus did.

• Dick Schaap, well-known as an author as well as a variety of network TV and radio work, received training from a specialist who taught accents to actors. "He had me read Shakespeare aloud to him, and I enjoyed that," Schaap says. "Then I studied under Lillian Wilder, who is well known. She taught me how to relax. When I first started on air, people told me my voice was raspy. Now they say it's distinctive, but that's the same thing."

• Tony Roberts, a smooth talker on Westwood One, says, "I haven't taken any voice training. I think I got my voice quality from my mother. She has a rather resonant voice. I don't particularly care for the sound of my voice."

• Jim Irwin, behind the mike almost three decades at Green Bay Packers football games, says, "Bless the University of Missouri. I had a wonderful speech teacher who taught me how to use my voice properly. So many of us speak from the back of our throats, rather than the front of the mouth where the words can flow out easily."

• Linda Cohn of ESPN Sports Center received the same invaluable advice from a college speech teacher at Oswego State University. "She told me to be aware that I had a strong New York accent, and that I should slow down a little, talk from the front of my mouth and not the back of it. It's the best advice anyone ever gave me."

THE OTHER COMPONENTS OF VOICE

Keep in mind, as stated earlier, "voice" incorporates several components. It is timbre, to be sure (i.e., the quality imparted to a sound by its overtones). In broadcasting, timbre is the resonance by which the ear recognizes and identifies voiced speech. Timbre is the first thing a listener or viewer is aware of when a broadcaster begins talking.

Resonance in speech is quality of richness. What you sound like—your "voice print"—certainly starts with the vibrations from the anatomy, in chambers (mouth), cavities (nasal), and so on. But your total voice, your sound on the air, extends far beyond the physiological explanations. Resonance also stems from quality or variety in speech. Therein lie the other facets of voice: pacing, diction, language, etc.

So, where do those come from? How do you determine how you're going to sound, beyond whatever birth rights your body granted you? The answers: Anywhere, everywhere, nowhere. Consider the contrasting experiences again of several who have made it in the big time. Kevin Harlan's development was complex, finite, and purposeful. Baseball greats Ernie Harwell of the Tigers and Vin Scully of the Dodgers, you will see, had simpler recipes.

• Kevin Harlan, another graduate of the University of Kansas, sprang into professional sports early in his career with the Kansas City Kings of the NBA. He moved on to Kansas City Chiefs football, and then Fox NFL network, plus the NBA Minnesota Timberwolves. He started developing style in junior high, literally copying three different "sounds"—one uniquely homey, one steeped in profound sound, and one built on solid preparation and description.

One night he would imitate Keith Jackson on college football. After listening for 15 minutes he would create a recording, aping Jackson's down-home delivery. The next night Harlan would do the same with a recording of John Facenda, that deep-throat voice describing NFL film features whose nickname among peers, stemming from his timpani sound, is "The Voice of God." The third night Harlan parroted the works of his college mentor, yours truly, on the call of, for example, a KU basketball game against UCLA, getting down pat the straightforward, polished and knowledge-driven.

Says Harlan, "Don't reinvent the wheel. Why is Keith Jackson where he is? Al Michaels? These guys have a certain voice quality. I would put a microphone by the TV and tape stuff, then rewind it, listen to it, and mimic what I'd heard. It put me on a road and gave me a map to follow . . . something in my mind that I wanted to sound like."

• Vin Scully, who also has worked extensively in pro golf, took the advice of another Hall of Fame professional who broadcast Dodgers baseball, Red Barber, who said, "Don't listen to anyone. Just be yourself." Scully parlayed the advice into what he terms a "natural" sound, rooted in storytelling, his trademark. "I lower my voice to be less strident. That way the voice lasts longer during a doubleheader, too, as opposed to speaking from the throat. I try to hit a certain tone and sustain it during doubleheaders."

• Ernie Harwell applied basic lessons of good manners to develop his style. Courtesy has always been his calling card. "You want to be like a guest in a person's home. You don't want to become a pest."

• Harry Kalas, possessed with one of the deepest, richest voices in the business (you ride dreamily on his words voiced over NFL highlights on HBO), nonetheless states emphatically, "You're talking for several hours. You don't have to be blessed with mellifluous tones. You need to be a conversationalist with your audience. That's much more important."

Kalas employs his philosophy on followers of Philadelphia Phillies baseball (and early in his career, the Houston Astros). A University of Iowa product, he says he gained both style points and command of language from his father, Harry Sr., who was a preacher.

• Jack Buck developed his style—in direct contrast to Harlan's method—on whom he did NOT want to sound like, specifically the legendary Harry Caray, who shared the Cardinals' booth with Buck in the early going. "Harry was so big, I thought I wouldn't last long in St. Louis. So I contrasted my style from his." Thus, while you received bombastic home run calls, punctuated by the legend of "Ho-lee Cow!" from Caray (and, later with the Chicago Cubs, leaning out of the press box during the seventh inning stretch to lead the crowd in "Take Me Out to the Ball Game"), you received even tones and laid-back comment from Buck. "I backed off and balanced the broadcast," Buck says. "We gave people two different sides. When you're on the air, you'd better weigh your words."

Buck's son, Joe, followed his father's footsteps not only into the profession, but also into the Cardinals' booth. Joe Buck says, "I tried not to sound like my dad. As much as I love and admire him, it was important to me to develop my own style and be my own guy."

• John Rooney works extensively in several sports for CBS Radio and Westwood One around his primary assignment as voice of the Chicago White Sox. He always gets requests to do impressions, because he can sound like many other broadcasters; his Harry Caray is a classic. But he didn't set out to find a sound. "Buddy Blattner told me it's more in what you say than how you sound," Rooney says. "It helps to sound pretty good, but I learned the sports . . . the technique of working a game, like giving the score and time after every basket, saying whether it's a zone or man-to-man defense . . . doing a good job technically to paint a picture for the listener. I tried to develop a style more than the voice.

Each broadcaster must develop a personal style. Clones don't make it. Much goes into the developmental stages: natural timbre, preparation, and knowledge of subject, diction, rhetoric (written verbal skills), pacing, and "feel" for the audience. A time-honored method for developing style is by using the tape machine, listening to yourself over and over and over until your "self" emerges.

I struggled with this in my early years at KWBW, a small station in Hutchinson, Kansas. At first I sounded like Curt Gowdy, because he's mostly who I heard growing up (in Massachusetts, where Gowdy worked the Boston Red Sox for 15 years). Then I started sounding like Monte Moore, whom I heard all the time on Kansas basketball and football.

I phoned Moore, distressed. He gave me good advice: "Don't listen to me for three or four weeks. Keep working, and someplace along the line you'll find yourself." One night driving home from a high-school game I broadcast in El

Dorado, listening to the tape, I had a breakthrough—I sounded like myself.
Cawood Ledford, forever, it seems, the voice of the University of Kentucky, recounts how he would drive all over the state of Kentucky to events "and I'd hear everybody on radio trying to sound like me. That's flattering, but it wasn't getting them anywhere. You have to be your own person."

Remember, we found only one example of a clone who made the big-time: Al Michaels, when he started out in Cincinnati, emulated Vin Scully. Sounded just like him. Eventually, Michaels found his own voice, and leapt to fame with his famous call of the close of the U.S. ice hockey victory over the Soviet Union during the 1980 Winter Olympics in Lake Placid, New York: "Do you believe in miracles? Yes!"

As Jay Randolph, of the Florida Marlins and formerly of NBC, puts it, "Mirror yourself. You're not going to make it by sounding like somebody else."

COPYING WORKS FOR SOME

Bob Costas, contrary to the opinions of many others, suggests that copying somebody good is the way to start. When asked how the Costas style emerged, he explained, "You start out copying people and you should not be embarrassed by that."

"The first sport I did on radio was basketball at Syracuse University and I copied Marv Albert, because I listened to him doing the Knicks as a kid. I went to Syracuse in part because he and Marty Glickman, an older New York announcer, had gone to Syracuse, as did Dick Stockton and some others. So, I just copied Marv.

"When I first started baseball, although I didn't copy the voices, I took a little from Jack Buck, and a little from Red Barber and Vin Scully. But over time, especially if you have a little success and you become comfortable, then your own personality comes out. As you watch tapes you see what's effective for you and what isn't. Once I develop my own style it is crazy for me to say, "Hey, I'm going to copy Al Michaels or somebody else." You find something you are comfortable with, that sounds like you and expresses your personality.

"On television you are trying to say things that are worthwhile. People know I don't shy away from an opinion, especially about baseball. But you have to say it in a pleasant, comfortable way so people don't mind spending

$2\frac{1}{2}$ -3 hours with you. If I have any criticism of myself, coming off the (1997) World Series, in some of the more dramatic moments I was so caught up in the moment and so wanted to do the best possible job that I could. And I am sitting there thinking, 'Gee, it is the seventh game and rights fees being what they are these days in baseball and all sports, who knows how many more World Series NBC will do. Only one more in this present contract, 1999. Who knows if I will ever get a chance to do a seventh game of a World Series again. So I'd better make this as perfect as I can.'

"And while I think I did a good job, in listening to the tapes afterward I thought I sounded a little bit more 'announcerish' than usual. A little bit more like a guy who was making sure that if they sent this to the museum that it would be a worthy inclusion. As opposed to somebody that's just doing it in his own style, the way he always did it. I think I actually changed my style in the seventh game just a little bit."

Kevin Harlan, at age 19, approached Larry King and asked what advice he might have for an aspiring teenaged broadcaster. King replied, "Son, please yourself first. If you don't please yourself, you won't please anybody."

ADDING SPARKLE TO THE VOICE

Twelve areas to work on in developing your sound:

Timbre

Some broadcasters, such as Harry Kalas, were born with better "pipes" than most. But even he will tell you, "To a certain point voice is important, but you don't have to be blessed with mellifluous tones. You have to be knowledgeable and conversational."

Speech instructors can teach you breathing, diaphragm and mouthing techniques that will help you make the most of what you have to work with. Marv Albert serves as a good example. "I have an odd voice, but it helped me," he says. "I did Knicks radio before TV, and people would imitate my call of a game and repeat the phrase 'Yessss!' on a basket like I do. That got me a lot of commercials, too."

Kevin Harlan suggests theater techniques: "Talk from the diaphragm, and more air in the lungs gives you a forceful, authoritative, confident sound."

Pacing

A normal tendency is to talk too fast. Bob Carpenter of ESPN basketball and St. Louis Cardinals TV says he was a motormouth when he started out in Fort Smith, Arkansas "Every time the general manager of the station saw me, he would bark, 'Bob, slow down! People can't understand you. Slow down.' "

Talking fast usually is caused by nervousness. Preparation builds confidence, which reduces panic and calms nerves. Kevin Harlan, although his pace is rapid, is careful, "You can't afford to tumble over your words because you're talking too fast. Besides, the slower you talk, the lower you sound. Some days you can talk fast and have every word sound crisp and clear. If they don't, adjust. Sometimes I will slow things down and get the entire production to downshift one gear."

Early in my 41 year career, when I was the voice of the Kansas City Chiefs, owner Lamar Hunt once introduced me as "a man who talks at the rate of 135 words a minute, with gusts up to 185." So, during my years as a classroom teacher, I've passed along to my students this credo: Slow down, and bite off the words.

Pitch

Squeaky doesn't work. You must be palatable for three hours. Women and young announcers tend to experience high-pitched voices the most. Again, speech instruction can overcome problems in this area. Both Linda Cohn, ESPN, and Jim Irwin, Green Bay Packers, cite examples of a speech teacher helping their pitch by getting them to speak in the front part of the mouth.

Andrea Kirby works with ESPN announcers on voice. She tells them, "Get a comfortable pitch. My voice used to be high and squeaky. I lowered it through practice because I didn't like the way I sounded, and my range increased enormously. Anyone can do that. Act like you are talking to someone, not announcing. Nerves factor in. Never let nerves and pressure take over."

Kevin Harlan adds two more elements: "You're high if you're talking with just your voice and not using the diaphragm. And learn proper breathing. Go to a voice teacher, a drama teacher, a music teacher—they immediately will talk about breathing the right way."

Personality

Conversational style bodes well, as Bob Costas illustrated so keenly with his late-night, non-sports television talk show, working one-on-one with a guest. Take to heart Ernie Harwell's tips on visiting people's living rooms in a congenial way. Costas says, "Eventually your own personality comes out. Mine has a little irreverence. I give the nuts and bolts, but throw a little humor in. And there's nothing wrong with opinion, if it's credible."

Conversational Style

Listeners and viewers love it when you're one of them, not a robot. What you convey is: I'm not announcing at you, I'm talking to you. Curt Gowdy says: that when he is delivering a broadcast, "I pretend I'm sitting on a couch with a friend, chatting, or I'm telling my mother what's happening as she works in her kitchen in Wyoming preparing supper. Arthur Godfrey had that knack; it always seemed that he was just talking to you from across the table. I was easy-going and had naturalness, and I always wanted to sound like I was talking to a pal while having some fun at the ballgame." Gowdy suggests listening to TV newscasters to develop a conversational mode, too.

In summary, keep in mind Cawood Ledford's belief: "The most overrated thing in announcing is the big voice."

These first five points are about wearability. From here on is about . . . .

Credibility

Whoever is tuning in, that listener is immediately wondering, "Does this announcer know what he is talking about?" You'll read it a million times in this text: prepare, prepare some more, and then dig up even more. Use the Bud Palmer theory: "When I was scheduled to broadcast the Knicks against the Celtics, Red Holzman knew more about his Knicks than I did, and Red Auerbach knew more about his Celtics than I did. But I knew more than either one of them about both teams."

Credibility also hinges on the perspective you create on a play or event. Herb Carneal of the Minnesota Twins said he sees a sea of young announcers who didn't make it "because they over-exaggerated every play, they had no credibility. People with transistor radios in the stands could see, 'Hey, this is a different game than I'm watching.' Those broadcasters were out of the business quickly."

Bob Costas points out, "The job could be a marathon instead of a sprint. After the first day of the Olympics in Barcelona, a producer told me I wasn't showing enough emotion, that this was the Olympics and they are emotional. I'm about to do 18 straight nights, five hours a night, and if I wear people out the first nights, where do I go from there? You can't always put the pedal to the metal. Some can . . . Harry Caray, John Madden, Dick Vitale . . . . but you have to remain believable."

Several pieces that add to credibility:

Diction/Articulation
Bite off the words for clarity. Slurring is totally unacceptable. Avoid lazy talking, a common malady. No mumbling. Slovenly speech is a turn-off. Speech or theater courses are superb for mastering this, as well as learning to project.

Bob Carpenter also cautions against speed. "People won't understand you, and they'll have the impression that you really don't know what you're talking about."

Pronunciation
Few things gall a listener as much as names of players pronounced wrong. It shoots credibility in the heart. A dark moment in the illustrious career of Curt Gowdy occurred at a 1978 NCAA regional basketball tournament in Corvallis, Oregon, when he called the Kansas-UCLA game for NBC-TV. Throughout the game, Gowdy referred to Darnell Valentine as Darrell, Clint Johnson as Jackson, and mispronounced the names Mokeski and Koenigs repeatedly.

He explains, "I worked a TV doubleheader that day, and I left the spotting boards up to an assistant, who wrote the names wrong [phonetically]. I had just finished the Weber State-Arkansas game, and I went to Kansas-UCLA and messed up on the names. I took the blame for it." After 25 years with the network, he never drew the plum assignments again. Moral: Do your own legwork.

Vin Scully recommends talking to the public address announcer at the home site for correct pronunciations, or the public relations director or announcer for the opposing club. "If you came in here [to a Dodgers-Cardinals game] and didn't know that Mark Petkovsek's name is pronounced 'pet-KY-zik,' you would be hopelessly confused," Scully says.

The best source is the athlete. Writer Michael McKenzie remembers when the Kansas City Royals had a rookie Dominican named Pichardo whose first name, Hipolito, sparked a variety of pronunciations—'e-POL-uh-toe' and 'ih-pull-EE-to' and others. Mike tape recorded Pichardo saying his own name, and then repeated it while listening until he got it down pat, like you would with a language tape. "Eventually," McKenzie says, laughing, "I just called him Pol."

You can use word or visual image associations to fortify correct pronunciations. Scully recalls from his days at Fordham University, "We had a guy who played football and basketball whose last name was Sjajna. If you just tried to fathom that on your own, it would be a bowl of alphabet soup. But when you asked him how to pronounce his name, he said 'shine-uh,' like 'Shina on Harvest Moon.' Then it was very easy. Just a little reminder like that means so much."

Having Fun

Give the impression that you're having a good time. And if you're not, don't fake it. In fact, if you're not, it's time to quit. Millions of people would love to be where you are, at the game, in the booth. They can't be. You're there for them. A bummer isn't what they yearn for. Ron Barr tells of a woman he met on an airplane who, upon learning who he was, paid him two of the best compliments possible: "You know what you're talking about, and you enjoy yourself."

Costas and many others mention the tasteful and timely use of humor. Banter between broadcast partners should sound fun, such as Bob Uecker of the Milwaukee Brewers, who has made a career as a baseball humorist, interacts with his cohort, Jim Powell. Or, the banter between Ken Harrelson and Tom Paciorek on a Chicago White Sox television network.

ESPN has the fun approach patented. Keith Olbermann and Dan Patrick made sly, clever quips and commentary the trademark of the ESPN Sports Center approach to news. They love puns and sarcasm. Teammate Chris Berman is renowned for his word play on athletes' names (Oddibe "Young Again" McDowell). Now the horseplay has even penetrated the promotions of the show, with announcers cutting up with athletes, using cheeky humor for copy.

Stay tuned: Several ESPN personalities amplify on their approach to delivering sportscasts in Chapter 12.

Tip: Make sure the fun, i.e., entertainment, doesn't become gimmicky to the point of overshadowing the main point, the information.

Vocabulary

Become verbally efficient. You don't have to be Howard Cosell, spewing fancy verbiage for its own sake. But become a word lover.

Misuse of words is as sinful as mispronunciation, perhaps more. Know the difference between *anxious* and *eager*, *uninterested* and *disinterested*, *effect* and *affect*, *historic* and *historical*, *imply* and *infer*, *lay* and *lie*; know that *irregardless* is not a word; discover how *hopefully* and *comprised of* are woefully misused terms by nearly everyone.

Further, develop a kit filled with proper terminology for various sports, at the same time avoiding cliches and too much jargon, or, as one linguist puts it, Sportugese. Mitch Holthus addresses this topic fully: "A common practice is to listen to other announcers and pick up many ways of describing the same thing. I talk with English professors, look at dictionaries and thesauruses. I keep my 'war sheet' in front of me when I broadcast—a list of synonyms and alternate ways of describing the same thing. This helps you avoid one of the pitfalls of extemporaneous speaking, which play-by-play is; you get into a pattern of saying the same thing over and over without realizing it. During timeouts I look at my 'war sheet' and it refreshes my mind."

Journalism Skills

Write well. Practice strong rhetoric. Report even better. Find out everything. And then pass along what is most important and germane to the story line, whether that's a sportscast, a feature, or a play-by-play description.

The late Bob Starr said he always told students, "When you are broadcasting, you are creating a story. Tell the listener what you are seeing. Tell a complete story. You can do things I can't do—fire facts at me that you've memorized—and I can't remember them five minutes. But I can do things you can't do—sit and watch a game, get the most important things that happen at a given moment, and make them come out the way I want them to in storytelling."

In the next chapter, Bob Costas and Marv Albert explain the importance of staying relevant and leaving some of that material in the briefcase, because you don't spend all of your ammunition in one shot.

Description

Details are a must. You provide all of your listener's senses (sight excluded on television, of course) although sometimes TV doesn't have good peripheral sight lines and you can see even more than the cameras). Bob Carpenter said,

"It is essential to be quick with your call, such as a 6-4-3 double play. If you get all caught up in verbiage, the listener hears the roar of the crowd and knows the play has been over several 5-10 seconds and that doesn't help. After the quick call, then you come back with details that embellish the visual image."

Kevin Harlan believes that many broadcasters are not descriptive enough. He offers this thought: "He makes the catch over his right shoulder, looking into the sun, with a cornerback right in his face with a hand—that's the kind of detail you strive for, instead of falling back on simple words like 'beautiful' or 'great' catch.

Jim Irwin says, "I can see things and tell you exactly what I see . . . I can capture the moment."

PEOPLE SKILLS

People skills are so critical that you will have an entire chapter (Chapter 13) devoted to the politics of the business, but it bears mention under the umbrella of fundamentals. Not only do you have to please listeners and viewers while you're on the air in this profession, but you also have to cope with fans, advertisers, management, co-workers, and other media professionals, just to name a few. Any and every one can be a critic, and you never know who among them might have influence in you getting hired and staying on the job.

Good listening skills are essential to dealing with people on every level. On one hand, Jack Buck says, "I never played the politics. Just be nice to people, listen their suggestions, and thank them." Vin Scully seconds the notion: "I just listen. I don't take sides. I don't get into office politics." Likewise, Jim Nantz, who didn't even have an office at the CBS headquarters.

On the other hand, as you will learn in Chapter 13, there are several general guidelines to follow to help you stay employed, and all of them filter down to your main strength in dealing with others: be a good listener. Bob Starr said, "The young broadcaster is better served to listen rather than talk. It will accomplish two things. One, you don't let anyone know how dumb you are, what you don't know. Two, you'll learn something."

Like what? "People will tell you," says Wayne Larrivee of the Chicago Bears, "what you need to get better."

And, again, always fall back on Ernie Harwell's back-to-the-basics approach of simply applying good manners and good will in your daily dealings with others.

EDUCATION

You will find one common thread running through the fabric of the careers of all who contributed to this work: Each opted for higher education. College is essential to your success.

You can go the route of the great university programs, such as Syracuse (Bob Costas, Marv Albert, Len Berman, Sean McDonough, Mike Tirico); Kansas (Roger Twibell, Kevin Harlan, Brian Sexton, and Tom Hedrick, Gary Bender, and Terry Shockley in graduate school); Missouri (Joe Buck, Bob Starr, John Rooney, Larry Zimmer, Jim Irwin); Iowa (Milo Hamilton, Harry Kalas, Bob Zenner, Bob Brooks); and many others.

Or, you can find a path through a smaller, liberal arts education, such as Denny Matthews (Illinois Wesleyan) and Fred White (Eastern Illinois) before they ascended to the Kansas City Royals radio booth, or Dick Enberg (Central Michigan) to start his path to major network assignments.

Chris Berman at ESPN says simply, "Get in the best school you can. You don't have to major in communications or journalism. I'm not saying that's bad. I knew Brown didn't have a 'J' school, but I knew it had a radio station. I majored in history. Courses that help you learn to communicate are as important as majoring in communications."

Berman weighs both sides of the issue further: "A major in communications at a large school might help you get that first job more than a major in history at Brown. Or maybe not. Maybe somebody would be intrigued with a person who majored in history. But once you have that first job, it's what you do on the air—the communications major doesn't get you the second job. Then it becomes my tape vs. your tape."

Among all the professionals who contributed to this book, the most-recommended course of study was J-school. The larger, specialized schools of mass communications often have an advantage in their state-of-the-art equipment, a school radio station, and availability of internships. Nothing is a substitute for job experience. I worked my way through college at a small radio station.

The workplace affords a wide variety of internships, and the broadcast student would do well to find one of those during every summer break. Harlan, who champions the strong educational background, nonetheless says, "Frankly, I learned more from my internships than from my classes." He worked more than 100 games of play-by-play on a school station in his high school in Green Bay, Wisconsin. At ESPN, he and Sean McDonough cut up baseball highlights for Chris Berman, Keith Olberman, and Linda Cohn and wrote scripts to match the pictures. Harlan also had internships producing his own 6-and-10 reports and play-by-play of high schools and Washburn University sports, and in Kansas City, where he was producer of "Chiefs Sunday," three hours of weekly programming. "All of that invaluable training led to me getting to work the NBA (Kansas City Kings) right out of college," Harlan said.

McDonough displayed great enterprise when he landed a play-by-play position at the Triple-A level of minor league baseball while he was still just a junior at Syracuse. He applied for an internship, and the Syracuse team liked his tapes so much they hired him as their voice.

Suzy Kolber comments, "The number 1 thing most important to me was the internship when I was a junior at Miami at an on-campus cable station. I pretty much never left the station, and I tripled my knowledge with that internship. You're out there getting real-world experience, plus people get to know you."

In many examples of internships, you'll notice a common thread of advice, one that Keith Jackson puts this way to aspiring young broadcasters: "Go to Boise." Many high roads lead out of tiny towns.

Virtually all announcers emphasize taking English and literature courses, to learn grammar, syntax, and vocabulary. Vin Scully says, "It will help you draw analogies in sports that will set you apart from others. You might want to quote Shakespeare and demonstrate that you're not a one-dimensional person."

Your spectrum of studies cannot be too broad. Theater and forensics offer invaluable training. Business courses will help in understanding the trends in athletics and in selling advertising. In sports today you'll indulge in economics and labor disputes. International studies are useful on an increasingly global sports scene. Psychology lends insight into the behavior of athletes.

Or, as Keith Jackson says with a laugh, "Study pharmacy . . . so you get a taste of how hard you're going to have to work."

A list of recommended curricula:

Journalism classes on reporting
English: literature and composition
Economics and business
Theater and forensics (debate, extemporaneous speaking, discussion)

Music and Art appreciation
Foreign language
Psychology
Sociology
Philosophy
History
Political Science
Law classes on labor and contracts

Terry Shockley, owner of six television stations in Wisconsin, who got his start primarily in sales, Tom Cheatham, who managed the Kansas City Royals radio network, and Brian Purdy, a sales manager for Evergreen Corporation in Houston, all stressed how varied a career in broadcasting can be. Suzy Kolber spoke of the value of working "behind the scenes producing, etc." Besides the announcing booth, many opportunities abound in producing, engineering, writing, researching, editing, or behind the cameras. Julie Smith, a producer of major motor events for ESPN, broke in as an assistant producer primarily in charge of rounding up facts as a foundation for Chris Berman's schtick.

Shockley says of education that he recommends a core of journalism courses. "Take every opportunity to be writing or in front of a mike," he says. "Make sure to develop good writing skills."

The message is clear: Absorb all the education possible, and be aggressive in pursuit of on-the-job training along the way. And throughout both experiences, wear out that tape recorder on events, real or imagined, and mock sportscasts.

COSMETICS

Visible nuances are vital to television—good posture, bright smile, smart dress (avoid overdressing for the president's ball!). Effuse energy. Convey that: a) you know what you are talking about and, b) you are enjoying yourself. Settle into the viewer's living room and talk to the viewer conversationally.

Sad but true, women have two obstacles to overcome: They must have better looks than men, and toearn credibility, they must work harder than men. Linda Cohn of ESPN said that the double standard is imposing. "Although it never was stated to me," she said, "women have to look more attractive than men."

Suzy Kolber says, "My mail usually says something about how it's nice to see an attractive woman on the air, but it also includes something about being knowledgeable. I think we're judged on a different standard cosmetically, with few exceptions."

Jim Kobbe, a TV sports director in Wichita, Kansas, says in general, "People going into TV have a certain look—a cosmetic look that is the smile, the teeth, the hair, and they are not heavy. Whereas people going into radio don't care as much about their appearance." However, good posture and a bright smile enhance enthusiasm and energy; so they are beneficial to remember on radio, too.

A viewer has to be comfortable with the person in front of a camera, but always remember that radio is "theater of the mind," so a listener has a visual image that is a frame of reference, too. Robin Roberts of ESPN and ABC-TV says, "When the red light comes on, do whatever it takes to make yourself feel more at ease. And remember to breathe!"

SUMMARY: CHAPTER ONE

Work Ethic

Prepare diligently for every broadcast, from the smallest 1- or 5-minute report to the entire play-by-play or commentary on a game, or you will fail your audience.

Voice

You needn't have the big voice, but develop a voice that a listener can enjoy for three hours in an informative and entertaining way. Work on pacing, diction, timbre, and style.

A caution flag: When trying to develop the good sound, avoid trying to sound like something you're not. The temptation is strong to strive for what you think you should sound like, instead of developing what you do sound like.

Writing

Develop effective verbal skills. In a world of 2-5 scripts a day, you will sound better in your own written style. Write your own scripts.

Cosmetics

Good presentation stems from good grooming (hair, teeth, makeup, etc.), sharp wardrobe, excellent posture and smile, and a warm, friendly, comfortable presence. Never underestimate the value of this, even on radio.

People and Political Skills

To make it in this business you must get along with all people with whom you work, from peers to management. Especially, learn to relate to and converse with persons that one day might hire you. Listen carefully, dress appropriately, and always be on time.

FUNDAMENTAL EXERCISES

• Make a 5-minute tape of a sportscast. Critique it yourself, and have three other persons listen to it and give you feedback. Have a broadcast professor or professional do the same.

• Tape a high-school football, basketball, or baseball game, or an amateur game such as American Legion baseball, or AAU basketball. Critique it yourself, and have three other persons listen to it and give you feedback. Have a broadcast professor or professional do the same.

• Listen to three announcers on radio and TV. Write down the things you like and don't like about their broadcasts.

•Read a newspaper sports section and rewrite some of the articles as scripts. Then tape them as you work on one of your weaknesses (diction, pacing, conversational tone, pitch, etc.)

TIPS

Read into a mirror, making note of your posture, facial expressions, smile, and overall look (dress, hair, makeup, etc.).

Read into a corner with one ear plugged to get an idea of how you sound to a listener.

APPENDIX I

Writing Tips for University of Kansas Student Station KJHK Sports (from Prof. Tom Hedrick)

1.   Every broadcast must have at least one or two KU Jayhawk stories.

These stories should contain actualities.

2. Make your copy interesting. Work on a strong, clever lead.
3. Type your scripts, making certain that the copy is clean and easy to read.
4. Leave your script and cue of the taped interview with a subject (such as Coach Williams) for the next person who has a sportscast.
5. Arrive at the studio one hour before you hit air.
6. Let the disc jockey know you are in the building.
7. In case of illness, notify somebody the night before you are scheduled to broadcast.
8. If you miss more than one assignment, you will be suspended until further notice.
9. Pace yourself. Avoid talking too fast.
10. Work on diction and articulation. Tape your broadcast so that you can critique your performance.
11. Find a mentor on the staff who can help you.
12. Produce shows that do not exceed 2 1/2 minutes in the morning, and 3 minutes in the evening.
13. If you want to do play-by-play, you must first do an excellent job on the daily shows and operate the board a few times.
14. Always behave in a professional manner.
15. Improve every time over the last time you were on the air.
16. Work on your weakest points, just one at a time.
17. Listen to other highly-regarded announcers and realize what makes them effective.

APPENDIX II

Sample Script for KLWN in Lawrence, on Monday Morning Following Weekend Action in December 1997 (By Tom Hedrick)

The Jayhawks will be playing for 3rd place today against Penn after their first defeat of the year, 86-83 to Maryland.

After winning 8 in a row, the nation's 3rd-ranked team bowed by 3 points to the best 3-and-2 team in the country.

Billy Thomas tried to send the game into overtime but missed a 40-footer at the buzzer. Billy went oh-for-9 from beyond the arc.

Paul Pierce had 26 points and played on a swollen ankle before he fouled out, and Raef LaFrentz had 24 points for the 'Hawks. Ryan Robertson had just 6 points, Thomas had 3, and off the bench Kenny Gregory and Eric Chenowith shot in 9 points.

After the loss, Coach Roy talked about it. (Roy Williams :31)

We will have the game broadcast today at 4:00 on the Sports Leader.

▲▲▲

The Lady 'Hawks won their own tournament 68-51 over Grambling, as Suzy Raymont shot in 20 points and was named the MVP of the tourney. (Marian Washington :41)

The Lady Hawks improved to 5-1 on the year.

Lynn Pride had a 20-point game on Saturday, and also made the all-tournament team. Nakia Sanford had 12 points and 14 rebounds in the win over Grambling. The 3-point shot was the key, as they hit 6-of-11 from beyond the arc.

The Lady 'Hawks hit just 40 percent from the field and made 21 turnovers to win their 5th game of the year.

▲▲▲

The Chiefs looked like a Super Bowl contender and the Raiders definitely looked like a pretender as the Chiefs blanked the Raiders 30-0. This win, plus the Denver loss, put Kansas City in the play-offs.

The Chiefs won their 11th game of the year, and they recorded their first shutout since a 34-0 blanking of the Browns. The Chiefs dominated—they had a 23-0 lead at the half, and they had 450 yards of total offense to the Raiders' 93.

Donnell Bennet led the rushers with a touchdown and he had 85 yards on 24 carries. Kimble Anders had 64 yards on 10 carries.

Rich Gannon went 15 for 21 passing for 225 yards and a touchdown, continuing to fill in well for injured Elvis Grbac.

The Chiefs held the hapless Raiders to 36 yards rushing and Napoleon Kaufman had just 7 yards on 3 carries.

The Chiefs next will take on the Chargers, who are 4-and-10.

▲▲▲

The Steelers had 5 touchdowns from Kordell Stewart, including three passing touchdowns, as the Steelers outscored the Broncos 35-24. This ties the Chiefs for the lead in the Western Division of the AFC. Both Denver and the Chiefs are 11-and-3, and the Chiefs will be granted home-field advantage if they win their remaining two games.

The Packers also made the play-offs with their 17-6 win over the Bucs. The 49ers bounced back with a 28-17 win over the Vikings as Steve Young had 2 TD passes.

The Ravens took the Seahawks 31-24.

The Rams won their second in a row 34-27 over the Saints, as Tony Banks had 3 TD passes.

The Giants bounced the Eagles 31-21 to win their division.

And the Dolphins outscored the Lions 33-30 on a 55-yard field goal. Barry Sanders had 137 yards and for the 11th straight week he rushed for at least 110 yards.

▲▲▲

K-State is headed for the Fiesta Bowl against Syracuse. The 'Cats are 9th and 10th in the national polls this week.

And M-U is headed for the Holiday Bowl to take on Colorado State.

▲▲▲

Lawrence High women will be in basketball action tonight. Coach Dave Platt will have a club that returns all but one starter and went 5-16 last year. They are led by Laura Rhodes and Katie Winter.

▲▲▲

The Free Men's won 73-33 in overtime over Washburn Rural on Friday night to win their first game ever. Paul Dillon had 16 points and Matt Heider had 14, with DiJohn Dillion snatching 11 rebounds and shooting in 10 points.

Topeka High won 76-48 on Saturday night as DiJohn Dillion shot in 15 points. The Free Staters are now 1-and-1 and will play Thursday at 5:30 against Bartlesville.

LHS will be in the Blue Valley tournament this week, and will play on Thursday night.

CHAPTER 2
PREPARATION

Bob Costas, on getting ready:
"All sportscasters share one thing in common if they're going to be
good—they're willing to prepare."

So, you have a grand voice? Tones that soothe the soul? Swell. That will come in handy sometime. However, keep this in mind: As a sports broadcaster, you will always be paid for what you are willing to find out, not just for sounding like James Earl Jones when you speak into a microphone. So, you will hear one worn-out term throughout the broadcasting industry: Prep.

Getting yourself ready with voluminous information to deliver to the listener or viewer is the key to success. When you leave the audience with a feeling of, "Wow, I just learned something I didn't know," that's your equivalent of a home run or touchdown. That's how you score points, the same way as the basics of Boy Scouts: Be prepared.

Good prep adds insight, perspective, depth and breadth, and value to a broadcast. Good prep endears you to an audience and brings them back for more. Good prep boosts your confidence, your credibility, and your ratings.

Costas, who has reached the zenith in many areas of broadcasting, developed his reputation on his versatility, and his willingness to indulge in exhaustive research in many areas of not just sports, but across the spectrum of entertainment, government, and current events. (This research created subject matter for his innovative "Later" interview program on network television). "You can't go in and get by on style alone," he said. "Even if you sound like Vin Scully or Jack Buck and you don't do your homework, you will not make it. If you don't have the necessary information, then the style won't be enough."

As an example, he cites the way he preps for a nationally-televised baseball game on NBC. "I've always thought of the telecast as a baseball conversation; so you have to know what's going on everywhere. The history of the game is so rich that you have to have a deeper amount of preparation than most other sports."

He taps into every available source. "I've always read the NBC press package, prominent newspapers that cover baseball thoroughly, and I also watch games on WGN (Chicago), TBS (Atlanta), and ESPN. Never confine yourself to the particular game you are working."

Costas' next point is as important as the preparation itself: Know how and where to gather the background, and then know how much and when to disclose it. Never force-feed information just because you took the time to gather it.

"Once you've done all that preparation (for any event or newscast) you don't know how much of it you're going to use," he says. "You should be well-prepared enough to use just a tiny percentage of what you have prepared. Often, you will finish the broadcast having not used most of it because it wasn't appropriate."

"The good broadcaster has a full briefcase, but also enough good sense to know when to close the briefcase, and not leave it empty. It would be arrogant to use it all."

Other voices on the subject of preparation:

• Gary Bender of the Phoenix Suns and St. Louis Rams says simply, "A well-rounded education and preparation have been the keys to my success.

• Folks marvel at the scope of NBC's Marv Albert's broadcasting duties. At the height of his career he seemed to be on airways everywhere doing every sport. He credits his versatility to a stockpile of assimilated information. He bones up on everything. "I'm one who always believes that it's what's being said that's most important in broadcasting," Albert says. "Listeners make judgments about announcers in terms of their knowledge, their sense of humor, and the entertainment value."

• Larry Zimmer, former voice of the Denver Broncos, talks about the value of prep in other terms: "You can't fool people out there. You have to be honest and informed, and if you don't know something, let the listener know that, too. If you're honest, you'll build your credibility."

And then, if you didn't know—go find out. That dance never ends. Preparation is ongoing, constant, and it requires tireless pursuit.

Mike Patrick, ESPN:
"If I can weigh the FedEx packages [of preparation notes] in pounds, I'm really happy."

Patrick often finds himself at the side of the inimitable bundle of energy known as Dicky-V—basketball commentator Dick Vitale. Patrick has a habit that helps him keep up with Vitale, whose frenzied pace could easily leave an unprepared sidekick in the dust. "I create files," Patrick says. "Reams of files. It really gets crazy after a while; you become so overwhelmed with paperwork. But I'm a glutton for punishment. I want the most information I can get."

Vitale, probably the most animated color commentator in any sport, knows better than anybody that he couldn't get by on his over-the-top phrasing ("Diaper Dandy!") and enthusiasm by themselves. He *must* know, *does* know what he's talking about, the result of countless hours of poring over information and talking to coaches, not only about their team but also their opponents for a different perspective. Plus, he adds his own knowledge of the game as a former coach at both the college and pro levels.

"The one thing I pride myself in more than anything else is preparation," Vitale says. "You can't survive 17 years at ESPN or anywhere else unless you do your job in terms of preparation. It's a tradition, and I believe in the old traditional things that apply to all of life."

Keith Jackson, the preeminent voice of ABC football through the years:
"My preparation for the next broadcast started in 1952 with the first radio broadcast that I did. It's never stopped… it's called wisdom."

A sage in the business, Keith Jackson, adds a twist that comes with 48 years in the territory. "It's never stopped," Jackson says of preparation. "What goes on now is simply an accumulation of all those years. Students today won't understand that entirely. I believe it's something called wisdom.

"Sometimes knowledge and wisdom aren't really related. I think to succeed in any business you must accumulate information and instinctively, somewhere along the way, apply it where it is appropriate. So I'm constantly on the lookout for information that I can apply. I look for things in January that I can apply in October."

That relates back to Costas's thought about the briefcase—knowing not to empty it all at once, and then recognizing the moment when you need to pull from it. You can never have too much information, but at any given time you can attempt to *use* too much information. Go find the inside dope, but don't become one. When just one more tidbit becomes tempting, just say no.

Once you get the info, peruse it, use it, but don't abuse it.

Jackson's perspective on life-long accumulation also reemphasizes a sector that is underscored in Chapter 1: Education, including the early self-imposed training and internships and part-time jobs, is an essential component of preparation. Pounding the pavement in the classroom and at the local ball fields and arenas sets you up for any given game or event down the road.

That's where the small market can be so handy, even though it might seem at the time a universe apart from where you want to be. In Keith Jackson's simply put suggestion to enhance your early preparation: "Go to Boise."

He amplifies, "If you go to Boise and sweep out the place, do a record show, do news, sell the games as well as do the games, you will prepare yourself well and develop. Go on, go to Boise."

In preparation, you cannot overdo it, from tip-off, face-off, kickoff, starting gun, or first pitch to the *denouement* of a game or event, from day one to career's end.

Jim Nantz:
"I'm often accused of over-preparation . . . ."

Two names synonymous with college basketball broadcasting are Jim Nantz and Billy Packer, the team that led off this book from the Final Four. Nantz is tireless, ceaseless in his prep setup of broadcasts, and it shows—from broad, sweeping strokes in the story-line opening, to the minutiae that crop up in relation to action in the play-by-play.

Nantz declares, "There is no such thing as over-preparation. I'd rather be accused of that than the other way around. I have the sports information offices of participating schools send me everything they have in their clip files. I go through the media guides for anything that could lend itself as a possible nugget."

Example: For the 1997 Final Four championship game, learning that Miles Simon, the Arizona team leader, had attended several Final Fours as a spectator when he was a kid. Or, tracking Coach Lute Olson's career roots in high schools in Minnesota. Or, at the regional finals, knowing the circumstances of why God Shammgod received his name, thus explaining why, by his family's religion, it is not sacrilegious.

Experienced announcer Bob Carpenter uses an elaborate color-code and numbering system in preparing for all broadcasts, regardless of the sport. As an example of how he prepares notes, he offered the following:

Required to comment on University of Kansas basketball '97, he summoned a clip-and-notes file from his briefcase and from them he could comment on: (a.) Jacques Vaughn, point guard, Academic All-American, turned down a probable $2 million draft slot to play his senior year for Coach Roy Williams; (b.) Jared Haase "will skin his knees" going after loose balls, also Academic All-American, transferred from Cal-Berkeley after playing against Kansas in the NCAA regionals; (c.) center Raef LaFrentz bolted from high school in Iowa because he was sold on the KU system, and because Williams convinced his parents that he would be treated "like a member of the family."

Nantz continues, "Billy (Packer) and I pride ourselves in being completely prepared. We go over things again and again and again. It's important to talk to as many players and coaches as you can to keep refreshing your material. There is so much to learn.

"The thing about it is, if you love your work—which I do—it's fun to do all this work. I do work very hard, and I make no apologies for doing what I do for a living—what I dreamed of doing when I was a little boy. And to stay in this business, to stay at the network, I have to stay on top of my game and put the hard work in."

Which brings us to another angle about preparation. Harking back to a credo that opened this book, to do whatever it takes, we find Mitch Holthus, A-1 announcer in pro football. Long before he pulled up a chair in that booth, we found Mitch Holthus, A-1 handyman—running the board and playing music at a tiny station in Pratt, Kansas, and on the side scheduling and selling advertising for area high-school games and 30 different coaches' shows.

"If it means I have to sell advertising to get on the air, that's what I will do," Holthus said. "If it means that I have to do the pre- and post-game shows free, or do the women's games to get a shot at WIBW (Wichita) to eventually do Kansas State football and basketball, that's what I will do. I will do what it takes."

Holthus recalls a telltale moment that represented all that he believes about his work ethic in preparing to call an event. He was the voice of the Kansas State Wildcats. Kevin Harlan, voice of the Kansas City Chiefs, received an NBC assignment in 1993, and Holthus got the call to substitute. "I gained the respect of Len Dawson [Chiefs color commentator] and everyone in the booth when I said that Albert Lewis picked off his third pass of the day, and it was the second time Lewis had done this against the Atlanta Falcons, that he had done it two years ago."

"Everyone kind of snapped their heads toward me, and Dawson looked at me as if to say, 'I'm impressed.' Doing your homework is vital."

That is a common denominator among our featured broadcasters: Commitment to the work ethic on all levels, never unwilling do what might seem menial or mundane at first blush, but holds value in training and preparation for the Big Show. "Don't ever think any task or job is too small," says Sean McDonough, who recalled handling play-by-play of the local Pop Warner girls' cheerleading competition on a local access cable TV as one of the first events on his resume.

Bob Carpenter, ESPN:
"I have four 'P's—Proper Preparation and Pacing keep you emPloyed. The last word really doesn't begin with 'P'—but it's a big 'P' you hear."

It's the double-P that opens his credo that Carpenter spoke of most. Not simply the gathering of clippings, notes and filler material, which, as you will soon read, is not as strong a point of emphasis in basketball as in football and baseball (because of fill time). Carpenter addressed the necessity of precise, thorough pregame preparation that goes beyond the collecting of material to talk about on his basketball assignments.

About half an hour before tip-off, you can find him looking all around. "I study the arena," he says. "I study the scoreboards—where are they located? Where are the foul indicators? Timeouts? What does the clock look like? Also, where are the benches? Anything, so that I'm never surprised once tip-off occurs. The worst thing in play-by-play is to have something happen that you weren't expecting. The more ready you are for anything, the better you will be on the air."

Joe Buck of the St. Louis Cardinals, where he succeeded his famous father, talks about a trait common to his trade: reading publications. Buck is a voracious reader of baseball publications, in particular, but also of non-baseball books and periodicals. "I read a lot during the day as I'm waiting around for a night game," Buck says. "I get *Baseball Weekly, USA Today,* and *The St. Louis Post-Dispatch.* I don't feel fully prepared unless I've read those publications each day. I'm not one who relies on statistic after statistic. I keep my head up and keep track of what's going on. And not just about sports. Know your vocabulary, and know what's going in the world around you."

Examples: During the summer of 1997, while the baseball race was unfolding, the Oklahoma City bomber got convicted, a manned space flight on Mir encountered difficulties that created human drama and the U.S. put a craft and robot on Mars, the stock market reached incredible record highs, and boxer Mike Tyson bit off a piece of Evander Holyfield's ear. Keeping abreast of these wide-ranging current events would not only bode well for a broadcaster's well-roundedness, but also could possibly lead to a story line. Hal McRae, a major-league coach and erstwhile manager, for example, was an avid tracker of stocks and bonds.

Former pitching great Vida Blue held a fascination for space travel and never missed viewing a launch, and current pitching standout Kevin Appier studies the planets through a high-powered telescope on his farm. You never know what interesting path your research might take you down.

Bob Costas says that knowing the rules is part of preparation, especially helpful in baseball. "There are a lot of arcane rules in baseball that even those that consider us knowledgeable probably don't know 100 percent," he says. "Weird situations that can come up once a season or once every 10 years. And at the very least it is important to know where to find that in the rule book."

He recalls how situations developed in which he didn't know for certain the interpretation of the rule while an argument ensued on the field. "I vamped long enough to find it in the rule book and then say, 'It's rule 506C,' and read it out loud on the air," Costas says. "The worst thing you can do is pretend to know something for sure that you don't. You might as well go right to the source and say, look, this is what it says here in the rule book, and read it verbatim."

Other random thoughts on preparation for various phases of broadcasting:

• Harry Kalas: "The way you prepare in order to know what to say correctly is vital, a lot more important than how your voice sounds."
• Terry Shockley: "You must have good word usage and proper grammatical usage. You must know what you're talking about."
• Steve Busby: "Read from a newspaper into a tape recorder."

You've got to work at it. If you lack content, preparation, if you didn't spend 12-15 hours to work a football game (attend practice), 4-5 hours to work a baseball game (go to the batting cage), 4-5 hours in a basketball assignment (go to a shootaround), frankly, you will fail. You've got to understand that it requires a lot of work to get ready to go on the air.

JIM KAAT'S LESSON ABOUT PREPARATION

A former left-handed pitcher of note during his long career, Kaat turned to the booth as a baseball commentator, working for ESPN, WCCO-TV in Minneapolis, and for the New York Yankees. Early on, he joined ESPN for telecasts of college baseball. One Easter Sunday he worked with me on an LSU-Miami game that ended 22-16. After the sixth inning Kaat turned to me and said, "Professor, I am out of notes."

I replied, "So am I."

"What are we going to talk about?" Kaat asked.

"We'll have a little Q-and-A time, and I will ask you questions and we'll just talk baseball," I said, and that's what we did, banter based on my leading questions to my color sidekick, 'til game's end. The telecast lasted 4 hours, 38 minutes. Jim Kaat learned a big lesson that night about being prepared.

"When I first started on high-school basketball and football games," Kaat said, "I was pretty bad. But I learned how to prepare and describe what I was seeing. I learned how to become a journalist. I learned how to form my words. In a word, I learned preparation, and that was a key to going from pretty rough in the beginning to having some success."

PREPPING FOR FOOTBALL

Several of our sources outlined their week of preparation preceding a football game. The strains run a similar course, with varying nuances according to personal preferences. But as you walk through a week with each of them, you get the sense of the invaluable preparation that courses through every live game broadcast. Let's start with Mitch Holthus, getting ready for a Chiefs Sunday:

Monday

"I use Mondays to start preparation even through the off-season. I keep a file on all the teams we're going to play. I look for little snippets from outside sources—Internet, *The Sporting News*, *Pro Football Weekly*, and daily newspapers. If I see something that will remain permanent for an upcoming opponent, even in June, July, August, I'll keep it in a file on that team. As the week comes up for a game, Monday intensifies for me. I do a television show on Monday night. I open the file on the opponent and get quick, important snippets of information. I'll do a lot of reading, underlining, and highlighting."

Tuesday

"[Head coach] Marty Schottenheimer holds his gathering with the media. So I'm gathering information coming from the Chiefs' perspective on how they view the opponent. In the morning I will talk to the public relations director of the opponent and get their impression of the upcoming game. Tuesday afternoon is film review. I go down in the bowels of Arrowhead Stadium, get video tapes from the coaches, and I watch the last two games against the opponent—on the big coaches' tape. From that I'll get the numbers, names, formations, tendencies, just like a coach would. I love to watch tape."

Wednesday and Thursday

"Chart preparation. I take all the information from Monday and Tuesday and put it into my chart information. I update my chart in progression. Wednesday I bring all the focus on the Lions. Then the next day I'll relate all the Chiefs' information to my chart."

Friday and Saturday

"If I'm in pretty good shape [with the chart] I spend time on review of my own tapes...over the last two games and listen to them twice. Now I focus on my preparation for the game. I will review everything on Saturday. I memorize the names and numbers, and I have someone quiz me on it. So they come up with, say, No. 84, and I'm going to feed back that No. 84 is Herman Moore, No. 87 is Brett Perriman, and No. 88 is Johnny Morton. I'll review that again on Sunday morning, too."

Go back for a moment to Holthus's Tuesday afternoons. "What I do more than other announcers, I've found, is watch video tape," he said. It's worth hearing him out on this subject and its value in preparation:

"I approach the game like a coach. Coaches need to be totally familiar with the opposition. I watch tape, first and foremost. It's especially important on an opponent I'm seeing for the first time. Then I can see not only the face of a player to go along with his number, but I can see his size . . . not just his height, but whether he is slender or stout. And the nuances of how he runs, different mannerisms he has. Watching tape helps me identify players better."

▲▲▲

Here is yet another example of one broadcaster's preparation routine—Brian Sexton of the Jacksonville Jaguars, leading up to a Sunday NFL radio broadcast (and a sample of his spotting board):

Monday

I go to the stadium in the morning, and visit with some players in the locker room. Talk about the game the day before. Get a feel for what's going on. I attend the coach's news conference. I read four newspapers, minimum, and then put together two "Jaguars Reports"—for Tuesday and Wednesday—and a Monday morning quarterback show. I watch Monday Night Football to find out as much about every team as possible.

Tuesday

"I'm at the office bright and early. On my desk is the Jaguars opponent's packet with articles, press releases, media guide, depth chart, and statistics. I spend most of the day going through all that and making out my spotting boards. I spend the evening with a video tape from the previous game. I watch at least one half."

Wednesday

"A very heavy prep day because I also have the [head coach] Tom Coughlin Show the next day. First I do detail work on the spotting board. Then I go to the coach's news conference. I talk to his players during the noon hour. It's the one day of the week I attend practice. In the evening I hunker down and finish my boards."

Thursday

"I spend the morning working on my boards and preparing for the Tom Coughlin show. I interview Tom for the pregame show. I write out 10 questions to ask. At noon I have a 10-minute chat with the head coach, and we do the interview that airs on our pregame package. Then I go to his news conference. I go to the locker room again. I might go to practice, but most of the afternoon is spent getting ready for Tom's show. That night I try to relax, because Friday is pretty intense."

Friday

"The boards are done, the shows are done, and it's reading day. I read clips. In the afternoon I build my own stat charts with the clippings, using the lead statistics. At night I do the Hooters Kickoff Show in Jacksonville where we talk about what's going on in the entire NFL."

Saturday

"I read a couple of newspapers. I go over my board. I make sure I've got all the details I need. I relax."

Sunday

"Get up and grab a couple of newspapers again. Visit with a couple of the players as they're having breakfast. I like to go to the ballpark early—at least three hours before the game. I visit with the head coach a few minutes, and three or four position coaches I like to talk to. I visit with the game officials. I like to spend some time with the opposing team's play-by-play crew. Then I head to the booth, and we kick it off. The whole week is built to that moment. I feel like, if I've done my best, there isn't a story that will get by me."

▲▲▲

Cawood Ledford spent many, many years as the voice of University of Kentucky Wildcats athletics—so long and so well that they named a street after him in Lexington, Kentucky, plus some network duties on the side. His approach:

"I go to practice every day after the team goes into pads in August. I want to familiarize myself with the team. Once the season starts I go to practice every Thursday, because the coaches have their game plan installed by then."

His weekly routine during the week of a football game:

Monday

"Listen to tapes of the preceding game, looking for ways to improve."

Tuesday

"Talk to opposing coaches. Make up spotting boards. Memorize all the backs and receivers."

Wednesday

"Study the media guide of the opposing team."

Thursday

"Attend practice and talk to the home-team coaching staff. Important: include the assistants; they often have key "inside" insight, whereas the head coach might be more cautious in divulging information. Assistant coaches generally will be more talkative, especially if you grant them anonymity (off the record)."

Friday

"More review of the opposing team. Before bedtime pack the briefcase, using a checklist of items you will need in the broadcast booth (spotting boards, binoculars, pens/pencils, note pad, media pass, media guides, production schedule, etc.)."

Saturday

"Meet with the sports information director of each school to check on any late-breaking developments on injuries or lineup changes, and to check correct pronunciations on names one last time. Quickly review the list of officials' signals for instant recognition. Quickly review the critique sheet of the previous broadcast (from Monday). Go to work."

A younger lion, Kevin Harlan, developed a diligent routine in his early work on college athletics while attending the University of Kansas, and he carried it over to his typical week of preparation for an football game (first he did Chiefs football on radio, and later NFL football for Fox on TV, interspersed with college football on Saturdays):

Monday

"I don't do much. I just had my brain fried on Saturday and Sunday."

Tuesday

"Prepare spotting boards, but just the skeleton, using one format for the offensive formation and one for the defense, filling in names and numbers."

Wednesday

"Peruse personal library of articles from *The Sporting News*, *Pro Football Weekly*, and *Sports Illustrated*, plus information from Fox Network's services. "I've accumulated articles for six months. I go through them and pick out what I think are the most useful pieces of information, and I write or tape them to a legal pad—one for each team."

Thursday

"Fill out the spotting boards with notes about each player under his name and number."

Friday and Saturday

"On about 13 pages of legal-size notebook paper, divide the accumulated information into quarters. Cull that which might be most useful in the first quarter, and then separate that which might work in the next three quarters. It's not that the game is scripted, it's just that you should have a road map. You must know the important story lines going into the game."

Example: "If the Chicago Bears have to stop Barry Sanders (of the Lions), I'll have that as a common theme throughout the game. Maybe I'll say to my color commentator— in this case, Jerry Glanville—'Jerry, the Bears had to stop Sanders, and sure enough, they've allowed him just 55 yards through three quarters.' That sets up Glanville's analysis of the Bears' defense."

Tony Roberts, heard worldwide on Notre Dame football broadcasts, gave a condensed rundown of his typical week:

"Monday is an off day. In college football everything is now FAX-back, so I might dial up some information to be transmitted to me from SIDs or conference offices.

"Tuesday I get a transcript of the news conference with Lou Holtz (the head coach). I'll access the team's media release and the statistics. Tuesday, Wednesday, Thursday and Friday I work on Notre Dame and its opponent— digging through media guides and press information sheets."

Roberts offered a good example of how the digging beforehand can set up an interesting segment to bring into the game broadcast, something fresh and original that takes initiative to uncover beyond a handout:

"A lot of times I find myself asking questions that I would as a fan. For example, Navy and Notre Dame, it was the last game of the year, and in each of the nine seasons that Lou Holtz was head coach he said that they don't play well at Notre Dame on the last game of the year. I was studying the media guide when I discovered that Holtz was down in the bottom third in last-game victories among Notre Dame coaches, 5-and-4. Going back through every Irish coach since 1900 I found out the guy who did last games best was Ara Parseghian, who won nine straight home finishes."

Sometime during the Navy game Roberts found a place to drop in that tidbit—granted, a nugget, but as golden as the dome at Notre Dame. And well worth the extra time in the panning. "It takes a lot of time to find it out, and I realize that it only takes 10 seconds to say, but it satisfies my curiosity and I figure that if it does that, then it might be something in the broadcast that television isn't getting. That makes it worth it to me because I have something that the other guy doesn't."

TIP: Work beyond the obvious. You must not rely solely on the voluminous work of publicity departments that have their best interests in mind. You have your listener's best interest in mind—and sometimes the two don't jibe. Anybody can recite back a passel of stats and notes that somebody else compiled for the masses. Only you can determine how fresh and original your material will be when you start talking.

SPOTTING BOARDS

Mitch Holthus and Bob Carpenter use elaborate color codes. Carpenter adds a numbering system. Veteran NFL announcer Gil Santos (Patriots) uses nothing more than a bare-bones sheet—the depth chart handed out by the team. To each his own.

The spotting board runs the gamut of variety and creativity among sportscasters. Go with whatever works best for you. Just make sure it serves the primary purpose: instantaneous player identification (number, position, size, etc.). It can provide more, much more, such as story lines, drop-in thoughts, statistics—on both the team and individual levels.

The one thing that all spotting boards share in common: instant information. No thumbing through record books, media guides, newspaper clippings, or interview notes. All of the above are condensed into formats that are easy to read and easy to find at a glance while you're making sound at the speed of light. (Just kidding. Remember: pacing, pacing, pacing. Slow down, bite off the words.)

But hyperbole serves a purpose here. With action taking place at sometimes frantic pace, while mixing constant description and interaction with a partner, as you're keeping abreast of a *huge* picture window of activity—you cannot afford more than one or two seconds to speed-read the spotting board for a fact or note to complement the play-by-play or commentary. Otherwise you wind up with a lot of *Uh* and awkward, disconcerting silence.

If simplicity suits your taste, try the Jim Irwin method. His board is Spartan by comparison, containing streamlined, bare essentials. It lays out on an 11-deep x 14-wide piece of cardboard. The data reads horizontally. Offense on one side, defense on the other. "I line up the players by position, the way they will appear on the field—like about everybody does," he says.

He draws squares across the top, moving from left end across the line to split end. Below them he draws squares for the backup at each position, sometimes even three-deep. He uses squares in the center of the board for the top three quarterbacks. To their right, wide receivers. Below, fullbacks on the left, running backs on the right. He lists kick returners along the left side, and punter and place-kicker in the lower right corner.

Irwin writes positions in red marker, player numbers in green marker, player names in black felt-tip, height and weight and years in the NFL and college affiliation in blue felt-tip. He uses little other information. Exceptions are players who probably will perform most notably.

Example: Barry Sanders, Lions running back. Irwin writes in his square: 5-8, 203, 7 yrs, Oklahoma State, 23-471-4TD, 5.1 (carries, yardage, touchdowns, yards per carry). Receiving stats appear under the rushing/scoring numbers. Irwin also writes stats in the boxes of quarterback Scott Mitchell and go-to receivers Brett Perriman and Herman Moore and tight end Ron Hall. The board shows kicking stats for the punter and place-kicker, and a few team stats—points, total yards, yards rushing and passing for Detroit and the opponent.

On the flip side, Irwin draws three rows depicting the basic 4-3 defensive alignment that the Lions use—linemen in the first row, linebackers in the second row, and defensive backs across the bottom row. He lists backups, and a few tackle or interception stats.

And that's it.

Now, compare that to Mike Patrick of ESPN. It is like comparing an O. Henry short story to *War and Peace*. We tested this, so take our word for it. A full description of Patrick's spotting board for a football game covers eight typewritten pages. He uses two pieces of cardboard section eight inches wider and three deeper than Irwin's (22 x 14). He merges the boards together, one on top of the other; so one team's offense lines up against the other's defense—putting a 22-wide by 28-deep spotting board before him.

In many ways Patrick's board looks like Irwin's, albeit much larger. The major difference lies in the amount and type of information in the boxes. And probably the most prominent difference is in the story lines that Patrick makes note of. Examples from a Kansas-Texas Christian football game:

1.   TCU defensive lineman Hayes Rydel—"No. 44, '94 walked on, 70 tax/3 sax (tackles and sacks). Used personal football gear. Attacked oak trees." (Patrick had gleaned stories about Rydel providing his own equipment, and practicing his techniques against trees.)

2.   TCU linebacker Tyrone Roy—"No. 41, Sr., 6-1, 240, Austin, Texas (hometown), #1 w/10 tax, off-season ballet work, committed to working with youth groups." (Patrick could couple on-field info—Roy led the team in tackles the previous week with 10—with off-field featured material on his dancing and community service.)

3.   Similarly, Patrick capsulated information on a TCU player who feared hip-replacement surgery ("auto accident, fears Bo Jackson surgery"); the difficult pronunciation of a player named Mikyha ("muh-KIE-yuh") and one named Ashundai ("uh-SHUN-day"); a quarterback who had bagged groceries while an injured elbow healed, and was "discovered" there by the Kansas coaching staff; a wide receiver who was considering a pro baseball career, and a player who had never seen snow until he went to school in Lawrence, Kansas. All of this was supplemented by countless statistical and awards information about players, plus team notes, quotes and anecdotes.

Given the contrast of the simple to the extensive, keep in mind that however you prepare a spotting board, it must make you comfortable in the knowledge that you are well-stocked for your call. A fountain of knowledge is only as good as its usefulness (remember the Costas don't-empty-the-briefcase theory), and if your obsession with telling the listener everything in the world gets in the way of good, solid description, then you are better off with the uncluttered board.

You will read about several examples of spotting boards in this book. Pick and choose what fits your style, or adapt from ideas you glean from them.

PREPPING FOR BASKETBALL

You have sampled the results of preparation by Nantz and Packer on the CBS telecast of the Final Four. And you have caught the gist of Bob

Carpenter's spotting board for basketball, which will be more detailed in Chapter 4 (TV play-by-play). While the commitment to prepare does not lessen, nor is any source of information left untapped, in hoops it usually doesn't play out in the same broad scope as football. No other sport does, in fact.

Kevin Harlan, who calls both pro football (CBS-TV) and pro basketball (TNT), observes, "Preparation for basketball is important, though not as important as it is for football. Not to make preparation sound secondary, but in reality it pretty much is. The attention span of your audience is so short that additional notes rarely stick with the audience. When you give notes or stats, they have to be very important to the outcome of the game or season."

During a basketball game, Harlan says, he doesn't " get bogged down with notes. I will pick up a couple of things and hopefully couple them with a story that will make sense to my audience. Avoid using statistics a lot, but if you can put a story behind a statistic, then it speaks louder. That makes far more sense and has far more sticking power than just blurting out a bunch of numbers. Since I follow one team, I am up to date with what is going on with them. To refresh my mind I look at the team's daily notes."

Following the same line of thinking, Cawood Ledford says, "Basketball does not require nearly the time that football does. The one thing I always made sure of was to pronounce the names correctly. You can get into trouble if you say the names wrong. In preparing I would memorize the names, and then watch the players during warm-ups. I can watch Kentucky (the home team) during shootarounds and it was helpful, but usually you are not allowed at shootaround by the other team."

Shootaround, like the batting cage in baseball, is a great "hangout" for picking up information. Virtually all college and pro basketball teams go to the game site the day of the game for that informal session called shootaround. It's a place to catch the coaches in a talkative mode, to get updates on injury situations, to catch the mood of the players, etc. Often, team or school officials also attend and will avail themselves to conversation or interviews.

Bob Davis, voice of Kansas basketball, says, "I listen to all the coaches on Monday (teleconference). I go through all the media guides. I read five or more newspapers a day to keep track of things—some of them on the Internet. Preparation is more of a pattern, rather than, 'Hey, I've got to get ready for this game.' It's a routine, with a little more prep when we play somebody out of the conference that I don't see all the time. I'll prepare a lot of things and only get a fraction of it on the air."

Other research sources commonly menioned by basketball announcers include daily newspapers, basketball periodicals such as *Basketball Weekly* and *Basketball Times*, media guides, interviews with coaches and players, and viewing the national sports programs and the studio shows that lead into large network matchups of top-rated teams.

Although basketball requires far less memorization of players' names and numbers, the closeness of the game (most broadcasts take place on floor level) and the small number of players make basketball plays easier to identify. Although jersey numbers can get lost in shuffles for rebounds and loose balls, or blocked from view by referees, it's easier to pick up on players' looks, quirks, and mannerisms. Many broadcasters use video tape to learn those visible traits.

"Recognizing names is much more difficult in college and high school than the pros," Harlan says, "because you see the schools only twice a year. Watch video and take notes on any tendencies that players reveal. In the NBA you see the teams so often that you can identify players basically by body type."

Mitch Holthus, a self-proclaimed "video freak," says that he absorbs the images of players' faces and body types. "I can see his size—not just height, but is he slender or chunky? I supplement that by studying the radio-TV chart, and by looking through media guides to get good visuals of the players and reference points."

Marty Brennaman, who long ago announced telecasts of Kentucky football and has been a longtime radio voice on NCAA basketball, says, "A tremendous asset to us in play-by-play of sports is the invention of the video tape machine (VCR). With the advent of ESPN, Sports Channel, and outfits like that we certainly have access to about everybody that we might become involved with on a broadcast. I can video tape a game, and it's like having an assistant coach sitting with me watching film to get ready to play that team. You see offenses. You see defenses. You identify players. You don't need spotters in basketball."

Spotting boards, yes. Streamlined and simplified, yes. Nothing like Mike Patrick's elaborate system in football. Only a fraction of that lode of information would ever be used during a basketball game because of its action and pace. So, spotting boards for hoops usually comprise the basics—height, weight, year in school or pros, scoring and rebounding averages (or assists or steals, depending). In Chapters 3 and 4, you will find detailed spotting boards as they are drawn up by radio and television announcers on basketball assignments. Generally, they are quite a reduction from football, as the basketball call relies on bare essentials.

PREPPING FOR BASEBALL

Joe Castiglione, coming to you from the Boston Red Sox booth, is one of your primary sources on baseball. He is the guest author of an entire chapter—Chapter 5—because of his incisive knowledge of how to recreate the sport for a listener. You catch a glimpse of that in Castiglione's thoughts about preparation:

"First, read sporting print sources—the local newspaper, *USA Today*, *The Sporting News*, etc. I make up a file card on every player in the league to help myself during the game. At the beginning of batting practice, go down to the dugout and batting cage, and just listen. The information you pick up there is invaluable, things you can't look up in a reference book. I look for scouts; I learn the most from them. Basically, just listen to what the people involved in the game have to say."

Virtually all baseball broadcasters, radio and TV, hang out at the cage. Baseball is the only sport that permits fraternization with the participants before the battle—during batting practice or B-P. From informal banter to formal interviews, the coaches and players reveal themselves and their game more during B-P than any other time.

The clubhouse is open at designated times before games, too, unlike football, basketball, hockey, and other sports. Managers and coaches in baseball arrive up to five hours before game time, and players arrive from 2-4 hours before the first pitch. Usually they are available for interviews or informal chatter about the goings-on of the day, the series, the season. Scheduling an interview is advisable, for a player might have early batting practice, treatment in the training room, or some other scheduled activity to work around. But often the players are available for impromptu conversations as they sit by their cubicle.

The second-generation announcer of the Cardinals, Joe Buck, points out, "If you're around a team 162 games a year, you will know things that most other people don't know. Plus, I'm 26 years old, the same age as a lot of the players, so

I know a lot of what's going on with them for better or worse—the way they think and the things they do off the field. Hanging around the batting cage is a big thing. Maybe you won't get stuff you can use on the air, but you can gather a lot of background information that lends insight and understanding."

This special place at the ballpark—batting practice and clubhouse—is for doing homework. It is where participants in baseball open the book—themselves—for you to study. So study long and hard.

Almost any baseball broadcaster eventually will get around to one basic way of summarizing the task: It's a conversation. To succeed in baseball, you must be conversant. The gift of banter is paramount to this sport, and therefore much of the preparation revolves around history, which can be ancient, or as recent as the night before. Here is a sampler:

Jon Miller, San Francisco Giants and ESPN Sunday Night Baseball, formerly Baltimore Orioles:
"When Joe Morgan and I call a baseball game on Sunday night, we are just talking baseball. There is always something interesting to talk about. Find it, and talk about it."

Miller starts every morning by reading the local newspapers wherever he is broadcasting plus *USA Today*. He then listens to a radio news station to pick up West Coast scores that didn't make it into the papers. He packs up his gear about 1 p.m. before a night game and heads to the ballpark. There he talks to scouts, other announcers, players, coaches, managers—anyone from whom he can glean just one more ounce of possibly useful information.

Ernie Harwell, Detroit Tigers:
"I talk to folks without using a lot of stats. Most announcers use a lot of statistics because they don't what else to talk about. Give the listener the history of the game you're calling, and the series, the rivalry."

Harwell gets to the park 3-4 hours before game time. "I start my preparation by seeing our [Tigers] manager and coaches, then a player or two that I know pretty well because they will speak candidly about things. I also try to see the opposing manager and a few of their key players. Finally, I talk to scouts at the game, other announcers, and the newspaper beat writers."

Harry Kalas of the Phillies:

"Understand the game. Talk with people about why things happen. You need a strong grasp of the game and how it's played . . . . because you're talking conversationally with your audience."

Bob Costas:

"I've always thought of it as a baseball conversation. The history of the game is so rich that you have to have a deeper amount of preparation."

Costas says that he's always waded through the material provided to the media in press packets, scoured newspapers, and watched a lot of games on TV. "I talk to the players, the managers, the coaches. I talk to the beat writers. I talk to the scouts, who always sit in front rows behind home plate with their note pads, stopwatches, and radar guns. Scouts are the great fonts of information in baseball; they can give you a very astute assessment of players."

"You have to be fully prepared to carry on that conversation knowledgeably."

A good example of special preparation to become fully prepared for fresh conversation occurred late in the 1995 season for Paul Splittorff, who divides time between the radio and TV booths for the Kansas City Royals, the team for which he holds the all-time record for pitching victories. The Royals called up eight new players one day in August, totally revamping the team and lineup with young, unproven players. And unknown.

Splittorff went to Kauffman Stadium at 1 p.m. even though start time was 7:30. "I visited general manager Herk Robinson and director of scouting Art Stewart to learn traits and prospects on each of the new players," he says, "and to double-check pronunciations." (New players included Vitiello, Fasano, and Jason Jacome, whose last name is pronounced "HAH-cum-ee"—prompting the joke, why isn't his first name HAY-son?).

Venerable Cardinals veteran Jack Buck has been arriving early at the park for eons. He says, "I go to the ballpark three hours before the game and do three interview shows—at least two with the Cardinals manager, and at least one player for the pregame show that's heard on KMOX and the Cardinals network. This, and hanging around the batting cage keep me informed and into the game."

John Rooney of the White Sox prefers time spent with the men running the club rather than the men they run. "I spend more time with the managers and coaches than the players," he says. "I establish a rapport with the players, and I get along with them because they know I'm fair in my assessments on the air."

Fred White, who did play-by-play of the Kansas City Royals for 25 years with Denny Matthews, goes through a similar arrive-early, talk-to-everyone routine at the ballpark that most baseball announcers follow. He adds one source that nobody else mentioned: a boosters lounge. "I get a pulse of how the fans feel from them," he said of the special booster group that sells season tickets, known in Royals country as the Blue-Coaters because they sport blue blazers.

A final footnote comes from Hall of Fame voice of the Dodgers, Vin Scully: "Be prepared not only relative to the game you're going to do, but in your own way of presenting it."

PREPPING FOR 6 & 10 SPORTSCASTS

Whenever you tune in to a newscast, whether it's a local station or a network program such as ESPN's *Sports Center*, *CNN-SI*, or Fox Sports, you don't see a talking head who dashed into the studio 30 minutes before air time and started reading. Nor do you find anchors who make it on glib, ad lib, or fib; they must have credibility, established through accurate and thorough prep. Believe Dan Patrick of ESPN when he says, "We never wing it."

Nobody does. The anchor or reporter who flies by the seat of the pants will crash land quickly. Or, more likely, never take off. Fran Charles of WNBC in New York says, "I'm not interested in having a gimmick. I want to provide you with information. My everyday challenge is to get my cast together and have something that the rival across the street I am competing with doesn't have."

Frank Boal joined WDAF-TV in Kansas City in 1981 after a brief career as an assistant football coach. He plans in terms of an entire week. "Unless there is something unusual breaking, such as Bob Boone getting fired by the Royals, we pretty well know what we will cover each day of the week in a given season. This industry is pretty well regulated," Boal says. "Everything is scheduled."

Boal's staff plans down to the slightest detail, such as featuring the highest-ranked team first in a series of rundowns of regional teams (UMKC, Kansas State, Kansas and Missouri). He says each of the three anchors decides on his own leads.

Mike Bush, a mainstay in the St. Louis market on KSD-TV since 1985, reiterates how preparation starts days in advance. "Monday we have a meeting about what's going on for the week," Bush says. "What are the biggest stories?" As sports director, he conducts the meeting. He arrives at the station early in the afternoon, and he supervises the building of the news shows. After the story board is created, he assigns reporters to specific stories or events.

The heart of preparation, whether at ESPN or the local TV station, is written scripts. Virtually every newscast anchor we talked to prefers to write his or her own script. One prominent exception is renowned Hall of Fame quarterback Len Dawson, a fixture on both the Kansas City scene (KMBC) and HBO's *Inside the NFL*. He has a writer, and he practices reading the script from a teleprompter before air time.

Most of the preparatory effort in television sportscasts goes into selection of the video clips that support the scripts. Anchors most often participate hands-on in the selection, editing, and scripting of the pictures.

As you can readily see, preparation for presenting a newscast is as fast-paced as play-by-play action. You will read in Chapter 12 more details from selected local and national figures who make a living delivering the news, including an inside look at the ESPN operation and a one-on-one with George Michael.

LISTENING TO TAPE SEGMENTS

A vital part of preparation in sports broadcasting is listening to tapes of your previous broadcasts. Many announcers become frustrated in the industry because they receive little or no critique or feedback from associates. Most of the top-flight announcers revealed that they listen to or view their own tapes at least once a week.

• Larry Morgan of the Iowa Hawkeye network says that playback of his tapes is a great equalizer: "You are never as good as you thought you were," he says, "but you're also never as bad as you thought you were, either."

Even though some might contend that you are your own worst critic—and certainly an objective, neutral source is better for giving you feedback from your tapes—there are many things you can listen for and ascertain on your own.

Brian Sexton of the Jacksonville Jaguars hired me, his former college professor, to listen to and critique his tapes for a more objective viewpoint.

After his first year in the NFL, I gave Sexton the following feedback: "Great job in the basics. Slow down a bit. Be more efficient verbally."

After that Sexton sent tapes on a regular basis, and he had his color commentator, Matt Robinson, listen to a critique of his work, also. As official consultant, I listen to each game twice, and then call Sexton on Wednesday morning of each week for a 15-minute "chalk talk." Sexton said, "I wait for two phone calls each week that are really important to me. One is from my mother. The other is from Tom. We go through the basics. We talk about the one thing I'm trying to improve on, and we rehash that quite a bit. And then Tom will pick up a phrase or two that could be better and I incorporate that into the next week's broadcast."

Robinson also remains in the loop every other week, receiving feedback on word efficiency, telling the listener why certain plays worked or didn't work, and repeating of phrases.

Renowned and versatile radio and TV announcer John Rooney will never forget a tape-playback experience early in his career that helped vault him to the top. He had broadcast a University of Missouri basketball game and didn't like it. "At three in the morning I went in [to KMOX in St. Louis] and listened to my tape and made some corrections. Nobody had to tell me, I just did it because I didn't like what I heard. So I became a better reporter. I was more descriptive, I had the score more frequently, and I had better life to my broadcasts [thereafter]. That really helped me land the CBS job."

Each announcer who habitually listens to and/or views his own work has a check list of things to determine. Following are several examples:

• Wayne Larrivee of the Packers has a check list that includes:

"…Down, distance, who carried the ball, who made the tackle, give the score often, and phrasing. I don't want to repeat a phrase too often. Then I make sure I painted the word picture for the listener."

• Mitch Holthus of the Kansas City Chiefs listens for the same basics, and for giving his color commentator, Len Dawson, enough air time. "I figure that fans dial in to hear their Hall of Fame quarterback," Holthus says. "I want to talk about 30-35 percent of the time, and Lenny about 60-65 percent. And the most important piece of the puzzle is getting the others on the broadcast—Bill Grigsby [score updates] and Bob Gretz [sideline reporter]—enough air time, also."

• Jim Nantz of CBS says, "The first thing I listen for is whether I had enough energy. I might have thought I did, but on the tape I might hear that I was flat. Then I listen for whether I set up Billy [Packer] well. Did I present the story line of the game? Did I talk too much? Sometimes we are all guilty of this. Nobody will ever be critical of you for not talking enough, but they will get on your case for talking too much. I make sure I'm giving pertinent facts. Did my comments match the pictures? Did I repeat a phrase too often? And finally, I check to be sure that I have given the score enough."

He gives a great example of an important result of his self-critique, germane to television: "Thousands of people who are visually impaired write to me and compliment me on giving the score often. Normal viewers can see the score on the screen. We take that for granted."

Here are a few more literal check lists used by prominent announcers:

Kevin Harlan:
1. Down and distance, ball carrier, tackle . . . the nuts and bolts.
2. Score every two minutes, and a recap of highlights every 5-10 minutes.
3. Did I repeat a phrase too frequently? Eliminate cliches and overused terms.
4. Did I get the correct story line and tell what was happening—a true picture?
5. My main complaint is when announcers are lazy and not descriptive enough. I want to know if the quarterback took a three- or five-step drop, if the pass was a spiral or had a flutter on it, that the receiver made a diving catch over his left shoulder at the 38-yard line.
6. If I get into a slump I don't listen for one game. You can be too critical of yourself.

Larry Morgan:
1. Did I know the players? Essential early in the game.
2. Did I give the score enough? TV has graphics, but people are constantly dialing in.
3. Did I talk too much? Recognize the difference between TV—a director's game—and radio. In TV, less is more.

4. Was I fair? Sometimes the coaching staff thinks I'm too fair. I don't want to be a homer. The other team is half of the story, too.
5. Did I work well with my color man? Emphasis on conversational. On instant replays I want to get out in time for the color man to do his job.

Tips for listening to radio football tapes:

I have worked more than 2,000 football games, from Chiefs to Kansas and Nebraska to the Cotton Bowl and Super Bowl. I listen to my tapes twice—once right after the game at 10:30 p.m. for an hour, and the next day for another hour to get a proper perspective. In football, here is what I look for:

1. Down, distance, ball carrier, tackle. The fans always wants this.
2. Giving the score frequently. You can never give it too often. Every 1-2 minutes is a good habit. I look to give it different ways—the lead is 14 with 3:14 to go in the third quarter, the score is 30-21 with 5:34 left in the game, etc.
3. Repeated phrases. Watch for "that time" and "now."
4. Talking too fast. If, like Lamar Hunt once said, I'm talking 135 words a minute with gusts up to 185, then I force myself to slow down.
5. Yelling and screaming. I did this early in my career. My first boss at KANU (Lawrence, Kansas), Ed Browne, said he would hire me next time around if I'd stop screaming. I did, and he did.
6. Good description, telling what is happening with an accurate picture. Be a reporter, not a cheerleader.
7. Correct calls on officials' calls. I study the rule and case books. I attend officiating clinics. I used to referee basketball five years.

Tips for listening to basketball tapes:

1. Did I know the players? I can tell in the first three minutes if I did enough homework.
2. The score. After every score, obviously, and going to breaks. But give it every minute during lulls in scoring.
3. Did I vary "good" and "no good" on baskets scored? I have at least 25 different ways of saying the shot was good.
4. Locate the ball—top of the circle, right and left wing, in the paint, etc.

5. Did I talk too fast? Basketball is up-tempo, and you can't let your tempo match the game sometimes. You can effectively eliminate some passes, but never the key pass or what the team is trying to do.
6. Screaming over the crowd. Especially at high schools, where voices are higher than college. Stay away from the band.
7. Was I a good reporter? Did I tell you what happened in the proper story line? Avoid homerism. Be fair.
8. Criticism of officials. Know the rules to avoid mistakes, especially the difficult goaltending and charging foul.

CHAPTER 3
RADIO PLAY-BY-PLAY

"Radio play-by-play is more challenging and more fun than anything in this business." - Mike Patrick, ESPN

Radio or TV? You can debate until doomsday which is more this, less that. The next chapter will cover the TV scene. Many sportscasters who have experienced both love radio. Patrick elaborates, "Painting the picture and describing everything is the greatest challenge in broadcasting. As a kid if I stood on my head in the corner of my room I could get KMOX in St. Louis, and Harry Caray was the best baseball announcer I ever heard. Somebody once wrote, 'He could make a chess match sound like World War II.' I love radio."

Kevin Harlan, whose career has spanned all of the air waves—audio and video—says, "I've found that the theater of the mind, the images that a broadcaster creates through description, is much more powerful than anything else. In radio you have to have description, energy, and you have to convey the emotion, especially during a local broadcast. You need a voice that conveys all these things in addition to being a good reporter and working in your analysis."

Another two-way announcer at ESPN, Bob Carpenter, avows, "I find radio much more refreshing. You have to provide more description. I find I'm always fresh when I come back from radio to TV."

And John Rooney, who works both for CBS Sports and Westwood One on top of his duty as Chicago White Sox play-by-play announcer, says, "The essence of radio is to do a good job technically and paint a picture for the listener."

Given the high amount of radio/TV crossover in the industry—such as Harlan and Rooney, Jon Miller and Joe Buck—you need to absorb the root values of broadcasting, applicable across the board.

Keith Jackson, the granddaddy of college football TV announcers, although admittedly loving what the tube provides for the fan, states, "I would encourage anybody, anywhere, any time, any color, any sex, anything, to do radio first."

Jackson elaborates: "You understand the value of the word so much more if you come out of radio. It helps enormously. First, you learn to write for a broadcast, so you eliminate a lot of words. As a result, when you transfer to television you eliminate words and become much more effective at putting a caption to a picture."

Regardless of which medium strikes your fancy most, the basics that underlie each are the same. And it starts with the score of the game.

"Everybody wants to know the score. They get mad when they don't get the score. Give them the score." - Jack Buck, Hall of Fame broadcaster

As we delve into the intricacies of providing radio play-by-play description of the three major sports, football, basketball, baseball, a recurring theme is to give the score...down and distance...position of the ball ...instant player identification...ball-strike count...vital statistics...recap—the nuts and bolts.

The same holds true in TV play-by-play. Keeping the listener up to the minute on the way the game has developed is paramount to a good broadcast. If you did nothing else, you would be good. Anything less is maddening.

Another Hall of Fame announcer, Pat Summerall, observes, "I am often conscious when someone walks into a room or the lounge at the airport, and the first thing out of their mouth is, 'What's the score?' You can't give it too much. Even with [TV] graphics, they want to hear you give the score."

The story of pioneering radio sportscaster Red Barber and his egg timer is the stuff of legends. He bought a three-minute egg timer, and when the timer went off he gave the score, regardless of whatever else was going on. Cawood Ledford told us, "When I started doing minor league baseball I'd heard that Red Barber used an egg timer. I figured if that was good enough for him, it was good enough for me."

Announcers use a variety of reminders, or they develop the habit. Vin Scully said, "I tried the egg timer. I'd give the score, turn the timer, and then get involved in the game. When I looked down the timer had elapsed—when, I don't know. So I just remind myself to give the score."

Tony Roberts adds an unusual twist to the theme: He broadcasts The Fighting Irish on the Westwood One network of more than 300 stations. So he not only gives the Notre Dame score with great frequency, but he also keeps listeners informed regularly of other scores involving top-ranked and big-name schools.

Whatever else you provide is whipped cream topping. You must, first and foremost and constantly, place the listener in a seat at the game. You are his eyes. Your words must paint the picture for him to see clearly. If he doesn't know where the ball is, and who has it, and what the player is doing with it, then the listener is lost. He might as well be wandering around outside looking for a concession stand, wondering what all that crowd noise is about.

Youthful Joe Buck puts it succinctly: "I relate what I am seeing in front of me."

A given listener might have just tuned in, or tuned in and out periodically—so give the score, give it again, and again, and again ….

Kevin Harlan, experienced at pro basketball and football and all college sports, says, "You cannot give the score enough. If I gave it three times during a series of plays in football, I didn't think it was too much. If you feel like you're giving it too much, then you're probably giving it the right amount. Because it's amazing how many people are listening casually, and they might not hear it the first four times, but the fifth time they'll hear it and you've covered yourself."

Other aspects of radio play-by-play that our experts cover include:

Credibility and homerism

Larry Zimmer of KOA and formerly of the Denver Broncos says, "You can't fool people out there. You have to be honest and be informed, and if you don't know something, then let them know. If you're honest about things, you'll build credibility. You can still find the positive side in a lot of things."

Another trap to avoid is that of becoming a "homer," a sportscaster biased in favor of the home team.

Milo Hamilton of the Houston Astros puts it simply: "You let it be known you want the home team to win. But a homer never tells you when the home team is bad, nor ever gives the other team credit."

Criticizing players, umpires, and referees

Gary Bender, a versatile announcer of several sports on radio and TV, says that he falls back on the human quality of people, and it has brought him criticism for not being critical enough of his subjects (especially by *USA Today* radio-TV critic Rudy Martzke). "We are all victims of our heritage," Bender respondes, "My dad was a coach, and my mother was a school teacher. I was taught not to be critical of coaches and teachers. By nature I am an optimistic person, and it isn't my nature to be critical. I like what I do and I honestly like coaches and players. Because of my background I cannot and should not be overly critical of them."

Lee Hamilton, who broadcasts the Seattle Seahawks, tries to strike a balance. "I realize that 99 percent of the people listening are Seahawks fans," he says. "But I'm not a homer. I call a big play with the same excitement, whether it's a Seahawks guy going 88 yards or the other team. I am complimentary to both sides. Or, if a guy makes a cheap shot and gets a penalty, I call it regardless of what helmet he's wearing." Also a talk-show host known as "Hacksaw" who is called on for pointed commentary, Hamilton reiterates, "I'm not a homer, but I am opinionated. I just report the game."

Style and pace, according to the sport

Versatile Kevin Harlan says, "Play-by-play in basketball is all rhythm. Football is more of a march." And baseball old-timer Curt Gowdy reminds us, "Baseball is a casual conversation with your friends sitting on a couch for 3 hours."

Relevant statistics

Ernie Harwell, Hall of Famer, says, "I talk to folks without using a lot of stats. Most announcers use a lot of statistics because they don't know what else to talk about."

Wayne Larrivee handles pro and college football, college basketball, and baseball. He says, "We all have a tendency to rely too much on statistics. You have to understand that people (tuned in) are relaxing, not taking notes on the edge of their seats. Keep it simple because many fans are not hard-core. Try to take numbers that support action that we'll see on the field."

Working with a color commentator

Kevin Harlan, who moved from the radio booth of the Kansas City Chiefs to the television booth with Fox Network, points out some differences. "In

radio it's more of a 55-45 percent relationship, with the color guy more domi-
nant. On radio you have to be much more the reporter than on television—
down, distance, location, and all that description—and get in and out quickly.
That leaves a lot of room for the color."

Recapping

Mitch Holthus, who replaced Harlan with the Chiefs, says, "Try to recap
at least every 10-15 minutes for later-tuners to the game." Larrivee takes notes,
and then every 10-15 minutes coming out of a break, he recaps the game. This
habit holds firmly in mind that listeners join and leave the broadcast constantly
in short-term intervals.

Varying the vocabulary

Connie Alexander, long-time voice of the Southwest Conference, prided
himself on writing down 180-200 expressions that he wanted to use in his
broadcasts. He would post them on a wall and cross them off as he used them,
and then recycle.

Virtually everybody we talked to said, a) vary the call but, b) avoid cliches.
In basketball, for example, get away from calling shots good or no-good every
time, yet keep from overworking cliches like "string music" or "nothing but net."

Knowing the rules

Lee Hamilton of the San Diego Chargers talks about a seminar that the
NFL puts on for announcers in the preseason to familiarize them with rules
changes. "They will explain the changes while showing video of some examples. For instance, they changed a rule one year about contact with a wide
receiver at the line of scrimmage. They showed us 4-5 video clips of what was
an illegal chuck and what was a legal chuck."

So, sport by sport, let's break it down. Recapping: The score, down and distance, player identification, describing the action, working the color commentator into an analysis, knowing the rules, dealing with homerism—all of which
add up to wearability and credibility. In each of the three major sports, we'll
examine the component parts and feature a one-on-one with prominent broadcasters.

FOOTBALL PLAY-BY-PLAY ON RADIO

> *"Football is the most demanding. By the end of a football*
> *broadcast I am physically and mentally drained."*
> —*Bill King, voice of the Oakland Raiders*

Bill King

King is one of the most well-rounded broadcasters out there. At one time he was the only person calling all three major professional sports—Raiders, Oakland A's, and Golden State Warriors—so his judgment holds weight. Others substantiated what he means—that football, with its six days of prep leading up to the weekly game, lends itself to researching exhaustive background on a single event. Basketball, baseball, and hockey move on quickly to the next in a long string of games.

Additionally, the game itself taxes the broadcaster more because of sheer volume. King pointed out, "The game is played by 22 people at the same time, and you have 90 or more people to keep track of. Any given play can suddenly expand to a great area of the field, and so much goes on in any given area. So you are dealing with distance, dealing with deception, dealing with such a great number of people—players, coaches, referees. My senses were almost totally exhausted by the time the game ended."

Adding to King's exhaustion, aside from the game itself, is his prep time, which, he says, "…is going on *all* the time." He works 2-3 weeks ahead on football games. "On a skeletal basis, that is. It's a matter of getting into my files. I have a file on each team, filled with notes. All the while, I work the names and numbers into memorization."

Mitch Holthus concurs with Bill King's assessment of the added challenges of calling football. "It has a pattern, but because it's not continuous action, the pattern leaves a lot of fill time. You have to know up to 106 players for an NFL game, 90 of whom will be active for that game, plus the game takes $3\frac{1}{2}$ hours. There's so much to talk about, and much time to talk about it." Plus, he has to juggle four guys, including himself, doing the talking on the Chiefs' multifaceted production.

Even with a multitude of topics, three *cannot* be overlooked under any conditions—*must* be not remembered, but must be habitual. As habitual as eating and sleeping: Score, down, and distance. Wayne Larrivee of the Packers and

Big 10 football force-feeds the habit. "I organize the most important information I give, starting with score and down and distance," he says. "I follow a list. Score, and then set the down and yardage to go, where they are, and then the formation. If there's time before the snap, I talk about who's lined up where. Then I describe the play. If it's less than 10 yards I'll say how much yardage they got, and who made the first hit. The final thing to mention is the down and distance coming up.

"We work with a three-man booth; so there is even more pressure on me to get the down and distance and ball location out more quickly than most."

"The minute I have the ball on the ground and the tackle is reported,
I shut up...Len Dawson is the star of the broadcast."
—Mitch Holthus, Kansas City Chiefs

Mitch Holthus
Holthus cut his teeth for nine years on Kansas State Wildcats sports before ascending to the booth at Arrowhead Stadium for the Chiefs. He said a mouthful in the foregoing sentence—about the nuts and bolts, and especially about using the color commentator. Former Chiefs quarterback and Hall of Famer Len Dawson, also is a television personality on Kansas City's KCTV and on HBO's "Inside the NFL."

"I will comment about 30-35 percent, and Len Dawson will talk about 60 percent," Holthus says. "The other 5-10 percent goes to booth-mate Bill Grigsby for quick-bite features, such as other NFL scores, and sideline reporter Bob Gretz.

"Football follows a distinct pattern. It's quick action, huddle, more quick action, another huddle. You have to follow that rhythm and get everything said between the huddle and the action. I know when to [let] Dawson lend his expertise."

As with everybody else who contributed to this book, Holthus emphasizes giving the score. "If you don't get disciplined to give the score and time on the clock every other play, you'll get caught going several plays without them. There's nothing more irritating to a listener than turning on the radio and going 20 minutes without hearing the score and time."

Holthus props small cards in front of him in the booth that bear the large words, "Time" and "Score."

Other Holthus insights:

• He is a stickler for preparation that gives an additional punch to the story lines of the game. An excellent example is a backgrounder on Chiefs running back Marcus Allen in which Holthus revealed, "He sat on 99 touchdowns in his career for several weeks because he went to coach Marty Schottenheimer and…. 'Listen, use me as a decoy. They know I have 99 touchdowns. Everybody in this stadium knows it. Fake it to me, they'll all tackle me, and then hit the tight end or [Steve] Bono runs it in.' Bono had five bootleg touchdown runs—a career record for the Chiefs. Allen's unselfishness was invaluable."

• Holthus likes to give listeners "inside" information about key people. For example, "Marty Schottenheimer is a general. The key in the NFL is to motivate players. Marty is terrific, and one through 53 on that team, from Derrick Thomas all the way down through the list, they'll tell you they'd follow that guy right to the gates of hell."

On creating the spotting board:
• Using an elaborate color-coded spotting board, he insists on it being "very user friendly." He starts by color-coding the teams: bright numbers of blue and silver on a Detroit Lions board opposite the red and gold of the Chiefs. "I place the teams as if you were looking down on top of the field at them in formation—the offensive line, the quarterback, and the wide receivers where they will line up and the running backs where they will line up."

He then follows with:

• Name next to the player's number in large, bold print.
• Pertinent information, such as school, years in the NFL, height, weight, draft round or free agent, hometown, etc.
• Write in information gathered throughout the week, color-coded. Purple is current season info. Red is career info. Green is NFL leader in stats, season, or career.

While Mitch Holthus prepares an elaborate spotting board, Bob Starr worked strictly off of a speed card when he broadcast the New England

Patriots—the quick-look roster and lineup sheet that the home team hands out in the press box before games. He didn't like the clutter.

On using statistics:
A keeper of statistics also contributes to Holthus's broadcasts, relaying information on 5 x 7 index cards for immediate use. Holthus says, "I meet with the statistics person about trends we will focus on during a game. For example, let me know immediately when Marcus Allen has 100 yards rushing, because when he does he'll be the oldest player in the history of the NFL to get 100 yards. I have to get that card in a split second so I can relay that information quickly on the air.

"On long plays, I need to know within a second or two that it was a 45-yard pass play, or a 39-yard punt with 17-yard return. Put it in my face. Give me pertinent information, like how a team has fared on third-down plays," says Holthus.

"Or, I will ask on demand for Grbac's passing stats, or Jim Kelly's, or Thurman Thomas's average running the ball. I will have information on my board that Thomas over the last four weeks had his average drop 50 percent running the ball, and how does that relate to today?"

On the pre-game routine:
• Holthus meets with the head coach, Schottenheimer, before taping his pre-game show. "I want to get into his head," Holthus says. "I have prepared pertinent information, but I have no predetermined notion of how the interview will go."

"We make a mistake trying to let people think, 'hey, I'm so smart because I've done all this research.' They want to hear what Marty has to say. Sometimes I'll hand him a list of questions. I'm trying to get how he views the game, not how I view it or to let people know how smart I am. I need to get into the brain of Marty Schottenheimer."

"Avoid the yes-no question, keep the questions open-ended."

Holthus's routine on game day:

1. "Arrive early. Go down to the field to get a feel and game conditions. Sometimes in the booth you get an antiseptic feeling. The wind can be

different up where we are. How cold or warm is it down on the field? I spend 15-20 minutes down there."

2. "Meet with my spotters, go over my charts, point out important things to look for. I go over the formations and point out that although they see one-back on my chart, the Lions have shown some zero-backs the last couple of weeks, so watch for Sanders in zero backs. Or, the Lions might put in a wide receiver, No. 84, who hasn't played in two weeks, but don't be shocked if he's in, and let me know immediately."

3. "Meet with the stats person and go over pertinent information. For example, the first game [of 1997] we'll follow Grbac [new Chiefs QB], his pattern. Bono was streaky—six completions in a row, and then six incompletions in a row—so how does Grbac's pattern compare? Give me that early in the game, he's three out of four, and then give it to me quarter by quarter."

4. "Spend some time with the public relations person from both teams, because they announce inactive players. Just 43 of the 55 players on a roster can be active for any one game. Eight players will be declared inactive before the game, and I need to update last-minute information. I'll mark them off my chart."

5. "Then I'll spend one more time period on memorization review. I'll take my spotter, or someone I know, and it's like a flash card review. They give me numbers, I give the names. They give me names, I give their numbers."

On the basics:

"I set up every play with down and distance, ball location, formation—because the NFL is very sophisticated and very few teams run the same formations in two successive plays—and situational substitutions."

Example: "The Detroit Lions are third-and-three at their own 42, 4:24 left in the first quarter, no score. The Chiefs are in their nickel package. With third and short they have five defensive backs on the field. They've taken Tracy Simien off and put Reggie Tongue on the field."

Samples of Mitch Holthus calls of Chiefs football:

"Just under way here at Arrowhead Stadium, Kansas City out of a split-back formation, first and 10 at its own 20-yard line. The fullback is Kimble Anders, lined up to the left side, while Marcus Allen lines up to the right side. Dive off the right tackle to Marcus Allen, and he dodges his way up inside to the 23-yard line. Three yard gain."

"Second down and seven for the Chiefs. Kansas City lines up in an I-formation. Marcus Allen goes into motion to the left. Three wide-receiver look here. Three-step, drop-back by Elvis Grbac, swings it into the right flat to Anders. He puts on a juke move and fights his way up just across the 30-yard line. Looks like it's going to be a Kansas City first down. Anders, last year, second leading receiver in the NFL among all running backs, second only to Larry Centers of the Arizona Cardinals."

"First down for Kansas City at its own 31-yard line, 13:22 remaining in the first quarter. This is Kansas City's first drive of the game after holding Indianapolis three-and-out on the Colts' first possession. Kansas City once again in split-backs. Now they shift to a quick I-formation. Tight end with a wing set to the right side. The wing goes in motion. Grbac wheels, and on first down it's a draw play to Anders right up the middle. Great block by Tim Grunhard, Anders scoots to his left and gains six yards up to his own 37-yard line where Kansas City will have second-and-short."

"In football it is a common mistake not to give the score and time enough. On radio, we see the game the whole three hours, but most of our listeners—I'd say 80 percent— come in and out of the game from the grocery store, from church, from a kid's soccer game, jumping in the car. They immediately want to know the score and the time of game."

Although Bill King works similarly to Holthus from exhaustive notes, he never overlooks the most basic tenet of his job. "I used to hear when I filled up at the gas station, 'Hey, I enjoyed the game last night, but, geez, you didn't give the score for five minutes and it drove me nuts.' I don't have a system. You have to constantly remind yourself to give it again, even if you think you're being repetitious."

Larry Zimmer formerly of the Denver Broncos comments, "You can't give the score and the time too much. My producer has a little card, and he'll show it to me if he thinks I'm not giving the score enough."

Wayne Larrivee

Wayne Larrivee has been radio voice of the Chicago Bears since 1985, and before that he called the Kansas City Chiefs for seven seasons. Larrivee's insights into handling football play-by-play on all levels make him the featured guest resource for this section, one-on-one.

Starting at the heart of the matter, Larrivee admitted, "I don't give the score enough. I'll do real well for a while, and then all of a sudden when the action heats up I'm not giving it at all unless we're breaking for a commercial. Fortunately, we have a lot of commercial spots. So I wind up giving the score quite a bit because I always give it going to a break. If I am not giving the score enough, my spotter points to his watch to remind me."

On preparation:

During game week he starts Monday by putting rosters on his spotter's board. He peruses the opponent's media guide and any source for notes to background the team. "I spend most of the time working on the other team, because I see and live the Bears every day, week in and week out, and absorb what they are doing."

On spotting:

Larrivee has a spotter seated behind him. But he relies on him mostly as backup. "I memorize everybody on both teams and do most spotting myself. If I see a number I know right away who it is. The spotter behind me might give me an extra tackler or two that I didn't see because I had to follow the ball." Mistakes usually occur, he said, because a jersey gets pulled and he can't see the number. "I use the spotter's board mostly as a study tool. In preparing it I memorize not only name and number, but information on the players as well. I hardly use any of the information, it seems, during the game...I don't necessarily look down on my charts to pull a note."

On sources for preparation:

Larrivee starts viewing tape of the opponent's games Monday night or Tuesday morning, and continues throughout the week, watching them two or three times.

A primary source is the advance scout. Larrivee follows a ritual every Wednesday of traveling to Bears camp in nearby Lake Forest, Ill., to visit with several sources. But the main one is the advance scout. "I sit down with him and go over the opponent's whole roster."

He relies very little on information from the public relations office. "Their booklets and clippings are useful, but otherwise they offer very little of substance you can use. The NFL used to be the best in sports for PR, but it is far from that now…the NBA has surpassed it by far."

Observing team practices can be helpful, but the Bears close their practices. The coaches permit Larrivee to observer from afar, through an upstairs window in a nearby building. "It helps during a year like the Bears had ['97] with several new players on the roster. It helped to an extent, but wasn't crucial. It helps in terms of anticipating something that might come up in a game, so that you are not totally surprised when you see a particular play call on Sunday."

Training camp is more important than daily practice. "I get most of my preparation handled there. You have an opportunity to meet the players, and they see you around. Travel and practice schedules during the season limit the exposure to players."

Hence, Larrivee's habit of visiting Lake Forest once a week. Along with the session with the advance scout, he hangs around the dressing room during lunch hour. "You'll see a player here and there, a coach or two, and maybe pick up a line or two from somebody that you can use during the broadcast."

The final piece to Larrivee's weekly preparation is a visit to the playing field before kickoff. "I visit with the offensive and defensive coordinators to get an idea of their last-minute thinking about what might come up. Occasionally they will say they are going to try this or that. They get comfortable enough with you to tell you something and know you are not going to go on the air and use it until and unless the play occurs."

On setting up the play:

Simple formula: Down and yardage to set up the play. "The yard line is the main thing. I set the formation if I have time, and who is where in it. Like, maybe Robert Brooks is to the right and Antonio Freeman to the left, and Dorsey Levens behind William Henderson in an I-formation, and go from there." How much information goes out depends on how much time the color commentators leave and how quickly the snap takes place.

On reporting the play:

"I focus on the ball, which somewhat limits the sight line." Larrivee believes in following the ball to be certain that a handoff takes place, or to determine whether the quarterback keeps it on a play-action fake. "With that kind of concentration on the ball, I don't see the rest of the field as well as a fan who can focus in on a wide receiver or offensive line. I describe exactly what I see happening."

On the importance of memorizing numbers:

"You absolutely must know the numbers, and see the numbers." Larrivee pointed out that viewing conditions at different facilities impact on that capability, especially at high schools and some colleges, even a few pro parks. "RFK Stadium in Washington, D.C., was the worst, and the press box is a long way from the field in Tampa. I always feel like I am half a beat behind the action in Tampa because we are so high that the satellite signal doesn't get to our booth quickly enough.[Tampa Bay moved to a new stadium in 1998.]"
In that situation Larrivee uses high-powered binoculars. "This helps me zero in on the numbers." Passes can create a problem, though, because through the narrow field of vision of field glasses, sometimes the view is distorted so that the commentor can't tell left from right. "In good locations, when the quarterback drops back to throw off of play action I'll drop the glasses and call the play from what I see [with the naked eye]."

On phrasing a call:

"I just react to what I see. I don't think about turning a phrase anymore. Also, some guys sound like they are shouting. That isn't bad as long as the listener understands what is happening on the field. I get enthused about the play whether the Bears are making it or the Green Bay Packers are making it."

On the three-man booth:

Radio is not analyst-driven like TV, so Larrivee insists that his two partners complete a comment by the time the team reaches the line of scrimmage. "The two color people have to work together on that, and they generally have to give more than I do because I have a basic framework to cover in describing a play. In TV, they can talk right over a play and it's not a big deal. In radio, I have to stick to the framework."

He said a color analyst gets frustrated sometimes because of unfinished thoughts, especially when there is more than one analyst. For example, one might want to amplify on the other's point, or counter it. "They have to hold it sometimes, and often that moment is gone, and so is the comment. The three-man booth is more frustrating for the analysts than for the play-by-play."

Example: Jim Irwin headed the Green Bay Packers broadcasts for 30 years with two color analysts, Max McGee and Larry McCarren. He devised a system of tapping the knee as a cue to the one he wanted to talk, and then he would look at that person. "That worked until we found a rhythm," Irwin said. "Eventually, we learned when one is going to speak and anticipated the comments of the other."

Lee "Hacksaw" Hamilton works a three-in-the-booth system for the Seattle Seahawks. "Most places it doesn't work. We are fortunate. I paint the picture. My color guys comment on the picture I just painted. The relationship is short and concise. One comments to the point, the other jumps in and jumps out, and I get back on when the offensive team comes to the line of scrimmage. Occasionally, during delays for measurements or injuries, we can have an extended conversation to talk about specific issues. Normally, it's on the yardage and play, and they add color to the picture."

Wayne Larrivee worked the Bears with a former defensive lineman, Dan Hampton, and former all-pro linebacker, Dick Butkus. More recently his partners were Tom Thayer and Hub Arkush . "The pressure really falls more on them," Larrivee said. "In radio, you're bound to the down and distance stuff. The color commentators have to analyze between all of that, and I like them to be done before the team breaks the huddle. So communication among us is vital; I let them know exactly what I want."

On being the eyes and ears of the listener:

According to Larrivee, the object is to constantly locate the yard line, determine the direction a play flows, and constantly update the down and distance, line of scrimmage, time and score. "As a listener driving in a car listening to a game, sometimes my attention gets diverted, and when my mind gets back on the game I am wondering where the ball is, what happened. Listener's attention spans are not very long, and many listeners join the game in progress…constant updating and recapping is essential - who is playing well, what trends are, etc."

On pacing:

"You never know what play is going to turn the game, and any play can make a difference, even in the first quarter. But you still have to let the game come to you. Have enthusiasm, yes, but avoid getting out of hand with it early. Make sure you have somewhere to go…another level to jump to in the third and fourth quarters when the game is really on the line."

On knowledge of rules:

Larrivee studies referee's signals. "I do not need to know the technical aspect of a rule like a referee, but I need to know basic information like how many yards for a particular infraction." Even though the umpire announces the call, an announcer should be knowledgeable enough to give the preliminary indication and penalty. Larrivee warns, "Sometimes officials get sloppy in their signals to the press box, hard to read. There is no excuse for not knowing the rules."

On accuracy:

Many fans watch TV and listen to the home radio broadcast. "You are held to a higher standard these days, from media to fans. If you make a mistake, correct it and move on. "

On homerism:

Larrivee gives the Bears players and organization the benefit of any doubt, yet does not gloss over the negative. "In a horrible season there are going to be coaching mistakes in play calls, or players don't perform well—mistakes, turnovers, penalties, play clock winds down and the team has to take a timeout rather than saving it. When those things happen, depending on the market you are in, you have to be credible."

He says that in strong markets like Chicago, Green Bay, and Denver, "you can't fool the fans. They are there for the show, they know what the game is about as students of the game. So you can't cover up bad stuff."

The trick is not to dwell on it. "Pick your words carefully. You can't keep coming back to something and ripping, 'Boy was that stupid.' You say, 'I don't know about that play call, I'm not quite sure what they were looking for.' The phrasing is important. But you can't say everything is going well when it's not, because you lose credibility."

Another approach, when things are really sour, is just to describe and let the listener judge for himself. "You don't have to say every time something is bad. It was third-and-four, and they ran the football on a drive. Obviously they were waving the white flag, but you don't have to tell people that. They know."

In terms of criticizing management and personnel decisions, Larrivee points out that "you don't have to agree or like it, but these are football people whose lives and jobs are on the line, so it's important to go to them and understand why they made their decisions."

He says that you probably will not use everything you know on the air, but having an understanding and perspective from the inside prevents you from saying something totally wrong about where the club stands on an issue or player.

On vocabulary:

Larrivee writes several terms on a manila folder and attempts to refer to each once a week. He starts collecting them in midsummer for the following season. "It helps describe a tackle or play in different ways instead of describing a pass the same way five or six or eight times during a game."

A trick for improvement: Larrivee practices using the terms out loud in a phantom play-by-play, and inserts names of opponents, thus aiding his memorization.

On listening to tapes:

He doesn't review tapes every week, only when he believes he was "off" on his game. He listens for basics: Description of location of the ball, down and distance, terms he uses, time and score. And he critiques his interaction with the color analysts. "The most important are down and yardage, the formation, and who is lined up where."

On importance of appearance:

This is not as critical as TV, but Larrivee believes that a professional air is important even to radio broadcasters. "Dress professionally. No shorts, T-shirts, golf shirts at games, even in warm climate. Training camp is different. A coat and tie are good, but at least nice shirt and slacks, never jeans. The way you dress and look tells people a lot about you as a professional.

On arriving early:

A must. Larrivee remembers getting caught in a traffic jam traveling from the airport to Arrowhead Stadium in Kansas City. Always anticipate possible delays. Early arrival allows time to talk to coaches, scouts, and other possible sources for last-minute information. "Also, you just want to get there and have a little bit of time to relax before your broadcast."

Advice on keys to success in football radio play-by-play:

"Practice. Go somewhere with a tape recorder, analyze your tape over and over. Develop style and pacing through practice, hard work, and study. Continue to work at it, improve, and look for ways to get better. Research the opponent thoroughly. Go to a game fully prepared. And finally, enjoy yourself… have fun, because it is a lot of fun to do."

And, going full circle, back to giving the score:

"Probably one of our biggest crimes is that we don't give the score enough. We have to understand that listeners come and go. I have my spotter and statistician both point at their watch if I have gone a little bit without giving the score, and that is a signal to give the time remaining and the score."

Example: Lee "Hacksaw" Hamilton has a system during football broadcasts of the San Diego Chargers: "I give the score once every series of downs, every change of possession, every timeout, and every other two minutes."

He gives the score at minute markers 13, 11, 9, 7, 5, 3 and 1.

"Be cognizant of it. You have to remember."

BASKETBALL PLAY-BY-PLAY ON RADIO

"The most important thing in radio (basketball) is to tell people where the ball is located." —John Rooney

"That's after giving the score, of course," Rooney added, laughing. Giving the score never stops, one sport to the next. But Rooney summed up well the main task at hand in describing basketball: "Where's the ball? Right of the lane to Pippen…left of the lane to Jordan…baseline right to so-and-so, free-throw line to so-and-so…shoots from 15 feet. Give [the listener] a point of reference."

Kevin Harlan

And for our main points of reference in basketball, we turn one-on-one to Kevin Harlan. He holds especially good insights because of his crossover from TV football to radio basketball—two severely different paces, both in the sport and in the on-air talking.

On the difference between TV and radio broadcasting:

"It takes a great deal of practice and knowledge of your new venue," he said. "Very few people make the jump. It takes a great deal of time. You must listen to people and study your own tapes. Find out your strengths and weaknesses compared to other broadcasters. The adjustment from local to network is difficult. The process is ever-evolving. I cannot stress the difficulty enough. There is no correct answer to the problems; adaptability varies from individual to individual…[but] even the individuals who are above water are always treading water. There is more uncertainty at the network level than you ever find with a local job."

Harlan also distinguishes a major difference between local radio and network television: "On network TV you are covering two teams you are not emotionally tied to. The color guy is the show in the booth. The play-by-play announcer is third, behind the picture and the analyst."

"On radio you have a completely different call—describing the scene and reflecting the excitement of the play," he said, pointing to the immediate difference in the mediums.

On preparation:

"To refresh my mind I look at the team's notes. The difference with the NBA on radio is that the action is ever-ongoing, and the need for a color analyst is the least of your priorities.

"College and high-school basketball is a little different. The action is constant, but not as fast, and more disparity increases the importance of the analyst's job."

In contrast to all the emphasis we placed on preparation in Chapter 2, Harlan points out almost apologeticaly, "Preparation for basketball is important, though not as important as it is for football. Not to make it sound secondary, but really it pretty much is. On radio your number one priority is calling the game. The attention span of your audience is so short that additional notes rarely stick with them. When you give notes or stats they have to be very important in the outcome of the game or the season."

With that philosophy, Harlan does not overload with notes before a basketball game, or at least not in the NBA. "I will pick a couple of things and couple them with a story line that will make sense to my audience," he said.

This theory can be used across the board in all forms of broadcasting. "If you can associate a statistic or note with a story line, it makes far more sense and has far more sticking power than just blurting out a bunch of numbers," Harlan said.

On the most important points in broadcasting a basketball game on radio:
• Number 1, make sure you are at the top of your game in description. Give the score. "That's the one thing every listener listens for. Give it in a natural, in-the-flow delivery. You don't want to sound like you've got this little card that says every 30 seconds you have to give the score. The key on radio is realizing many people are mowing the grass, taking the kids out for ice cream, jogging, not listening on a continual basis, so you have to be the consummate reporter and give the score."
• Continually give the score and a recap of the game. "Going in or out of a break have one sentence recapping action, or one statistic that sums up the game, and the quality of the broadcast will improve greatly."
• Gain some perspective and look at the game in terms of the big picture.
• "All I ever worry about is the call. That is the first and foremost thing on my mind. Painting the picture. From the color of the uniforms to the position of the ball."
• Statistics are secondary. Ask yourself, how can they enhance the call?

The three most important areas to address are: Description, score, and time.

It is important to point out that although Harlan had a strong opinion on the difference between prep work in basketball and other sports he does not take getting ready for the game lightly. In fact, he pointed out that on the pro level of basketball, the pace of action off the court can be about as swift as the game, and you must be prepared. "You must read something every day and stay in contact, even on days off," Harlan said. "So much goes on with transactions, with guys who are hot, and you've got to have those things upstairs, uppermost in your mind. It's an every day process. People who want to get into this business have to know that."

On player identification:
"It's much more difficult in college and high school than the pros because you see the opposing teams only once or twice a year. The best method is to gain access to a video tape of the visiting team. Often these are available in high schools, and almost always in colleges."

"Take notes on the players as you watch the videos. Look for tendencies in their game."

In the NBA the teams play each other so frequently that you can make player identification almost strictly on body type. "That makes it easier to call," Harlan said, "because you can't always see the players' numbers. The more successful you become at identifying certain players by body type instead of a number, the smoother your broadcast will be."

Because of the emphasis that Harlan places on description, we want to focus on his technique explicitly.

For example, does he follow every pass in the call?
"It depends. It isn't important if two back court guys are throwing it around to eat the clock," he says. "You can paraphrase, especially in college. In the NBA, the shot clock is shorter than college, so the action is faster."

How about the call on made and missed shots?
"I go by the credo of saying what you see. It is easy to become cutesy in your description. Be aware of that. Since every play is different, no two calls should be the same. You might have a couple of similar jump shots, but if you give a different description on the location it makes it sound different, distinctive. This should be the least of your concerns, though. What should concern you more is the description leading up to the basket."

Other phraseology:
"Never go in with a plan. If it goes in planned, it will come out sounding planned. Concentrate on the game, on all the things you must do, and know that if a big play comes up you have a bullet in your gun [a catch phrase of de-

scription, such as his well-known, *Oh, baby, what a play!*] and you're ready to shoot it when it's time. But you can't overuse one or two favorite phrases, either, or they lose effect."

On letting a color commentator interject:

"You facilitate the broadcast. You'll develop a rhythm with him, but you make the bridge easier to cross. You can never be too involved with him. Never be afraid to use body language in the booth to communicate."

On the subject of credibility, one of the most critical areas in basketball is officiating. Harlan has a distinct viewpoint on that topic. "Say the head coach is disputing a call, and the crowd is worked up," he said, "in a frenzy over a play that could have gone either way. When you start worrying about referees, I think you have lost some credibility. You are a reporter first and foremost, and you must report what is going on. More times than not, the referee is right. All the calls even out during the course of a season. You have to be diplomatic about things."

He points out that you must remember where you come from, where you work. "On the local level you answer to the president and the general manager of your club," he says. "You have to be very aware of that because you don't want to step into a bad area. The way around that is to report. Get excited when something calls for it, but leave the really tough comments to your color commentator—that's his turf. Just be down the middle, call the play, give the position of the ball, the score, identify the players—it's not that tough."

On spotting boards:

Finally, Harlan has one of the most readable, functional spotting boards in the business. It stands as a good sample among our files of spotting boards:

1. On a piece of paper 12 inches long, allot an inch to each player.
2. Down each side draw a yellow circle for each player, and draw a line down the middle of the paper to separate the teams.
3. In the predominant color of the team, write in names and numbers of each player.
4. Below each name and number write the main statistics of the player and a couple of story lines. Where is he from? How tall is he? Weight is only a factor for extremely large players. Does he lead the team or league in a category?

5. If the player has an interesting off-the-court story line, write it down.
6. On a separate sheet of paper write the story line of the game. Include the teams' overall and conference records. Are they on a hot or cold streak? Jot down team leaders in scoring, rebounding, and assists. Is anyone missing from injury or suspension? How is a new starter filling the void?
7. It is important to keep good notes as the game goes along. Know the story line. Recap often. During commercial breaks, make notes on the perspective of the game.
8. Write everything down so you won't forget anything relevant.

As a post script to the note-taking and preparation, Harlan adds, "Remember that the stuff you come into the game with is only fresh for about the first 10 minutes. After that, rely on what you write down as the game progresses."

Harlan has a different approach to listening to tapes for improvement. He doesn't just listen to his own. "You usually aren't smart enough to know what you're doing right and wrong," he says. "Have someone else listen to you, too, and have on hand a couple of tapes of guy who sound like you want to sound. Put yours in for five minutes, and then theirs for five minutes, and it becomes pretty darn clear what you are lacking."

He wraps up his views of basketball on radio with a perspective on...perspective. "The most important things to know are the names and numbers and a couple of headlines. You've got to know the players, and if you don't you're in trouble. If you can give one sentence going in and out of a break that summarizes the game, gives it perspective, that's part of being a good reporter. You've always got to be sharper on radio because everything happens so quickly. Description is paramount."

BASEBALL PLAY-BY-PLAY ON RADIO

> *"I could spend 5-6 hours getting ready and call a basketball game pretty... 10-15 hours and call a football game... You spend your entire lifetime getting ready to call a baseball game well. And that is no hyperbole."* —Joe Castiglione, Boston Red Sox

Several sportscasters echo Castiglione's sentiments about the buildup to baseball and its unique character among the major sports.

As Ernie Harwell aptly pointed out, "It's a conversation....and you're invited into people's living rooms to share it."

The viewpoints vary on how you lead up to that casual, yet excitement-filled conversation. "A cup of coffee and a couple of good newspapers in the morning isn't a bad start," former Kansas City Royals announcer Fred White says. And not too long after he finishes the java and the sports pages, White is where they all are—all the good ones—at the ballpark, in the dugout, at the batting cage, spending a lifetime getting ready.

Marty Brennaman of the Cincinnati Reds keeps a journal, a book on day-to-day achievements of each individual player. "That way I don't get just the positive stuff you get from the public relations departments, plus I can track trends. I read a lot of newspapers, too, but the really invaluable stuff simply comes by communicating."

The guys who spend a lifetime talking baseball on the air do the same off the air—in the dugout, at the batting cage.

"Baseball is an everyday thing. Read the papers in the morning, "says John Rooney of the Chicago White Sox. "Go to the ballpark early, 2-3 hours before the game. Go down on the field, talk to people. I listen to the former players who are analysts, pick their brains. I talk to the people I know from the other team, broadcasters and beat writers, to see who is hot and who is cold, and try to apply that to the game.

"You have to paint a picture for the audience, so I try to stick closely to the game. The more attention I pay to the field the better the broadcast. But you can't do ball one, ball two all the time. That gets boring."

As Castiglione will discuss in detail in a later chapter, "The key to a good baseball broadcast is what you say between pitches."

Everywhere we turned—and we turned everywhere, to every American League visiting team booth at Kauffman Stadium in Kansas City—the refrain is the same: Give the score often, track the ball, stick to good description, avoid too much homerism even though you work for the club, stay off the umpires' backs, pace yourself through 21/2-3 hours (sometimes more), and prepare for many interludes of conversation between pitches and pitching changes.

For more details on the ins and outs of performing play-by-play of baseball on radio, we take you through the doors of the Baseball Hall of Fame, into the broadcasters' wing, to have your own conversation, of sorts, with five of the all-time greats: Jack Buck, Herb Carneal, Milo Hamilton, Ernie Harwell, and Vin Scully.

Jack Buck, St. Louis Cardinals

"I've been here since 1954 so it doesn't matter if I have a style. I have the job. Having the job is my style. I didn't think I'd last long in St. Louis because Harry Caray was so big. I contrasted my style to Harry's. I backed off and balanced the broadcast. We gave people two different sides. When you're on the air, you'd better weigh your words.

"Other than that, I think my style came from my mother. She was Irish. Her name was Katherine Fox. A Fox married a Deer and they had a Buck. In fact, they had seven of them. She was very good with language skills. Not only can the Irish talk, sometimes they talk too darn much, and frequently they say the wrong thing. But they can talk. I've had the pleasure of attending the Irish Derby several years, and when you meet those people you realize they are the boss of the language. It's fun to listen to them. So I think I inherited that from my mother. My grammar has always been quite good.

"I don't prepare very well or very long. I prepare better for football (he handled Monday Night Football on CBS Radio for many years). With baseball, I could walk in here 30 seconds from the first pitch and be OK, since we have a producer and engineer. But I do several pregame interviews, and that helps me. I also read the newspaper cover-to-cover. Talk, listen, learn. If people trust you, they'll tell you things, knowing you'll make good use of them. Aside from a formal education, nothing is more important than common sense. If you see a player out at 3 o'clock in the morning with a woman other than his wife, and you're not capable of forgetting it, then you shouldn't be in this business.

"I smoked, I'm ashamed to tell you, for 53 years. Don't do that. I finally quit.

"Where's the ball? What's the score? How many on, how many out? What's the score? That'd be a good title for your book."

Herb Carneal, Minnesota Twins (since 1963)

Herb first worked in the minor leagues for the Springfield Cubs three years, went to Philadelphia and worked both the Phillies and Athletics on one station while doing five sportscasts a day on another station—probably a first and only—and then worked with fellow Hall of Famer Ernie Harwell with the Baltimore Orioles before joining the Twins booth.

"I probably got the best advice I ever had from the owner of the Twins back when I started with them, Calvin Griffith. He told me, 'Young man, your job is to tell the fans what is going on the field.'

"I do an hour or two of preparation at home before I leave for the ballpark. I make out a score sheet for the game and read some publications. I have found that if you read something about a ballplayer that you are going to be involved with regularly, you'd better check it out with the player. There often is a big difference between what you read and what actually is. Get to know the guys one on one.

"One of my favorites was Brooks Robinson with the Orioles. When he was 19, a rookie, and everybody knew he was the third baseman of the future, we had a day off in spring training in Scottsdale, Arizona. My wife, Kathy, and I decided to have lunch, and we invited Brooks. He was killing some time. I told him that this place, Meg's Hambun, had great ham sandwiches. He couldn't get over that we were driving a one-year-old Oldsmobile, such a plush car at the time. That's hard to believe today, because he probably has three or four new cars sitting in his driveway.

"I would talk 500-600 times a year about Harmon Killebrew. Eventually you run out of things to say about him. So one time our program director said, 'Maybe you should tell the people that he's right-handed.' I assumed people knew that.

"I think it was far better to tell a human interest story about Harmon, who loved poodles. He gave my daughter, who was 5 at the time, a poodle and she named it Kicky-Boo. We called it Killer. That was a little thing we had some fun with on the air. It's hard to keep talking about the same players for an entire season and come at your audience 162 times.

"Sometimes someone will say, 'Oh, you're a celebrity.' I say I'm a working stiff. I just paint a word picture of a game. The most gratifying thing to me is getting letters from shut-ins who really look forward to hearing a baseball broadcast. Sometimes I ask myself: Why I am doing broadcasts of a kid's game for 40 years. But celebrity? One day a few years ago a man stopped me on my way to the booth and introduced himself, asked a few questions about the ball club that I answered, and when I excused myself he said, 'Sure been nice talking to you. I really enjoy your column in the paper every day.' That takes you down a notch or two.

"I try to be honest and truthful and paint an accurate word picture. I worked with one announcer who really embellished the game. On a routine fly ball, he would have the outfielder going back to the wall. A lot of people bring their transistor radios to the ballpark. They would be wondering what game this guy was watching. He lost his credibility. Once you lose that it's very difficult to get it back.

"I'm not a cheerleader. That's something people want to bag on me about. I'm more upbeat when the Twins win or score a big run. But to be cheerleading I feel I'm insulting the listeners' intelligence. If the listener wants to cheer, let them cheer. They don't need someone else doing it for them.

"I use an egg timer to remind me to give the score, like Red Barber did in the '40s. Listeners don't object if you give the score every minute or two.

"I've covered a lot of last-place teams, and a lot of championship teams. I remember 1982. We lost 102 games, but that team was still exciting because we had Gary Gaetti, Kent Hrbek, Tim Laudner, Randy Bush, Frank Viola—the nucleus of a pretty good rising ball club that added some excitement.

"But the way I always approach the game is, today is another day. Once the game is over I forget it. I can't do anything with it, so I immediately start looking forward to the next game.

Ernie Harwell (Detroit Tigers)

Ernie broadcast the Tigers from 1964-91, and returned to the Tigers on TV after getting fired by new ownership and doing a brief interlude on CBS radio for the playoffs and World Series. The only major-league announcer ever traded for a player, he joined the Brooklyn Dodgers booth in a trade for a catcher who went to the Atlanta Crackers. He has written two books. Now, at the age of 81, Ernie is calling Tigers games on WJR radio—and he never sounded better.

Jon Miller says this about Ernie Harwell: "He is so popular because he is so humble as a broadcaster. He brings you the ball game, paints a great picture. He always said to remember that everyone is not hanging on our every word and not with us through the whole broadcast. Ernie had the humility to know that people tune in and out all the time, and when they tune in during the middle of a game the one thing they need is the score. I figured once every 2-2 1/2 minutes, but Ernie told me one day, 'No, really more like once every minute.' I'm sure fans never thought of it, but Ernie was always updating a listener very quickly after they tuned in. That's why Ernie Harwell has his niche as one of the great baseball broadcasters of all time."

"I still love coming to the ballpark. God has given me good health and I enjoy being around the game. Preparation is still fun and has been pretty much the same my whole career. I do most of my research during the winter, reading newspapers and magazines. I keep a card file on every hitter that I put together during the winter months at home.

"When I get to the ballpark, things are pretty well set up for me. We've got the stats, the averages, all that. So they're pretty much taken for granted. A lot of the stuff I use is taken off the top of my head. It comes from all my years of experience. I just say what comes to my mind. But I do add to my little files on each player.

"I get to the ballpark early and sit around and listen to war stories. If I pick up anything usable, fine. If I don't, that's OK, too. You've got to be a good listener in this business because you're not learning anything if you are talking to yourself. If you sit down and listen a little bit you will learn something you can use.

"I think my style pretty much evolved by itself. My style is one of a reporter. I had a background in newspaper work. That set me up to be a neutral announcer. I'm not what you call a homer. I like to give the other team a lot of credit.

"I'm not excitable. There are times to be exciting. But baseball is a game of peaks and valleys. If you're excited all the time, then when you are really excited it's meaningless. On the other hand you don't want to be dull all the time, either. Because you can't say ball one, strike one all day. My style generally is low-keyed and neutral.

"I like to tell stories…make references to things that happened in the past that might pertain to what's taking place on the field now. I don't use stats unless I absolutely have to. I think they are a burden to people. A lot of announcers use them as crutches because they don't know what to say. And if I don't have anything to say, I don't object to remaining quiet 10-15 seconds and letting the crowd noise come up and letting people rest their ears.

"Everyone does it differently. My style isn't necessarily the best. It's the one that suits me the best, and that's what all young announcers should do—be themselves. When you're on the air as long as a baseball announcer is to talk, you can't be anything but yourself. If you try to be anything but yourself you won't be a success.

"I try to be fair with people and have some integrity and credibility. I don't go off the deep end and make a lot of goofy statements. I try to be realistic and put an optimistic spin on things. You can't be Pollyanna completely, sunshine all the time. You have to tell what really happens. In baseball we're lucky, we don't have to beat a dead horse. Let's say a shortstop makes five errors in a game. I don't have to say he's having a bad night. All I have to say is he's made five errors, the most he's ever made in a game, something like that. The listener knows he's having a bad night.

"That lets us off the hook to some extent. We're not like writers—we don't have to ask why the ball went through his legs.

"I don't use a system like Red Barber's egg timer that he turned over every three minutes as a reminder to give the score. I don't think three minutes is a short enough time. I give the score 2-3 times during every batter because I know that people are getting out of cars, getting out of the bathroom, looking up from a book or magazine, and the first thing they want to know is, 'What's the score?'

"That way they set themselves to listen to the game. If the score is 13-0 and a guy hits a grand slam and makes it 13-4, it's not a big deal. But if the score is 1-1 or the home team is behind 2-1 and their guy hits a bases-loaded homer, it's a lot different. The listener has to set up psychologically, and the only way to help him do that is to give him the score.

"When you listen on radio, everyone knows where left field and third base are, and the announcer tells you that they made a play at third. You can see it in the mind's eye.

"I have a style where I don't have to change when I move between local and network broadcasts. I use the same techniques on a game between the Braves and Twins that I do between the Tigers and Twins. I really don't see much difference. The only difference is in a big game you don't have to work as hard because everyone has read so much about the players. I don't give as much information as usual. I lay it out there even more simply than during the regular season.

Vin Scully (Los Angeles Dodgers)

Vin has broadcast the Dodgers in Brooklyn and Los Angeles since 1950 and has announced a number of World Series on both television and radio.

"I really don't think I'm a wordsmith. I don't think I have any greater ability than the next man or woman. I perhaps have my own particular style, my own imagination, which was the thing Red Barber told me when I first started. He said, 'You bring something into the booth that no one else does.'

"I couldn't imagine what that could be, so I asked him. He said, 'Yourself. There's no one else quite like you. So don't be afraid to listen to other broadcasters.'

"And although I'd be the first to agree that I can learn a great deal by listening to others, I have maintained that as a rule that I don't listen to anyone else. So whatever comes out of the other end of the microphone is me. Good, bad, or indifferent as far as words are concerned, I guess I have always enjoyed using words. I hate numbers and I love to read, and perhaps that combination has helped me, along with the good Lord, who has certainly helped me a tremendous amount.

"Traveling with the Dodgers every day, preparation is osmosis. After a while you get to know almost anything and everything there is to know about the team. Then, because of the computer, this computer age we live in, we are overwhelmed with notes and statistics for every game.

"So the important part of preparation, since you already know one team exceptionally well, is to cut away the fat, the extraneous material, and get down to the nuggets on those (handout) sheets and perhaps use some of those. But if you spend your whole pregame reading all those notes and planning to assimilate and use them, it would be a nightmare.

"I do use the PR person or the PA announcer for the home team to check out pronunciations.

I remember trying to lower my voice, not so much to get a richer sound, but to be less strident. [Scully gets a lot of attention because of his smooth speaking voice and style.] I found that in doing doubleheaders, which we don't do often anymore, if I could get my voice down somewhere in the vicinity of my abdomen, it would last longer in the course of a 7-8 hour day. That's as opposed to speaking from the throat, which will wear out. So it's a conscious effort to keep the voice down for less wear and tear.

"It takes a lot of confidence when you first start in this business, just to be yourself instead of a little bit of Scully, a little bit of Buck, or this or that guy. Don't do that. Just be yourself."

Milo Hamilton (Houston Astros)

Milo was the voice of the Atlanta Braves who called Henry Aaron's historic 715th home run in 1974 that broke Babe Ruth's record. He was approaching his 50th year of announcing baseball when he was interviewed for this book just before his 70th birthday. How does a voice hold out that long?

"I grew up in the Depression in the '30s [in Iowa]. My father made $12 a week, but my mother found a quarter every week for me to have a music lesson. All the PTAs and every little one-room country schoolhouse heard me from the time I was 14 either sing or play the coronet. The good Lord gave me timbre, but the singing lessons helped. When I was in the Navy at the end of World War II I sang in the blue-jacket choir. I went on the air on Armed Forces Network right after my 18th birthday.

"I hear a lot of young announcers misusing their voices…doing things with their vocal cords not meant to be done. They have throat trouble and have polyps taken off their vocal cords. All because they're trying to be somebody they're not. I love Bob Costas, but one Bob Costas is enough. I hear 10 clones out there, which means they're doing something that isn't natural with their voice.

"I listened to Bob Elson growing up, and he was probably the best interviewer of all of us. I hear so many interviews that are planned, and the next question has nothing to do with the last one. They don't play off of anything. You have to be a good listener. I won't say I am the best interviewer, but I'm in the top two because I listen. I have an idea where I'll start an interview, but after that it depends on what the other guy is saying. I don't force anything.

"Recreations in the old days helped you develop a style. [Hamilton, like many, would make up a broadcast while reading results of a game off of a wire, like former President Ronald Reagan also did in Iowa.]

"I prepare a lot, mostly just before the game I'm going to call. Sometimes I'll work ahead a series or two…defense cards and so forth. Then all I need is a starting lineup when I get to the next series. I keep a lot of books and records that the league or Elias [Sports Bureau] or the P-R department don't keep. I get a kick out of saying something, and 15 minutes later they announce it over the PA system. An example, we hit four home runs and I had it right in my book and said that it was the first time that had happened since last year at Chicago. I get a kick out of having that as the ball goes over the fence. It's important, though, if you keep a lot of extra books not to use them unless it fits.

"Some young broadcasters have a 3 x 5 card with 15 items on it they put into the game, no matter what. Like ESPN or Fox, who try to put 10 pounds of feathers in a two-pound bag every game. My books are a library. I don't use it unless it means something to an instance in the game. A lot of stuff I don't use—like who has stolen how many bases off left-handers. But I'll have that a guy scored after seven of 10 stolen bases, so they are quality steals.

"I keep extensive pitching and hitting records. The old announcers generalized—Nellie Fox is really good against this club—and I prefer to pin it down and say he is 10 for 18, something the fan can directly relate to. If you say pretty good, the fan can think that's anything from .300 to .500. If one of our relievers comes in facing a club for the eighth time this year, I can say he has two wins and a loss, two saves, and seven of the eight appearances have been quality, with only one shaky one. That tells me and the fan, hey, this is a pretty good guy to bring into this game. If it only takes you an hour or two to prepare, and you have it and nobody else does, that is a bonus I've created for the listener. I give the score, or an indication of the score, on every hitter. That is, if it's 5-0, you can't keep saying 5-0. A listener is in his workshop, out in the yard, driving home, he might come into the game in the fifth inning. He wants the score when he turns on the ignition. I might not give him the score when he turns it on, but I will say we are in the fifth inning and the Astros lead by five. Now he's got an idea, and next hitter I might say 5-0 again.

"First rule of thumb on credibility is to be honest. When Drayton McLane Jr. bought our club and came to Denver, and we had just stunk up the place at Mile High Stadium for two days, he saw me at breakfast and asked me how I described it. I had to tell him we didn't play very good. He said that is exactly the way I am to do it on the air. Our fans know. That's been my premise all along. If I don't say it, and they read about it, they wonder where the heck Hamilton was. I am not going to be scooped by a beat writer

"If you tell them when the team doesn't play well, an error costs a game, a guy misjudged a fly ball, or a guy isn't pitching well and hasn't for five straight starts, then when things, do go right they'll say, 'He must be doing pretty good, because Milo says he is.' It cuts both ways.

"Here's another rule that lets you stand in good stead: after a game when I recap and say, "The shortstop, Bogar, made an error tonight and it cost us the game," that's the end of it. If he plays shortstop the next game, that is not mentioned. You can't let it build. Every day is a new day. When the national anthem plays, yesterday's game is in the book. You cannot ride a player, or he gets a burr under his saddle.

"I absolutely do not predetermine what I'm going to say. My strong suit has always been spontaneity. Even on the Aaron home run, even though there were similarities—he and Ruth were the same age, they both did it in a Braves uniform—I was determined that *Holy Toledo!* [Hamilton's trademark call] would not be part of that call. It was Aaron's moment, not mine.

"I don't tape myself anymore because I hear myself every night on the highlights, and the next morning I hear it again because I have a morning show. So I've heard everything twice before I do the next game. I recommend it [listening to tapes] for young people starting out. But when you've done it for 50 years you have a pretty good idea.

SUMMARY OF CHAPTER 3

FOOTBALL

1. Learn the players both by numbers and by physical characteristics for immediate recognition.
2. Give down-and-distance and yard line before every snap, and the ball carrier or passer and receiver, and the tackler on every play. If you can pick up a key blocker, that's a bonus.
3. Give the score at least every 1 1/2 minutes, and recap the story line every 10-15 minutes so that the listener dialing in and out will know what has happened when he has just joined the broadcast.
4. Work in advance with your color commentator and define your roles specifically. Determine a system for knowing who will talk when.
5. Describe every play so the listener can visualize explicitly what is happening at the stadium.
6. Check your tapes after the broadcast to be sure you have covered the basics on each play. Determine whether you gave the score enough. Listen for cliches.

BASKETBALL

1. Know the players on both teams by name and number. Learn a characteristic other than the number, too, because the players often will be moving sideways in your view.

2. Describe the action precisely as you tell what is happening. "Vaughn dribbles to his left, stops, puts up an 18-foot jumper from the side of the key, and it's good."

3. Vary the terms "good" and "no good." Examples: "hits it," "net," "that's two." Have 18-25 different ways to describe the same thing.

4. Discuss techniques in advance with the color commentator, working on a routine of when to talk, because basketball affords only brief interludes in the action for comments. Examples: Trips to the foul line offer a decent time to talk, whereas the time following a made field goal does not.

5. Know the rules.

6. Avoid sounding like a homer.

7. Check your tape after the game to be sure you are giving an accurate and entertaining account of the game. You are to be both informative and entertaining at the same time.

8. Check your tape after the game to be sure you did not talk too fast, that you gave the score often enough, and that you are not repeating a certain phrase too often.

BASEBALL

1. Know the players. Arrive at the park 2-3 hours early and chart the pitchers and hitters.

2. Learn as much as possible about both starting pitchers and the bullpens. They are at least 50 percent of the story.

3. Glean information from coaches, managers, and players. Read all you can, and then use only what is pertinent to the story line.

4. Review any game notes that the teams provide, and use only what pertains to the game.

5. Weave the stats, the strategy, and the stories into an informative and entertaining broadcast, maintaining a conversational style.

6. Entertain, because listeners will join you up to 162 times during the year (in the major leagues, less in college and high school), and you are a guest in their home for $2_{1/2}$-$3_{1/2}$ hours a day.

7. Give the score every 1-$1_{1/2}$ minutes, and recap the story line every 15 minutes. People dial in and out all the time. If you don't give them the score, they'll grow angry with you.

8. Get the players' names right. Wrong names will irk the listener, too.
9. Check your tape after the game to be sure you were accurate, you described the action well, and you gave the score often enough.

EXERCISES

1. For a Friday or Saturday football game, go to practice on Monday and obtain rosters of both teams. Make up a spotting board. Watch scrimmages throughout the week, identifying characteristics of players besides their numbers, and talk to the coaches to gain a perspective on the team offensive and defensive formations, and on the opponent. Tape the game. Critique your tape afterward.
2. For a Friday basketball game obtain the rosters and numbers and draw up a spotting board on Monday. Attend practices and pregame drills. Call a scrimmage session out loud, using your spotting board. Tape the game and critique your tape afterward.
3. For a baseball weekend series check with the sports information director (college) or public relations director (pro) and obtain probable lineups and starting pitchers on Monday. Go to the field every day, hang out at the batting cage during pregame, gather information for story lines. Simulate a few innings of game sometime during the week. Tape the game and critique your tape afterward.

NOTE: You can do the play-by-play from a video of a televised event (with sound turned off) if you have a problem attaining access to a game, but realize that you lose some perspective by not being there.

CHAPTER 4
TELEVISION PLAY-BY-PLAY

"Tell me something I can't see. Don't tell me what I can already see."
—Ray Scott

"On TV, shut up and let the picture do the talking." —Harry Kalas

Get the picture? The soul of television sports is simple: shhhhh. Never has the adage about a picture being worth a thousand words been any more applicable.

There is irony in becoming an announcer on TV. They are referred to commonly as TV talking heads. Yet, the art of learning when *NOT* to talk is the hallmark of the best in the trade. Any and all talk on the tube revolves around the pictures on the screen, whether that's a one-on-one interview, a newscast with highlights and scores, a feature, or game action. The choices of venue are many.

The world of sports broadcasting wears a drastically different face than ever before in its history. A face you can see because of TV. Many faces, actually—the faces of the game and the players, but also the faces of those who inform the world about the game and the players.

Network coverage has exploded. In a simpler time, we could tune to ABC, CBS, or NBC for our *Wide World of Sports* or *Game of the Week*. Now, we have FOX, ESPN, and regional cable systems.

What all these sources of news mean to the aspiring student or young professional is a world of opportunity. Cable and satellite dishes that bring some 300 channels into homes mean a job market that is vast. Choices range from play-by-play to sideline or courtside reporting to the traditional anchor and feature reporting tasks, either local or network.

Not all jobs are on camera. Keith Jackson points out, "Television is a director- and color-driven medium." Directors and producers come at a premium, too. More on that in Chapter 12: Getting the Job.

This chapter focuses on the handling of play-by-play and color commentary. And the play-by-play announcer still drives the cast. As Jackson said, "Nothing is worth a damn if you don't have definition. The whole thing has to be blended. Basically, the lead announcer's job is to frame everything and to keep it collective so the viewer can understand it. Don't let the viewer wander off."

At the same time, while there is more and more television sports, you work them with less. That's the credo that all the announcing stars live by on the tube: "Less is more." We'll call it Scott's Law.

Although the late Ray Scott led the radio broadcasts of Minnesota Twins baseball for many years, he made his mark on TV football with the Green Bay Packers, and, later, network telecasts of the NFL. As one of the pioneers of TV play-by-play announcing, he became the main reference point for television sportscasting with his classic descriptions, such as on a touchdown pass play: "Bart Starr...Max McGee...touchdown."

During that sequence, the viewer saw a flurry of action as blockers clashed, receivers ran patterns, Starr dropped back into the pocket and flung the ball to his tight end in the end zone, and heard the crowd reaction in the background. There is a contrast between TV play-by-play broadcast, and radio description that paints a mental picture CBS veteran Jim Nantz says of the craft: "We are supplying captions. Let the telecast breathe, like a nice, red wine."

Nobody let it breathe any easier, sweeter, or more appropriately than Ray Scott. He measured his words concisely and precisely to accommodate the bombardment of visual images flooding into the viewer's living room. His technique, the industry standard, was derived from listening to a friend.

Scott explains, "A high-school football coach once gave me a tip when I was in Pittsburgh. He said, 'Ray, do me a favor. I can see that the quarterback completed the pass. So tell me who caught it, how many yards he gained, and who was trying to cover him. Tell me things you have access to that the average fan doesn't. But, for heaven's sake, don't tell me what I can already see.' That was the best advice I ever received in this business."

Scott's Law is the best advice you'll ever receive in determining your future in handling sports on television. All the sportscasters say it, in one way or another. Gary Bender says: "The less you talk, the better you will be on the air."

Or, more bluntly, says Keith Jackson: "People blabber on television when they don't need to blabber...because they don't understand the value of the proper word at the proper time."

Contrasting radio and TV coverage, Kevin Harlan, with extensive credentials in both worlds, adjudges, "Radio description is much more powerful than sitting there and watching on TV, because you get more involved."

Despite the prevailing perception that TV is more glamorous than radio, some veterans don't think so. Cawood Ledford grew his legend and gathered his legions primarily on radio, both at the University of Kentucky and on network NCAA Final Fours for almost three decades. He dabbled in the world behind the camera. "I never liked doing TV," he says. "Doing TV is like being a public address announcer."

If television is your medium of choice, here, you will delve into the absolutes of play-by-play in the three major sports—football, basketball and baseball—learning from the masters about:

• The nuts-and-bolts (score, down and distance, location of the ball, player identification).
• Working with the color commentator(s) in teams of two, three and sometimes even four.
• Using the monitor in balance with watching the live action
• Knowing the rules.
• Developing a story line.
• Criticizing the referees/umpires, or the home team.
• Style and varying the terms used for description.
• Score sheets and spotting boards.
• Wearability and credibility

In each sport, you will hear from several sources on these topics, plus go one-on-one with a featured announcer: Joe Buck in college football, Pat Summerall in pro football, Bob Carpenter in college basketball, Bob Costas in pro basketball, and Sean McDonough in baseball.

Regardless of the sport, though, some general guidelines prevail. For three of the most important areas of concentration, we turn to Kevin Harlan, Marv Albert, and Keith Jackson before we cut you loose to go sport by sport.

Regarding preparation, Harlan points out how you must step it up a notch for television. "It takes a great deal of practice and knowledge of the venue," he says. "Even in moving from local TV to network, TV the adjustment is difficult. It takes a great deal of time. The process is ever-evolving. Very few people have made the jump. It is a completely different set of circumstances, covering a local team vs. two neutral teams you are not attached to. Even the announcers who are above water are treading water because of the pitfalls of the network job where there is more uncertainty. Listen to people and study your own tapes."

Albert reminds us that in TV, second-most important to not talking too much is working with the analyst: "In TV, it is really the announcer's job to set up the commentator. The color man in TV is much more important than in radio. You must gather a lot of information to be prepared for the telecast, but in the end maybe I'll have used just 20 percent of the information. If you use too much, it's not good. It means you're talking too much."

And you know the sin of that.

A major difference on television, Kevin Harlan says, is that "you develop more of a story line than on radio." He draws a terrific analogy:

"Think of an hourglass. It's very wide at the top, and then it tapers to slender and narrow in the middle, and finally broadens back out at the bottom. Take football. Think of each half an hourglass.

"On top of the hourglass is your headline. As it narrows, you find your secondary headline. As it continues to narrow, you throw darts, talking about players and their impact on the game, making it very specific through the first quarter. As the second quarter begins, the hourglass broadens out again. At halftime, you go back to your original story line.

"This analogy works for basketball and baseball, as well. Think of your game perspective in those terms, and by using this system you provide your audience with a grasp of what's going on. I don't give my audience credit for anything, because I need to reach all of my target audience."

Jackson is the granddaddy of college football on TV, but his remarks on style carry across the entire spectrum of sports. "Remember that in the television business, you are talking to one or two people at a time. You might have 30 million watching, but you don't know that. In most instances, when people turn on their television sets, it's with just one or two watching.

"So, generally speaking, you are talking to one or two people. And, often they will be doing other things during the telecast, so you simply have to keep reminding them of what's going on."

Jon Miller, is a former Orioles radio voice now with the San Francisco Giants. He also handles national network television of baseball games. Miller agrees that although TV is analyst-driven and baseball is conversation-driven, the announcer still must keep the very basic tenets of broadcasting at the fore of the call: "We are telling you what happens. I hear some announcers sit there and not tell you the score, and not talk about what is going on in the game. If you are the announcer, and the game or the play is not important, then you should not be there."

FOOTBALL PLAY-BY-PLAY

Preparation

Although giving the score, down, distance, and immediate player identification are at the heart of strong, descriptive enhancement of what the viewer is seeing, preparation is the soul of the telecast. Preparation includes not only assembling and organizing of material for story lines, but also the planning among the people in the booth and the people in the production control truck.

Unique to television is the power and influence of networks. That is, networks—either national networks owning rights to the league or sporting event, or team-controlled networks—mandate much of what happens when. And television revenue impacts so mightily on colleges, professional teams, and organizations (NCAA, Olympics, etc.) that the teams attend to whatever needs arise for a telecast.

The TV infrastructure opens more doors for preparation with people involved in the sporting event, such as special one-on-one interview time, live shots from locker rooms, wired managers, coaches, or umpires—things that print and radio media normally wouldn't experience.

Marv Albert, NBC football broadcaster outlines his typical preparation for a Sunday game. "We not only talk to the head coach, but also the offensive and defensive coordinators and five or six players the day before a game." (Coaches often make players off limits for interviews with the press after Wednesday or Thursday the week of a game.)

"When I first started, that wasn't the process. Maybe then we would come in on Saturday and talk to the head coach and the public relations director. You could do a game like that, but we find the modern way very helpful in getting a lot of insights. In past years of radio, I would not have had access to all those people. With the network, you're fine."

Television announcers have other possible advantages by the nature of the medium, regardless of the size of the market or on what level.

One is the quick-hit appeal TV has to the player or coach getting interviewed. The subjects know they will need just a quick interlude to give the TV interviewer enough for a clip, whereas a print interview usually usurps more of their time.

Also, "mugging" has become popular, especially in football where the athlete during competition is more covered up and distant. So the on-camera interview, sans helmet, offers the opportunity to get face-to-face with the adoring public.

Public perception might be that you are, indeed, living on easy street. Keith Jackson said, "In our business you are somewhat of a celebrity. People might think you are partying and raising hell, and they would be surprised to learn that on the night before a game you are locked in your hotel room. Most of the week you invest your time in watching tapes and preparing yourself to tell a story as it happens."

Ray Scott, the North Star on our compass point for this chapter, sums up preparation: "I would pay them to *do* the games. They will pay me to *prepare* to do the games."

The Score

Keith Jackson says, "Sometimes we get lax on scores. You have to poke yourself and remember, hey, I haven't given the score for a while. Maybe you don't give it until you go into a commercial. Often it's given so briefly on the screen you don't see it. So, even though we're in a visual medium of graphics, keep people apprised of the most important thing. Giving the score—that is something that all announcers must remind themselves of."

Marv Albert says that the score is the first thing he listens for during an air check, regardless of the sport. "The first things I think of are whether I'm giving the score, and the time remaining in the quarter or game. There is no set system, it's just something triggered in my head. I have always believed in constantly giving the score."

Down and Distance

Also important is placing the ball to supplement what the viewer is watching. Albert suggests doing that every play. "On TV they have the down and distance posted on the screen almost every play, but you still have to give it."

Pat Summerall he points out the unique quality of television that an announcer must always be on the alert to—graphics. The viewer might be seeing "3rd Down, 7 to Go" on the screen while the announcer is saying, "Third and eight." Uh-oh. Not good. Summerall's tip: Be patient.

Working with the Color Commentator

When sports announcers talk about their analysts, they aren't referring to shrinks. But, to a person, they all agree that on TV they must shrink into the backdrop against the sweeping commentary of the color analyst.

The networks load up on "expert" commentators. Former players and coaches dominate the booths. Viewers salivates over the access to these football minds to supplement their armchair quarterbacking—Madden, Maguire, Millen, Mm-m-m-m. The fan can guess right along with not only the coach and quarterback on the field, but the expert in the booth, too.

For that reason, you find Fran Curci and Mike Gottfried and Phil Simms at the mike to enhance the play with explanation and exclamation points. "I don't think you can do color in football if you have not played it," Paul Maguire says. "As a former player I know what they're doing on defense and the keys to their offense. You have to understand the mechanics of the game."

The play-by-play announcer must recognize and accept gracefully the star quality that color commentators bring to the telecast. "The color guy is the show," Harlan says. "The play-by-play man is third behind the picture and the analyst. He has to pick his places. Working with Jerry Glanville, I know that right after the ball is down he will start talking. While he is talking, I set up in my mind what I'm going to say during the down time or instant replay."

The Pat Summerall/John Madden team—*both* former players—is unique, and they never seem to step all over each other, flowing in and out of their running patter with exceptional results. "The regimentation of the past has disappeared," Summerall says of early broadcasting when play-by-play announcers dominated. "If I happen to be talking when the play begins, that's OK with John, and if he happens to be talking when the play begins, that's OK with me. We share much more equally than [duos] did when I first started in the business."

Likewise, Keith Jackson works in seemingly perfect synch with his main sidekick, Bob Griese. "Bob works hard at what he does," Jackson says, "and I think he's the best in the business because he gets to the point so well. He understands TV. He works very hard with the producer and director. They sit down and plan the isolated shots. I just sit there and take it in. Bob participates in setting up the graphics."

Mike Patrick sums up the teamwork in the booth: "One of the main problems in broadcasting is people getting out of their job description. Even though I feel I know football, I do not have the background for someone to sit at home and say, 'Yeah, that was a great point he just made.' It's better coming from the analyst."

"The fan will take what Mike Gottfried or Joe Theismann has to say for gospel, much more than if I said the same thing. Now, if I do know something, I can lead the analyst into it, set him up to make the point—especially if it's something we've discussed before."

Marv Albert reflects, "I've loved the guys I've worked with. NBC matched me with someone who could play off my style and sense of humor—Paul Maguire, Bill Parcells, Phil Simms, Cris Collinsworth. Getting it right involves a sense of feel-it-out, work-it-out. Looking at each other. A nod. A touch. Knowing when to talk is very instinctive. In TV it is my job to set up the commentator. In TV he is much more important than in radio."

"Simms does his homework. He wasn't sure how to prepare when he first started, and then how to use the information at the right time when he was on the air, and do it succinctly. To get in and out and say something that has meaning, something that is not obvious, that's the toughest thing."

At the University of Kansas, Gary Bender became an unofficial tutor for rookie color commentators, helping them feel comfortable as they broke in. "

Bender remembered one such situation vividly, when he helped a new guy named Madden feel at ease. "We were doing a Detroit Lions game when suddenly John's headset mike went out. The assistant producer handed Madden a stick mike. For 10 minutes Madden wasn't emoting or colorful on-air. During a break I decided John couldn't talk without using his hands. So we switched:

I took the stick microphone, and John used the headset mike, and he was back to his normal, colorful, outgoing self once he could wave his hands around."

Using the Monitor

Have you ever watched your TV screen and seen a play develop, and the announcers seem to overlook something that you saw? That's because most often they are watching the action on the field and not the monitor. Sometimes the announcers seem to have multiple sets of eyes.

"I watch both the field and the monitor," Albert says. "I'm always glancing at the monitor, and I'm still learning. It's amazing how much you can pick up that you wouldn't otherwise see. Particularly in football, where often you are a victim of location. You often will see things much better than if you're watching the whole expanse of the field, because of the obvious close-up. Mainly, you are seeing what your audience sees."

"If I want to point something out that is not on the monitor, or if I'm going to talk about a particular play, I use the talk-back button so I can speak to the production truck. I warn them. It works smoothly. We're always setting each other up. There are various vignettes and features when we roll in and after timeouts. It's all rehearsed beforehand. You try not to have many surprises for the guys in the truck."

Harlan is a rarity; he leans to the monitor so he can relate better to his viewer. "I see what the people at home are watching," he said. "I want to relate to that. I don't get blocked out if I happen to have a bad angle or sight line. I watch back-and-forth, monitor to field to monitor, when the color man is making his comments."

Jackson also keeps an eye on both monitor and field. "The TV camera is just one eye," he explains. "The picture you see on the TV set is coming from just one eye. So I don't watch the monitor at first. When the play starts and develops I'm looking at the field. If I don't see something, or if I need some help, I go back to the monitor especially on replays. I watch the defense as much as the offense. Once I see a guy with the ball, then I look at the defense."

Maguire watches the field. "The weak-side guard takes you to every play except two—bootleg, and reverse. It's the only time he goes away from the play. The only time I look at the monitor is when I hear Tommy Roy [director] say, 'Replay.' I then have to tell you what you are seeing. One thing I keep in mind while looking at the replay is that I'm not telling you what you're seeing. I'm going to tell you why you you're seeing what you're seeing."

Wearability and Credibility

Much of an announcer's credibility on TV hinges on how he interprets what the viewer is seeing, not only as it developes on the field but repeatedly on replays, commonly several times from several angles. The instant replay now and again reveals a goof by an official. Often it reveals a botched tackle or block or catch or handoff or any assorted other erratic action by a player or set of players.

How will you call those?

Criticize or can it? Candidly, Jackson forewarns, "If you are honest, it will cost you money. Sooner or late you have to take a chance. Salesmen in the business are management. I'm too blunt and honest. That's hurt me, but that's me. I still have to get up in the morning and look at this player or coach—and they [ad sales reps] don't. I always felt that if you just told the truth and you were fair, you were doing your job."

One of the great color analysts, former player Paul Maguire says, "I would rather say a guy made a great block than a guy got his rear-end knocked off. It's more important that a player made such a great move that he got behind the tackler instead of saying a guy got faked out of his jock strap. It's a lot easier for me to do it that way because I played the game for so long."

The officials underwent wide-open scrutiny for many years with the use of instant replay on controversial plays to determine whether to reverse the call. Fans watching television still benefit from it, and they count on the announcing team to comment whenever such an incident occurs. Some announcers jump the officials, many do not.

Jay Randolph, who called NBC football for 25 years, says, "I never get involved in criticizing officials because it's counterproductive. It doesn't get you anywhere. They're out there doing the best they can. I hate the instant replay. I've always been an advocate of letting players play the game and letting the officials call the game."

"When we put instant replay in the NFL, I was vehemently against it. The human element [of officiating] is part of the game. Sometimes you get beat on a bad call, sometimes you get beat on a good call. I don't get into criticizing players to any great degree, either, except I might say, 'He should've made that play.'"

Wayne Larrivee points out in 1996 that "…officiating has reached an all-time low [quality]. I will point out if an official is being inconsistent, and I also will say what other people believe about his call. Officiating goes through good and bad cycles. You have to be aware of an officiating crew's tendencies, because they are significant in how a team plays. Officials don't win or lose games, players do. If they make a bad call, I simply say it and move on."

Tip: If you choose to be critical of officiating, be certain that you know the rules fundamentally well and have a rule book at your grasp at all times.

The criticism cuts both ways. "You'd better not be thin-skinned in this business," Maguire says. "It's just like the player. I've seen so many players worry about what the press says about them. I feel sorry for them, but they get so caught up in it. Most of the people who report this stuff have never been there anyway."

Nor have the fans. Most criticism leveled at a broadcaster is highly subjective. One man's fancy is another's curse. Same voice, same style, personality—one viewer loves it, another hates it. Often there's no middle ground for an announcer. You simply must take the good graciously, the bad with some grains of salt, and grind on with solid preparation and descriptive, accurate, and entertaining reportage.

Jackson bristles at the mention of those who get paid to evaluate broadcast talent in newspaper columns, such as renowned radio-TV critic Rudy Martzke in *USA Today*. "All these pain-in-the-rear TV critics sit around and second guess us," Jackson said. "There is no one who writes for a newspaper who can tell me how to do a TV show. I don't need to wait until Monday morning to find out if we had a good telecast.

"I feel I know more about it after 45 years in the business than they do. But if you get caught up in that show-biz syndrome, it will drive you nuts. The old-timers don't pay any attention to it."

A final piece of the credibility puzzle is reviewing videotapes of telecasts—yours and others. That is, always strive to improve your work. Basically, you check to make sure you gave the score often, reported down and distance correctly, avoided cliches and redundant phraseology, and called the event with high energy, enthusiasm and entertainment value.

Jay Randolph emphasizes, "Check the basics. What's the score? Where are we in the game? It's also important to distinguish between radio and television—talking too much or too little, depending on the medium. And you've got to recap for people who join you throughout the broadcast."

Kevin Harlan offers some pointers for reviewing TV tapes:

1. Scale yourself way back. Did I let the picture breathe enough?
2. Did I make sense of the pictures and graphics so the viewer could easily understand them?
3. Did I make sure the color commentator was clear to the listener? Did I set him up well enough?
4. Did I keep the audience informed about the significance of a possession, a play, or the game in general?

Harlan comments, "In TV you are developing more of a story to supplement the pictures."

Style

In terms of pure style, Pat Summerall comes immediately to mind when you think of who's silky in the TV booth. He's fluid, easy to listen to, and he sticks to the basics. He says he took it from his mentor, Ray Scott. "Ray was known for his simple delivery," Summerall says. "He never seemed in a hurry. His aim was to take his time and be accurate. I patterned my life style and my announcing style after that credo."

Hot, young talent Joe Buck patterned much of his style after a legendary announcer, too—the one in whose home he grew up, and whose name he carries as a Jr. For contrast, in football, we offer you some one-on-one material from the old guard, Pat Summerall, and from Joe Buck Jr.

JOE BUCK JR. ON FOOTBALL PLAY-BY-PLAY ON TV

In our society, things are so politically correct that I put almost everything through a filter in my head to make sure I don't offend anyone. You have to be a little guarded, and I think maybe things come out a little watered down.

"I got to deal with the day-to-day circumstances of being a broadcaster when I was growing up, of course. You have to know how to deal with athletes, when is the best time to ask them questions, and so forth, and I learned that as a little kid. I got a feeling for what life is like around the booth.

"The first thing my father talked to me about was rhythm—when to talk, and when not to talk. His advice, which I have followed, was, 'Don't talk every minute, let the crowd carry it sometimes.'

"Plus, diction was something he steered me toward and made me listen for. I worked to enunciate every word and get every syllable out there. Try to get to a point in as few words as possible. In football (and in basketball) you've got to get in and get out."

More on style:

"I went into this trying not to imitate my dad. I get enough grief about being his son that I don't want to sound like him. I may have a similar rhythm, but I avoid saying the things he says. When you listen to guys from the older era, they get away with things that I could never get away with. Harry Caray pushed it to the limit."

On giving the score:

"That is the vital part of the broadcast. I don't have a system, though. Whenever I remind myself of the score, I remind the fans of the score."

On working with the color announcer:

"At the network level, the color guy is the star. Just give the nuts and bolts, and let the other guy go nuts. I think we're graded as a group on the effectiveness of the color guy."

On being critical:

I learned that from my father, too: Don't criticize a player unless you think you can make the play yourself. You have to respect these athletes and what they're able to do."

On officiating:

Don't get on the officials, especially in the NFL. The rule book is so thick. We always go down before every game and talk to the officials, ask what to look for, what announcers are butchering that they shouldn't. They appreciate that you're not there to blast them. But if it's a judgment call, you have to put your judgment out there, too. My dad told me they're right 99.9 percent of the time, because they know the rules better than anybody.

On preparation:

"I'm the same age as a lot of the athletes I cover, and in some ways that helps me. I understand more what's going on with them. Maybe I don't learn things that I can use on the air, but I learn a lot of background.

"I'm not one who relies on statistic after statistic. I keep my head up and keep track of what's going on, and describe it.

"Know your vocabulary. Know what's going on in the world around you, not just sports."

Joe Buck's week leading up to an NFL telecast:

• Monday: Day off after a Sunday game.
• Tuesday: Watch tapes. The game we just did, and the games of the upcoming teams we'll cover next. I also work out to stay in shape, and I watch tapes during the workout.
• Wednesday: Spotting boards. It's a two-day process. Offenses one day, defenses the next.
• Thursday: Watch the tape of each upcoming team with their spotting board in front of me, working on memorization and familiarity with players.
• Friday: Leave for the game site, and meet that night with producers and others involved in the broadcast. We go out together for dinner.
• Saturday: Attend practice of the both teams. Meet with the offensive and defensive coordinators of each team, informally with no cameras or microphones. The production team and announcers get together again that night and discuss story lines, graphics, other visuals, everything about the broadcast.
• Sunday: Do the game, and by the end I'm worn out.

PAT SUMMERALL ON FOOTBALL PLAY-BY-PLAY ON TV

"I worked with some all-time greats—Chris Schenkel, then Jack Buck, and finally Ray Scott—and learned a lot from all three of them. Here are some of the finer points… On nuts and bolts—score, player ID, down and distance:

"You can't give the score often enough. It appears often, sometimes constantly, on the screen graphics, and that's fine. But the viewers still want to hear it. They might have gotten just a glimpse of it.

"First the Fox network sends me tape at home. Identification of the players is in my head from Tuesday on during the week before a game.

"I've been around football so long I can pretty much tell how many yards they gained. I say the back or receiver got about 5-6 yards, and I know what down it is. I don't want to say how long they have to go for the first down before the information comes to me from the production truck, so I know what yardage they are going to put up on the screen graphically.

"One of the toughest things to get used to is making sure you're not saying second-and-seven, and they're putting second-and-eight in the graphics. So that patience pays off. Wait until you're sure that what you're going to say is correct.

On working with John Madden, color commentator:

"I used to be an analyst myself. We didn't have the tools they have now. The analyst then was the secondary character in the booth. That's changed over the years. The play-by-play man was totally in control before he took over. Now the play-by-play man and the analyst share time more equally than when I first started.

On being critical:

"Number 1, we don't have a home team. We cover the NFL for the Fox Network. We're supposed to be more objective. So if that means being critical, then we have to be critical. We're supposed to be. Madden doesn't mind that, and I don't mind that if we think something is a mistake (either player or official). I don't go out there to make people look bad or to be critical."

On using the monitor:

I have developed a system over the years. I watch the monitor between plays. Once the ball is snapped, I watch the field. Then I come back to the monitor for replay."

On wearability and credibility:

"Not everybody is going to like you. Nobody likes criticism, but you take it constructively. If the person criticizing is correct, you rectify the mistake. I try not to overreact to what is being said, but you certainly are conscious of what people say about you—if they like you or don't like you. Whether you missed something, or made a mistake, you're always aware of it.

"Anybody who says they don't care about what somebody says about them, I don't believe they are telling the truth. The key is not to overreact if it's negative and to react constructively."

BASKETBALL PLAY-BY-PLAY

Preparation

Setting your stage for a basketball game involves the same basic steps as the other sports—digging up information on both teams, putting together spotting boards with TLC, and so on. "The homework aspect is very, very important," says NBC's Marv Albert. "I beat myself up on preparation."

A couple of sources were strong on this subject regarding the immediate pregame setup.

Jim Nantz describes how the CBS crew prepares an opening. "The on-camera open is dictated by our producer, Bob Deikas," he says. "He lays out what we do during those short first three minutes. For example, at the 1996 Final Four it was about great Cinderella stories in recent NCAA tournaments—how North Carolina State toppled mighty Houston and Olajuwon, Villanova had beaten Georgetown and Ewing."

"The opening is carefully planned and formatted. It's not like, 'You guys have three minutes, Jim…OK, go!' We have all the material coordinated with a script matched to the picture the director wants to cut to, or the vignettes the producer wants to roll in, or sound bites from the coaches. All of it is very carefully and appropriately measured and produced."

Larry Morgan, TV voice on the Iowa Hawkeye network, takes us through pregame prep with finite definition for practical application. Starting with arrival at the arena 2 1/2-3 hours before tip-off. "You've thoroughly researched the game," he said. "You've studied media guides and updated news releases, current rosters and statistics.

"And now it's show time."

Begin with a production meeting, usually just after the teams' shootaround but still several hours before game time. The producer leads the meeting. "He talks to the play-by-play and color announcers about the game coverage," Morgan said.

"It's an open exchange of ideas about story lines, like this team likes to press, so watch for backcourt steals. Cutaway shots, like so-and-so wears an unusual knee brace, let's get a close-up. Personalities, like keep an eye on coach Bob Knight who could go crazy on the bench. This discussion revolves around the format of the entire day—what time you will rehearse, what you will say, and what the audience will see during the stand-up, on-camera intro, and when and how you will take commercial breaks, including cue lines. We also cover what to do at the half and after the game."

The production meetings last between 15 minutes and an hour, depending on the producer and the familiarity of the broadcast team with one another from previous work. "We make sure everyone is on the same page," Morgan says. "The meeting is vital to having a smooth and well-coordinated telecast. Pre-planning with good communication are essential here."

Morgan also believes in a pregame checklist:

1. Broadcast location. Angles of the vantage point, proximity to players bench and crowd.
2. Location of scoreboards, sight lines, and location of information they display (team fouls, timeouts, etc.).
3. Player identification review during pregame warm-ups. Associate numbers and physical characteristics with players.
4. Away from home, always check the route to the game site and parking. Determine adequate time for departure the next day, factoring in weather, road conditions, and unforeseen circumstances such as traffic jams, road construction, or a flat tire.
5. Relax as game time approaches. It is difficult to remain calm if you have rushed to a location.
6. "Finally," Morgan said, offering one last sage bit of advice, "visit the restroom during your pregame prep. It is impossible to do your job right when you are uncomfortable."

Giving the Score/Recapping:

Basketball on TV is unique in many ways. First, the score is almost always on the screen for the viewer to find, certainly after every made basket. Second, the score changes continuously, so it serves as a constant reminder to say it, as opposed to the score that stays static for long periods in football and baseball.

Still, the TV announcer cannot let it slide. Viewers drop in and out casually, take breaks during commercials, have running conversations or are busying themselves with other activities while the game plays in the background.

Jim Nantz uses the rule of thumb to offer the score every other trip down the floor. Larry Morgan isn't as concerned because of the picture. "I don't give the score as often on TV because people can see it," he says. "I caption the pictures. I say the score as it's flashed most times, but not every time. I might vary it with something like, 'Iowa leads by nine.'"

Kevin Harlan recaps scoring segments in recapping. "If you gain some perspective and look at the game in the big picture, the telecast will come across better," he said. "I keep a tablet close to me and write down trends, such as the scores during each timeout. I can immediately refer to a team's big 18-2 run, or a 10-0 spurt, and repeatedly give the listener the story line of the game."

Player Identification:

Nothing is more annoying to the viewer, nor more detracting from the announcer than to misidentify or to mispronounce the name of a player who just made the big play. It happens, even to the best, but not habitually; nobody ever gets the chance to make it a habit.

On one hand, basketball provides the easiest setting for proper player ID, given that just 10 participants are in the mix at any given time, and the announcers generally are at floor level or midway up in the stands (occasionally, broadcast booths still exist near the top of the arena), and the players' faces are visible throughout most of the game action. On the other hand, uniform numbers and entire bodies can be blocked from view frequently, depending on your angle. Referees move in and out of the sight lines constantly.

The challenge is to be quick, stay with the pace of the game, and be accurate with certainty. Wayne Larrivee, who works the Bulls games for WGN in Chicago, suggests the use of video tapes for familiarization. "You have to know the physical descriptions of players," he says. "I review tapes of every team before we play them, at least a couple of times."

This also firms up the roles they play, the substitution patterns, and other nuances of the game to anticipate. Larrivee also spends significant amounts of time with assistant coaches to hear their scouting reports of the opposition. "I receive a lot of information from that," he says. "I know how they want to defend certain players, or break up the rhythm of an offense. A knowledge of the game plans allows me to set up my color commentator easier."

Attending practices and shootarounds is the best surefire way to embed images of the players, coaches and others in your memory bank. Marv Albert says, "I worked college games two weekend days for NBC, and we'd attend practices, sit with the coaches and a couple of players, because sometimes you never see these teams before they play each other. One day it's Arizona-UCLA, and the next day St. John's-Louisville. But basketball, by nature, is much easier and less taxing in terms of research and memorization of player identification."

Nantz reminds one and all of the age we live in. "I store player information in a laptop computer, which pays dividends down the road," he says. "Take the four teams the week of the Final Four [1996], for example Mississippi State. I stored generic notes about the school, anecdotes about the participants into files on each player and the head coach."

LOCATION OF THE BALL/CALLING THE ACTION

Style

Shhhhh.

That's the style a television play-by-play announcer strives for, and basketball is as challenging to that end as anything because the constant flow of action tempts the constant flow of chatter. Games don't take on the rhythm of football or baseball, with their routines between plays.

"There is entirely too much talking on TV," Nantz says, "and I'm as guilty of it as the next guy."

Carpenter said, "When I review tapes I hear a lot of verbiage."

Larry Morgan asserts. "Play-by-play has become a misnomer for what we do in college basketball. We're a host and a setup person for the analyst, who is the star. We must not overstate the obvious. Play-by-play talks about 40 percent of the time, and color 60 percent."

Because you are visiting people face-to-face in their living rooms and dens, Larrivee suggested talking with, and not to the audience. "The more television you do, the more conversational you become," he says. "I tone myself down on TV because the importance of the color commentator increases. You can be more laid back. It's a cool medium. Radio is a hot medium, requiring a hot call. An announcer on television takes a step back and lets the audience hear the natural sound of the game."

Varying Terms (Good/No Good):

Most of our expert sources agree that in calling basketball to keep two things in mind: Vary the way of describing made and missed baskets, and go easy on statistics.

Especially the latter. We are inundated with statistical categories in sports today. While some are age-old staples, fans still want to know scoring and rebounding averages, assists and steals.

"But any stats that are not pertinent to the story line have no business being on the air," Jim Nantz says. "It's incumbent upon the broadcaster to edit. We work with a statistician directly on my left, which is standard in the business. You weed through the mine field of gobbledygook the stat person provides, and deliver only that which is meaningful.

"My stats person is under demand to feed me numbers constantly. But sometimes you don't use them. Do not clutter a broadcast with a bunch of minutiae."

Kevin Harlan works the production truck through the cue microphone for numbers that he wants displayed on the screen. "I will tell them what numbers I want that I'm not getting, yell to them during breaks," he says.

The king of phraseology, of course, is Dick Vitale. He breaks the mold on cliches, because he creates them and thrives on them. "A lot of them I got out of the locker room when I was coaching," he said. "I just transferred them over to television—things like P.T. (playing time), and Diaper Dandy (freshman). I can't believe the way they've worked."

Working with the Color Man:

One of the stiffest challenges in TV basketball is working in the color commentator. Greg Sharpe of Kansas State points out, "About the only openings you have for anything other than a quick hit is when they go to the foul line and coming out of breaks."

Wayne Larrivee reiterates what we have learned about all sports on television, most especially on the national network level: "TV is analyst-driven. A play-by-play guy cannot have a huge ego and be successful in television. I struggle with being effective in setting up my analyst in basketball because I am so wrapped up in what I'm doing. You have to be versatile in your call of the game because of his importance."

Partnership is vital, in the strictest sense. Jim Nantz and Billy Packer form one of the most renowned, and smoothest, partnerships in the realm of basketball booths. Nantz said, "When I'm working with Billy, it's like two friends calling a game together who happen to have a true love for the game.

"When I have a question I never pretend to know one-tenth the game that Billy knows. So if I want some clarity brought to the picture, I ask him a question, speaking on behalf of everyone who is watching.

"If I'm a little unsure what the strategy is—why did the coach make this kind of move?—Billy is so outstanding at responding immediately to anything fired in his direction. I ask because Billy can explain it."

The two of them talk about how they build rapport in their "down" time, off the air. They attend practices together, shoot baskets, stroll around campuses, talk over meals. "I hear what's in Billy's head," Nantz explains. "I take mental notes on it. When a situation arises in a game where a given thought is appropriate, I prompt Billy. I've already heard what he feels about it. So many stories come out of our time together that later pay dividends. None of it is contrived. It just materializes and sounds natural.

"It's amazing. People talk about how we work at it, but we don't feel like it's work. We feel like it's fun."

Let's go one-on-one with the most famous of all the basketball color commentators. Hey, bay-BEE, it's Dicky Vee with some Eye-Tee (interview time)!

On sustaining high energy:
"Never a problem. I've always been this way. The Detroit media labeled me Mr. Enthusiasm when I coached there (college and the Pistons). The bottom line is, once I walk into an arena like Bloomington, Indiana, or Lawrence, Kansas, or Cameron Indoor Stadium at Duke, if I can't get excited there's something wrong with me. The one thing you know when you work with me is that I'm going to give you everything I have."

On being yourself:
"I try to transfer from the locker room what I learned in high school and

college and the pro ranks to the broadcasting booth just being myself. I don't truly consider myself a sportscaster like the guys I work with. I'm strictly an analyst. I tell you why a team is winning, why they're not. I try to entertain. I try to have fun. I love the fans, and they've been great to me."

On preparation:

"The first thing is long-term preparation. Short-term I zero in on a given game. Talk to coaches when I get to the arena. Find out little tidbits. Who's hot and who's not. I did the very first game on ESPN, and I've survived 17 years; you don't do that there unless you do the job in preparation. I'm punctual. I'm may be late because a plane is late, but never because I'm sitting around the room. I believe in the traditional values that apply to life."

On style:

"If I tried to be a low-key guy I'd be kidding people, because people who know me know that the person they see on the screen is the real me. Writers who covered me on the high-school coaching level who see me now say it doesn't shock them. I'm the same person they saw back then. I've tried never to change that. I don't think you can. You have to be yourself, and build from there."

Using the Monitor

Again, basketball would appear on the surface to be a cakewalk compared to football and baseball because the arena that contains the action is much more compact (easier to survey in its entirety) and involves so many fewer players on the stage at one time. Most announcers watch the action on the floor at all times, reverting to the monitor only for replays.

Bob Carpenter explains later in his one-on-one how the referees can alter that plan. Jim Nantz talked about the typical combination: "In a live-ball situation, my eyes are on the floor at all times. As soon as the whistle blows my eyes are fixated on the monitor. So I will watch the monitor through the duration of timeouts or commercials, or coming in and out of commercial breaks, free throws, and instant replays. I work all of that material in concert with the monitor.

"Once the ball goes back in play, my eyes are back on the floor."

Packer has to be prompted, sometimes commanded to use the monitor. "I hate to tear myself away from the court unless the director cues me," he says. "I watch the court until the director tells me there's an instant replay. The reason is simple: I might miss something. When they cue me and Jim winds down, I watch the monitor and comment on what I am seeing there. Sometimes the director wonders if I ever watch the monitor. I stay on the court so I can see the strategy and what might be coming up."

Wearability and Credibility

Take note of the thoughts of three professionals regarding: handling homerism and comments critical of players, coaches or referees.

Larry Morgan: "I will be honest. Never shilling for the home team [Iowa]. If they're bad, and you say they're good, you have no credibility. I back up things I say with statistics, or by stating someone else's opinion, too. If I say a guy is not a very good free-throw shooter, I should have a number to back that up."

Wayne Larrivee: "On television a fan can see when a player is struggling. You mention the fact he is struggling, and give a stat to prove your point. Often when a player struggles, another teammate raises his game to a new level, so you can talk about him, too, in the context of the critical comments."

Marv Albert: "I have always believed in broadcasting objectively. You have to say what is happening because if you're not honest about things when they're bad, the audience isn't going to believe you when things are good. I've had my share of controversies. I don't mean you go out to take shots at people—that's not my style, I don't believe in that.

"Sometimes by injecting humor you can make points in a subtle fashion to bring the message across. I couldn't broadcast any other way. You have to tell what's going on, good or bad. If general managers or coaches get upset, they're overreacting. And you can't fool the fans. In certain cities they want to hear a so-called 'homer' telecast, and I understand that. But I'm uncomfortable with it."

BOB CARPENTER ON COLLEGE BASKETBALL PLAY-BY-PLAY ON TV

For one-on-one in college basketball, we turn to Bob Carpenter, who also has extensive background in baseball with the Texas Rangers, Minnesota Twins, New York Mets, St. Louis Cardinals, and ESPN. He has worked for over 10 years on ESPN college basketball. His spotting boards are especially valuable.

Tips on preparation:
• Talk to the sports information directors of the teams about 10 days before the game.
• Tape games involving those teams.
• Every sportscaster should have a FAX machine at home.
• Get your spotting charts finished well before arriving at the game site. I do charts nicely, but spend as little time as possible, because I'd rather spend my time talking to coaches and players. I color code everything and pay a lot of attention to detail.
• Go to assistant coaches and grill them for any information they can give. Assistants love it when ESPN wants to talk to them. A lot of them become head coaches, and then you already know them.
• I keep score for myself during the game. You can't be looking for the stats guy to give you everything.
• My motto is: Proper Preparation KeePs You EmPloyed.

On the routine before a game:
"Let's take the Kansas-Virginia game. I talk to the SIDs up to two weeks before the game. I get a media guide for both and study them. I talk to at least one assistant coach 4-5 days before the game and find out what players are doing what, their roles, how the starters are faring, what the system is. With Roy Williams [Kansas] it's motion offense and pressure defense, with multiple defensive looks.

"Virginia is known as a physical team. They'll play tough defense. They have great guard play with Cory Alexander and Harold Deane.

"I let the analyst talk to the head coach and develop that relationship closer. I just listen in. I like learning how the head coach thinks. Keep the time with the coaches brief—between 10-20 minutes. I'll ask, 'Coach, I need one thought on every guy we're going to see in your rotation Saturday night. Tell me their role and how they're playing.'

"I also ask for any personal stories that might come into play. By the time I arrive on campus I've had that conversation with the assistant coach. I enter his thoughts into a notebook, which I have handy at all times, and which is color-coded. I transfer them to a player's box on the spotting board so I can instantly recall what a coach told me. That's important, because I believe that when a player comes off the bench, people don't care that's a 6-3 junior out of

Alexandria, Va. I think they're more concerned that he's an instant-offense guy who comes into a game shooting. And if he's hot, he'll stay in, but if he misses two shots in a row we might see him for just a few minutes."

On spotting boards/score sheets:

"I have a score sheet that I've revised five times. I have the basic information at the top: Univ. of Kansas 28,000 and Allen Fieldhouse 16,800.

"In another box, team info: last year's Big 12 record, won-loss record, field goal and free throw averages, three-point percentages, scoring average, etc. Also, in that box a note that tells me that KU traditionally has been a good shooting team. I can immediately look at their record of 29-5, went to the Elite 8 of the NCAA, and yet shot only 45 percent from the field, which is unusual for a Roy Williams team.

"Next box: Big 12 tournament results, NCAA results—that they beat S.C. State, Santa Clara, and Arizona, and then lost to Syracuse.

"Next box: Players lost from the previous year. KU lost no starters, and the only loss of significance was a guy who was seventh all-time in three-point shooting. That leaves some room, so I'll write that KU won five of the last six conference titles. I'll write in KU tradition—Phog Allen, Wilt, Clyde Lovellette, Danny Manning, NCAA titles in 1952 and 1988.

"Next: Early in the season, preseason poll position of teams in the conference. Later in the season, conference standings. Below that, their current record and team stats.

"That box leads straight down to a column filled with current individual stats on each player. Some guys do five starters first, and subs below that. How can you do that ahead of time? Things change and you don't always have the same starters. I got in the habit years ago of doing my charts numerically.

"The left-hand side of the box has each player's number, name, biographical information, and anything interesting about him. Example: Ryan Robertson, academic all-conference with 3.75 GPA in business administration. Jacque Vaughn conference player of the year, academic All-American. Billy Thomas, all-conference bench team.

"On the right side of the box, current statistical information and notes. Example: Vaughn, torn wrist ligament... B.J. Williams, married with son and daughter. Out there I keep score for that player. You cannot rely on statisticians for accurate information. I tell the stats guys that I'll track points and fouls, and they can give me other meaningful things—like shooting trends.

"Every time a player scores a field goal I write in a 2 or 3. I put a slash behind that number so I know how many points he scored in that half. Same with fouls, represented by red dots. I can look at a game Paul Pierce had against Virginia in Maui and see he scored 11 in the first half and had four assists. In the second half he lit things up and had 16 for a total of 27. Scot Pollard had 10 of his 17 in the second half. Those things tell me who delivered in crunch time.

"Now, if I do another KU game, I apply self-adhesive, rectangular white labels to each box, covering them perfectly, and completely whitewash the used boxes and start all over again with current charts. I can use the spotting boards over and over without having to redraw them.

"I color code everything—Roy Williams information in powder blue, because he was an assistant at North Carolina. If he'd been at Missouri I'd use black. I list current assistant coaches, even the trainer, because you never know when Mark Cairns might be on the floor, and I list former assistants under Roy who have become head coaches—Steve Robinson at Tulsa, Jerry Green at Tennessee, Kevin Stallings at Illinois State.

"Finallly, there's a box for schedule highlights, mainly a team's non-conference opponents. As much information as possible without cluttering too much."

On giving the score and recap:

"Whenever the score flashes on the screen, say it, too.

"I have three things in front of me during a game: spotting charts, coaches notes, and play-by-play of the game. I write the score at every timeout—regular, 20-second, timeout, TV breaks. I can look back right now (February) and tell about a game last November, that when Kansas played Virginia in Maui they led by three at the first timeout, that Virginia put KU in the bonus with 9:07 to go in the first half with the score tied 14-14, that KU gave up the lead and came back to tie at the half 30-30, that the half had five ties and five lead changes.

"I can tell when Ryan Robertson got his third foul, when Metheny of Virginia got his fourth, that Virginia called a 20-second timeout when KU went up by eight on an 8-1 run. I mark some of those things with a highlighter. This is a way to give a recap at any time. I can also wade through that notebook for reference points if they relate to a game I'm doing later in the season.

"In the right-hand corner on this sheet I have the three officials' names, who's in the studio—Gary Miller and Digger Phelps—the results of our earlier games that night, what's coming on next, and under it all I write *Sports Center.*"

On player identification:

"It helps to see guys in advance on TV, so I tape as many games as possible involving teams whose games I'm going to work. But I attend shootarounds, and in pregame warm-ups, I concentrate on faces, mannerisms, haircuts, funny-looking legs, socks, earrings, anything that distinguishes a player that will help me identify him without his number.

"I do 35 college games in a season, covering more than 50 teams. I have to know a lot of different people. During the first five minutes of the game, I try not to do too much except concentrate on the players, because identification is still the number 1 thing an announcer has to do right along with giving the score and time of game."

On style:

"A lot of guys try to describe every single thing they see. Pick your spots. Some things you ignore, and some things you cannot mention. Nothing burns me more than to hear the crowd react before the announcer tells me what's happening. That crowd reaction does not lie. Those people don't care squat about your performance, they're at the game cheering. And if I hear them cheer, and two seconds later the ball goes through the basket, that does the viewer no good whatsoever. I'm not saying be ahead of the crowd, but I am saying that you've got to be up with them, because the viewer won't feel like he's at the game unless he can react at the same time the crowd reacts."

On wearability and credibility:

"Do everything possible to avoid a mistake. That's one of the most important things. Mistakes hurt your credibility.

"The viewer has to know that the announcer is in control. If you sound hectic it hurts your credibility in the mind and eye of the viewer/listener. Impart information to them in a relaxed but sometimes urgent and exciting manner.

"You must have what one of my professors at UMKC, Dr. Gaylord Marr, described as economy of words. I've had that phrase in my mind a long time. If you talk too much you get monotonic—your voice and inflections work like an ocean wave, and you go up with the high moments and down when nothing's happening. If you are the same monotonic level all the time you're going to be very boring to listen to."

On working with the color analyst:

"I set my analysts up as much as possible ahead of time. That way we're always on the same page. One of my pet peeves is play-by-play guys who come out on camera with a two-shot, standing next to his analyst, and talking for 30 seconds while leaving the analyst there to pick his nose. I like to make a quick, pertinent comment—in the open, or during the game—and immediately turn to get the analyst involved. There is nothing more embarrassing than seeing an analyst stand there forever before he gets to say something in the opening, or go long periods with no chance to talk during the game.

"At the network level you work with a lot of different people. At ESPN we work with the most knowledgeable guys in the country—Dick Vitale, Bill Raftery, Larry Conley, John Albright, the late Jimmy Valvano. They all played or coached the game. You must recognize your role with them. If I go on the air intent on impressing people it's a big mistake. Nobody is tuning in for the play-by-play. Like, 'Oh, yeah, there's that guy Bob Carpenter, he really works well with Dick Vitale.' You can't assume people know who you are.

"I reestablish myself every time I'm on the air. Your time on the air is very precious. It's a small percentage of the time you spend in your career getting ready for a game, traveling to a game, sitting in the hotel room working on your notes, working on your charts. Your two hours on the air are a precious few. So you'd better be ready to work with your partner to make that time beneficial to the viewer.

"Something that endeared me to ESPN is that I work well with any analyst. I can take charge of the show when I have to, but if I'm sitting next to Dicky V. when some guy has a slam-jam, double-pump, dipsy-do, dunkeroo, then I'm going to sit back and let Dick do his thing. When things settle down, I'll get us back on track.

"You have to adjust. You can't make that adjustment if your gums are flapping all the time. So, pacing is critical. Sometimes I'll get stuck for quite a while if Vitale is making a point, but that's different. He's Dick Vitale, and he's who he is.

"Working with guys like that taught me a lot about handling certain situations. It's a key to working at the network level—to get along with and work with a lot of different people. To do that you check your ego at the door and you go back to square one every night when that ball is tipped off."

On objectivity and officials:

"There's a way to be objective without being overly critical. There's also a way to be critical without ripping someone.

"I very seldom see referees have a bad game. Fans get emotionally involved. They think officials from certain conferences stink. These guys are the best in the business. I'll report it if something controversial happens, but I immediately lay back and let the analyst take charge.

"I've heard announcers who like to sit there and moan and gripe about the officials. I don't like that. I think it cheapens you. You become some homer announcer who hopes never to get off campus and never to have a nice job somewhere. I'd rather turn it over to my analyst, sit back and watch the replay. If there's something I can add to his statement, I'll say it, like how that call impacted on the game."

On using the monitor:

"The only time I watch the monitor is when I'm blocked out by the perimeter official. In this day of three officials, announcers get blocked out more often. Otherwise, I watch the floor.

"Whenever a whistle blows or play stops I go immediately to my monitor because I know ESPN is going to have a score, a promo, or a studio cut-in. You have to be ready for those situations."

On using stats:

"I round off everything. I don't give a squirt that a guy is averaging 8.2 points a game. He's averaging 8. If it's 8.5, he's 9 a game. I don't have time to deal in decimal points. Pick out only significant stats that tell a story line. I don't avoid them, but I'm choosy.

"Like in a Tulsa game, the career stats of All-American Shea Seals. He was a 1,600-point, 600-rebound, 300-assists guy, and to me those are important numbers. I don't care one iota that he had 30 points against Prairie View two years ago, but I care if he got 20 against North Carolina, 22 against Duke. Put everything into context. The fact that Seals got 20 points in 23 minutes against the [Olympic] Dream Team in their exhibition game and went 8 for 11 from the floor, 4 for 5 from three-point range—that's on my chart, an important historical item.

"Stats must be kept in perspective. We have too many of them."

▲▲▲

BOB COSTAS ON PROFESSIONAL BASKETBALL PLAY-BY-PLAY ON TV

Calling the game in professional basketball has different nuances than the college game. Extensive travel, agents, high-salaried players and coaches all make the landscape very different. So we tapped six-time Emmy winner Bob Costas to reveal his methods on NBA telecasts, which he took over during the 1997-98 season.

How do you prepare for NBA basketball on television?

"I use a manila folder that opens to either side and I put one team on the left and one on the right. I use red magic marker for the numbers, and then in a black or blue magic marker I put the names beneath the numbers.

"I write the center and backup in the middle, the forwards and their backups on the sides, and the guards and their backups beneath—so it corresponds roughly to an outline of the floor. Then, in ballpoint I write the height, the weight, number of years in the league, the player's college, scoring and rebounding averages, and any other important statistics, plus additional notes—games missed recently with an injury, or some sort of anecdote. I write the anecdotes in shorthand—three or four words that remind me of a story that is already in my head. Write neatly. I put little check marks next to each anecdote so at a glance I can see how one story or one note is separate from another.

"Basketball poses a little bit of a problem in that you don't have the natural space between pitches that you have in baseball or plays that you have in football. Very often, lets say Michael Jordan makes a basket, you might want to note something about him, but as soon as he makes that basket, the Lakers have in-bounded that ball and Kobe Bryant is streaking down the floor the other way. So, you have very little time to put in background material.

"You have to pick your spots very carefully and you don't really have time to look down at that sheet and fumble around—oh, where was that Kobe Bryant note? —because by the time you find it the moment is lost. So, once I have written all that preparation down, I read and reread that sheet several times over so I have committed most of it to memory. Then when the moment happens I can just spit that fact or that story out instantly. Otherwise, the best moment for it probably slipped away and something else is happening on the floor."

Do you note physical characteristics for player identification?

"I don't write down the physical characteristics, but as I watch the players go through their lay-up lines and pregame drills, I make a mental note of their physical characteristics. That becomes especially important for a college game where you might see a team only one time, or they might not be nationally known, and other than one or two players you might not be familiar with the rest of the guys on their roster. That is less of a problem in the NBA where you are familiar with the teams from having covered them, from watching games on television. Except for a few guys at the end of the bench, you should be able to identify them by sight, even without the numbers."

A difficulty in television is to avoid radio play-by-play, quickly identify and carry on a conversation. How do you do that?

"Use short-hand notes, and remind yourself that on TV you absolutely do not have to say, 'Jordan brings the dribble to the side of the circle, looking now inside, finding Pippen, Pippen turns, puts it on the floor....' You could very well say, 'Jordan finds Pippen...he's got eight (after the basket goes through), and the Bulls lead by six.'

"A viewer can see the movement of the players, and you want your comments to become captions beneath a picture as opposed to word pictures themselves, which is required on radio. Meanwhile, you are also concerned about leaving enough time for your partner, the color analyst, to make a comment. You might be listening to him or posing a question to him.

"But, straight play-by-play description is maybe only 5 percent of what you need on television. It's more writing a caption beneath a picture and drawing out the thoughts and opinions of the person you are working with."

When you work with Isiah Thomas, do you have a gameplan of what you are going to talk about before the game?

"Because Isiah is new to this [in 1997] and still finding his way, I tell him before each game to give me about 10 topics or opinions that he would like to get into during the game, such as a point about Scotty Pippen or perhaps an area where Michael Jordan is declining a little bit. Something that is not dependent upon the specific happenings in that game, but something we could get into no matter what direction the game goes.

"We usually won't get to all 10 points, but I will be familiar with them, so if he starts in on one on his own, I will be ready for a follow-up question or to lead him in a direction that will let him finish the thought effectively. Or if the game hits a lull I will draw on one of those topics. He has thought about it beforehand, and he can express himself clearly and concisely. That gives him a little confidence boost, that at least in those moments he is not going to be caught off guard, and he can definitely do a good job with those points.

"Also, it is important to have that for any broadcast, even if the person you are working with is a veteran, in case the game is a blowout. You need that safety net in any sport, something to fall back on if the game gets dreary."

Curt Gowdy said, "you have to get a hook." You two talked about how good the Lakers could be when they get Nick Van Exel back and whether Michael Jordan might come back. You become a journalist don't you?

"You need an overview. Sure, the Lakers and the Bulls, in your example, played an exciting basketball game. But the real story was how that game fit into the story of their season. The Bulls were a veteran team playing their fourth game in six days. They would then play two more games in the next three days before the all-star game. What does this segment of the season tell us about where they might wind up in the playoffs? Is this the end of the Bulls dynasty, or can they extend it with another championship? And are the Lakers not just a good team this year, the team that could step forward when the Bulls decline and become the team of the next decade? How good can Shaq be ultimately? How good is Kobe Bryant—the next great player in the NBA?

"Those kind of over-arching questions are just as interesting as what is happening in the game. A good game broadcast is a combination of what is happening at the moment on the floor and some thoughts and stories about what is happening in the past and what is likely to happen in the future."

Do you watch the monitor or the court or both?

"In basketball, I watch the live action more so than in any other sport because I am sitting right there court side and I can see it very clearly. With few exceptions the camera angle has to be pretty much the same as the angle at which I am watching with my naked eye. You know the director can't possibly cut to close-up shots, except when the ball isn't in play—immediately after a basket when a guy is back-peddling into defensive position, or right after a foul when you see the guy who committed the foul.

"Except for those rare occasions, or maybe a little cutaway of the coach on the bench, 95 percent of the time the viewer has a wide shot of the floor and sees all 10 players. So, you don't have to sit there worrying whether the audience sees something at home that I am not commenting on. You are just better off looking at it that."

What about the score even though they give it and a recap on the screen? Do you have system?

"You shouldn't let very much time go by without mentioning the score. Producers have gotten hip to that, so the graphic is usually up there. Fox displays a continuous time and score. NBC puts both in after two or three minutes. So, each time I look up at the scoreboard after a basket, if I am inclined to mention what the time remaining and the score is, I quickly glimpse at the monitor. I don't want say it if it is already on the screen. If it is, I may say something like, 'Lakers by 12,' rather than saying, '73 to 61.' I will do some other version of it. But if I take a quick glance and the information isn't on the monitor, then I say it all."

What about knowledge of the rules?

"The various leagues put out booklets or supplements whenever rules change. This year the NBA changed the definition of charging, once a player gets underneath the basket, and they changed the rule about calling a timeout while in the air flying out of bounds. And they moved the three-point line back to its original. So, we must keep up with those things. I am also in touch with the head of officials in the league office. I have known guys who travel with a rule book and on a plane or bus, they leaf through it. At the very least, it is important to know where to find situations in the rule book. The worst thing you can do is to pretend to know something for sure that you don't."

When you evaluate your tape, what do you look for, what you critique, and what do you want to improve on?

"With Isiah Thomas, a huge part of my responsibility is to make him look as good as possible. He has a lot of good things to say, but he has to work on the craft. So I make sure that I listen carefully to what he has to say. If he leaves anything hanging, I can clean it up for him, or if there is something that needs to be clarified or a follow-up question that needs to be asked. In my own case, I am looking for timing and pace. I had been away from basketball for a long time. For example, Utah played the Bulls in Chicago on one of our early telecasts. And with about 30 seconds to go, Utah was in front by four and Karl Malone went to the line for two free throws. A statistician handed me a note that said the Jazz were something like 25 of 32 from the line and the Bulls were 10 of 13. It struck me how the Jazz had shot two-and-a-half times more free throws than the Bulls, and the game was in Chicago.

"So as Malone shoots the second free throw, I say, 'There is a huge difference between the number of free throws attempted by the Jazz and the Bulls,' and I give the numbers. While I'm talking, Scotty Pippen races down the floor, pulls up and takes a three. And I am completing my thoughts about the free throws as he misses the three, Malone grabs the rebound and the Bulls have to foul him instantly. I won't make that mistake again. I will think it through and realize, well, since the guys are in front, the Bulls are going to have to foul them again. And the time to make this point is when someone is walking to the free throw line, so I have plenty of time to make it and so that I am not making it over potentially exciting action.

"What if Pippen had made the three? Not only would my point about the free throws have been diminished because people would have stopped listening to it, but a very exciting moment—where the Bulls draw within two, with a three pointer and their crowd reacts—that moment would have been underplayed because I wouldn't have had the excitement in my voice. So those little pacing things—how to say something in five words, instead of in eight—are what I watch for. On the air, economy of words is important in play-by-play.

"Think of ways to say things effectively, but concisely, and use some of the pauses in the game for emphasis. There isn't just silence when the announcer isn't talking. There is a moment of anticipation, when the ball is in the air and the crowd is watching and wondering if it will be good or not. It is effective to be done talking while that ball is in the air, and then to punctuate the call just as the shot goes through the net. Or, to let the viewers hear the squeaking of the sneakers and the dribbling of the ball and the hum of the crowd.

"Not speaking is actually part of the orchestration of a broadcast. It is not just the two voices. It is also the sounds of the game and getting the right rhythm."

▲▲▲

BOB COSTAS ON PROFESSIONAL BASEBALL PLAY-BY-PLAY ON TV

Bob Costas, although he loves variety—from the Olympics to interview host—holds a special place in his heart for baseball. He shared some insights into handling TV baseball, especially in dealing with three in the booth:

Talk about working a three-man booth with Joe Morgan and Bob Uecker. How do you define what you are going to talk about?

"A three-man booth is difficult no matter how much the three guys like each other, no matter what the traits of the three people. A three-man booth is tricky and it doesn't always work. I think Paul Maguire-Phil Simms-Dick Enberg really works. Other situations are trickier than that.

"Joe Morgan is very straightforward. He has a good sense of humor in person, but doesn't joke around very much in the booth. Bob Uecker is obviously very funny, but at the same time he has more baseball knowledge than a lot of people realize because they associate him with some of the comedic things he has done. So, Bob has some baseball things to say too.

"My job is to set them both up, but at the same time handle narrative of the game. We don't do any regular season baseball on NBC. Every other year we do the all-star game and then each year we show up for some portion of October. So by the time we get the hang of it after four or five games, then there are only a handful of games left. We always feel that frustration at the end, where you say hey, now we got it, we just got into the rhythm, and, boom, it is over with.

"It's tricky and you can't manufacture chemistry. Either it is there or it's not. Some broadcasts I feel it is there, and others sound like three capable people, but they may as well be talking on three separate tracks."

When do you lay back and just watch the game and let the game breathe?

"When the game is very dramatic, you want to make your words really count and not get in the way. If you watched the last few innings of the seventh game of the World Series, I probably said fewer words in those innings than in any other time of the post season. A whole game and the whole series was on the line and that made all the close-ups of the pitchers' faces, and the managers in the dugout all the more dramatic. Everything had been said in terms of background and history, and I just tried to write captions beneath those pictures, but make those captions as concise as possible.

"If I had a historical note, I inserted it coming out of the commercial before the half inning began. But since the series could end or the decisive play at least could happen on any pitch at that point, I didn't dare risk being in the middle of a point that wasn't absolutely essential while the pitch was on the way. The last thing you'd want is to have a guy hit a home run while you were making a reference to some background fact. All that stuff becomes secondary when the game is on the line. That is when you really pull back."

You quickly talk about every pitch, but you don't over-describe it do you?

"I don't think you have to. You have got the center field camera, it's right there. In fact I think sometimes you can say, 'Here is the two-one pitch to Chipper Jones,' and it is clear that he fouls it off. I don't even think you have to say fouled off. I think you can just let it sit there. Or you say, 'Curve in the dirt, two-and-two.' In baseball, it is often helpful to be thinking, 'I've got this good observation about Chipper Jones. I am going to make it as soon as the next pitch is complete.' That gives you the maximum amount of time. Now, obviously if he hits the ball, then you abandon that plan, but if he fouls it off or if he takes the pitch, you then want to be ready to tell your little story because now you know you are going to have a few seconds. The catcher is going to throw the ball back to the pitcher, he is going to walk around a little while Jones is going to step out of the box.

"It is better to start a story then than to start it when the pitcher is in his windup. So, here comes the pitch and I might just say, "One-and-one," and then launch into the next point or get out of the way so Joe Morgan or Bob Uecker can make theirs. I think when you describe the pitch is if the pitch sequence is unusual or very important.

"When Livan Hernandez was throwing his masterpiece in game five of the

[1997] LCS for the Marlins against the Braves, he was throwing that big curve ball and using it very effectively. But Eric Gregg was giving him so much of the corner that the Atlanta hitters were swinging at pitches that they otherwise would take. And he was continually setting them up with a couple of breaking pitches and then he would blow them away with a fast ball high and away. You need to comment on that pattern if it is an important part of the story of the game. But if it isn't, I don't think you have to say on every pitch, especially on television, slider for a strike, fast ball, ball one. Because there are so many pitches in a game that it just becomes kind of drowning if you did that on every pitch."

How do you develop the conversational, talkin' baseball style?
   "If I have developed it, it's from everything that I have done. It's from doing baseball primarily, but it is also from interview shows. It is also from hosting the Olympics, from doing the non-sports things, like 'Later' on NBC. Also, an understanding of television that, for example, as much as every one of us admires Vin Scully or Red Barber or Mel Allen, we are not doing on network television the same thing that we grew up listening to those great announcers do on the radio.

   "We might like to take our crack at doing that, but the time to do that is on the radio. On television, you're secondary. As Red Barber himself put it when he did the first televised baseball game—I think in 1939—he was a visionary in how he perceived the whole thing. He walked out of the booth, and he said to the other people who were there and wanted to know what the experience was like, 'I am not number one anymore, I am number two. That camera is number one.'

   "The best thing you can do is to complement the pictures. You can't compete with the pictures. The technology is so good now, so vivid. The replays are so wonderful. The quality of the direction and production are generally so good that the best thing you can do is provide some kind of background that makes the viewer feel as if he's sitting alongside some knowledgeable people who care about baseball and can give him some insight and some tidbits of information that will help him enjoy it.

   "But if you think you can compete with the pictures by describing better what the director has already laid out with his cameras, I think you are barking up the wrong tree."

SEAN MCDONOUGH ON PROFESSIONAL BASEBALL PLAY-BY-PLAY ON TV

Our other featured announcer in a one-on-one discussion of baseball on TV is Sean McDonough, play-by-play announcer on Boston Red Sox telecasts.

On preparation:
"Being prepared to provide commentary means gathering enough information to span the entire game, organizing it, and knowing when to use it.

"The process starts long before you set foot into the ballpark, and it means gathering more than just statistics. It's easier to omit information than to stretch if you don't have enough.

"On game day I arrive at the ballpark about three hours before the game. Most importantly, spend time with each team. Get into the clubhouses, seek out the managers and get their thoughts about the upcoming game, the way the teams have played recently, injuries and their effect on the lineups.

"Find the pitching coaches and discuss the starting pitchers, how they've fared recently, their repertoire of pitches, who might be first out of the bullpen in long relief, who will set up the closer—anything that offers insight into the pitching possibilities.

"Have random conversations with whichever players you run into. You never know when you'll strike up a conversation that leads to an interesting player story that can be useful on the air. That's very important because baseball on television lends itself to storytelling. There's a tremendous amount of dead time between pitches.

"We're required to fill that space with interesting stories about players and others involved in the action. Seek out sportswriters who cover the visiting team, and the visiting announcers. Pick their brains for interesting stories or trends. I can't stress enough the importance of spending that pregame time downstairs. After that, you're pretty well set. Head back to the booth, have a bite to eat if you're so inclined.

"Time now to fill in your lineup cards and tape things where you want them to be for ready accessibility when you're looking for anecdotal or statistical items during the course of the game.

"Then the game starts."

On rehearsal:

"We tape the on-camera opening about 15-20 minutes before the game. Some broadcast teams do it live. Our production crew in the truck prefers tape so that if there's a mistake—either by one of us on the air, or by one of them in the truck—we can do it over again.

"We have a production meeting before the game with the producer and director and the announcers to discuss the subject for the opening of the show. We also talk about other story lines we want to get to as the game goes along. The producer and director let us know what they have for production elements—sound bites from the managers or players, interesting graphics or taped vignettes, flashbacks, and thing such as that.

"Knowing what they have available, as we're talking about something on the air we might think of one of those elements, get on our talk-back button to the truck and cue them that it's a good time for that particular item."

On game plan/theme for each game:

"When you get late into a season, most often your open pertains to how this game affects the two teams in the standings and their position in the playoff races. Over the last month or so of the year [1996] it seems we were putting the wild card standings up on the screen because that was of most interest to Red Sox fans. It reflected how many games the team, or both teams, were behind for the wild-card berth, what the other teams were doing and where they were playing that night.

"Generally, the races have to be incorporated into the telecast. Otherwise, we look for the one topic that is most important that night pertaining to both teams. If we only have time for one subject, generally it is a subject about the Red Sox."

Routine through the first two innings:

"The first time through each batting order, almost everything you say is statistically-based. You want to be talking about what the viewers see, so when they see a player's batting average, home runs, or runs batted in, you want to make some comment that refers to that graphic.

"That's the time to mention that the hitter might have a little hitting streak going, or he might be in a prolonged slump. Give whatever numbers pertain to the streak or slump.

"When the batters come up the second time I say what they did in their first at bat. The second or third at bat lend themselves to tell the stories you might about that player. Generally there's too much business to take care of the first time they come to bat, not time to start launching into stories."

On giving the score:

"I give the score after every batter. I give it a lot, comparatively. I get frustrated when I turn on a game and go two or three outs, or the whole inning sometimes, without knowing what the score is. Only once in my nine years have I had someone tell me I gave the score too often."

Tips for success:

The most important thing is to be very well-prepared. There is so much dead time within a baseball broadcast that needs to be filled in an interesting fashion. You can't just fill it up with interesting statistics, because you can whack people over the head with stats. Gather interesting stories that are pertinent to the game.

"Second, know when to stay with the game, remain with the action, and know when it's OK to tell stories and deviate from the action a little bit. There's nothing worse than the game coming down to the critical point in the eighth inning and ninth inning, and the announcer is talking about other things."

Sean's Pointers:

1. Know the teams. Use radio and TV news, newspapers and other periodicals to stay abreast.
2. Take notes. From all that you gather, write down primary items of interest, organize them for use during the game, and tape them where you can get to them quickly and easily while on the air.
3. List questions. Write down what you want to find out at the ballpark.
4. Talk to the managers, pitching coaches, players, other announcers and sportswriters. Look for unusual angles to story lines.
5. Set up the booth. Make out lineup cards. Organize stats and notes.
6. Rehearse. Practice the show opening, and outline and prioritize the story lines.
7. Have a bite to eat. It sounds funny, but you don't want to be on the air with a growling stomach.

8. Pre-production preparation includes discussing graphic elements and the main "theme" of the game.
9. Let the game begin: start with stats, save the stories.
10. Know when to deviate from the action.
11. Defeat the dead time. Discuss the defense, field and weather conditions, attendance.
12. Locate and identify each pitch.
13. Give the score frequently, approximately every two to three minutes, or at least twice every half-inning.

SUMMARY

• On television, baseball is the hardest sport to work, because you can see it all and there is so much to see—so much going on in many places all the time, such as positioning of the fielders with every hitter, variety of pitches used by a pitcher, weather and other elements affecting the game.

It's also the hardest because of the fill time. The ball moves a few minutes, and you have to talk three hours, blending stories and strategy and statistics.
• Football is next hardest. You have to simplify a very complex game. You become a mental mathematician. In baseball and football you really earn your pay.
• Basketball is the easiest, a one-foot putt comparatively, because of the continuous action. It has special challenges because of the pace, but it's the easiest to prepare for and the easiest to work, simply because of the logistics of fewer people involved and a continual-action game.

CHAPTER 5
HOCKEY, GOLF, TENNIS, SOCCER, AND OLYMPIC SPORTS

"Do play-by-play for any sport you can. It is important to be well-rounded in the area of play-by-play." — *Roger Twibell*

We covered the importance of broad-based knowledge of sport, and touched on the versatility factor. Now we hear from noted broadcasters whose range takes them into the rinks, the links, the netted court and 5-ring sports around the world.

Although these sometimes are referred to as non-major sports, their audiences do not regard them that way, nor do the persons selected to give play-by-play or color commentary at the events. Those broadcasters are not lightweights or afterthought choices of producers.

The Stanley Cup is major. The Masters, British and U.S. Opens, PGA and LPGA and Senior PGA Tours are not minor. Wimbledon and the U.S. Open tennis venues overflow with the world's best talent. And the Olympics stand at the zenith of what all of sports is supposed to be about—and as the most coveted, plum assignment for any journalist on any level.

So, when you fortify yourself in these sports, you become value-added as a possible hire. Hockey announcers tend to be specialists who don't branch out much further than the ice arena. But many heavyweights from baseball, football, and basketball booths cross over to golf, tennis, track and field, and other general assignments, not to mention feature-story interviewing and reporting. Roger Twibell is one of the most versatile broadcasters in the industry, bouncing between radio and television on virtually every sport. You can catch him on preseason NFL football, golf, soccer, golf, track and field, college basketball, you name it. He believes firmly that his ability and willingness to cross over has endeared him to network bosses.

But he also throws up a caution flag. "Never lie about what you can do, because, trust me, it will catch up to you. I did say I could do play-by-play for soccer when I never had, but I had confidence in my ability to handle it. I prepared for the next month to do it, and I did it well when the time came."

"Do you believe in miracles? Yes!"

Al Michaels stands as a monument to what can happen with the willingness and preparation to broaden your scope. Primarily a baseball announcer in the 70s, Michaels received a request from ABC-TV producer Roone Arledge to lead the hockey broadcast team during the 1980 Winter Olympics in Lake Placid, N.Y. Michaels had not called much hockey. But he prepared in earnest, and—timing is everything—a golden moment catapulted Michaels into more prominence than he had ever experienced. He made a call for all time.

Circumstances set him up. The underdog but dogged United States team, under brash coach Herb Brooks, pulled off one of the grandest upsets in sports annals. The game was rife with warm-fuzzy personal stories and charming personalities, such as Mike Eruzione as the U.S. skaters defeated the perennial-gold Soviet Union.

As Michaels counted down the final seconds of the game, he exclaimed, "Do you believe in miracles? Yes!" And it registered as one of the most-referred to calls in sports broadcasting. Michaels' stock went up as he springboarded off of the Olympics assignment to a sport he previously had all but ignored.

Eruzione, who scored the winning goal, later became a prime color commentator on hockey.

When circumstances call for it—or, more specifically, when your program director or producer calls for it—will you be ready, steeped in enough background knowledge of rules and nuances of the sport, to make the call on the "other" sports?

HOCKEY

"Hockey probably is the most difficult for play-by-play description, and certainly the most taxing."—Marv Albert

Al Jaffe, the main talent procurer for ESPN, points out that his network is constantly scouting for announcers who are knowledgeable beyond the Big Three, especially in ice hockey because of its popularity in major markets like New York, Chicago, Detroit, Boston, Los Angeles, and even Denver.

One of the greatest hockey announcers of all time was the late Dan Kelly, who called the St. Louis Blues for many years. He once told me the two key elements in calling hockey: 1) instant recognition of players, and 2) accurate description of every pass, every movement of a game filled with rapid and swirling movements.

The two experts we relied on for insights into hockey, Ken Wilson and Marv Albert, reiterate those points.

Hockey presents unique challenges in description. It features rapid, continuous action but light scoring (like soccer) and audience unfamiliarity (the game mostly is associated with Canada and a few specific climes in the United States).

Also, the puck is small and often hidden from view. The late satirical columnist Jim Murray of the *Los Angeles Times* once wrote that all goals scored in hockey were figments of the imagination. "I defy anyone," he wrote, "to tell me that they actually saw a hockey puck go into the net."

What's the score?

The starting point for calling hockey is no different from that of any of the other sports: What's the score? If you don't literally see the score, you can always see the scoreboard.

Ken Wilson is a preeminent on-air TV talent for hockey for the St. Louis Blues. Do his words on the score sound familiar? "You can never give the score too much. I give it whenever I go to commercial break, and whenever we come back from commercial break. I set it up at every face-off—name all the players, and give the score and time of game. Continually. I even give the score when the play is flowing from one end to the other whenever possible.

Marv Albert, who has called the New York Rangers on the Madison Square Garden radio network, gives the score every time play stops. "When the puck deflects to the crowd, after a good save—as much as possible," he said.

KEN WILSON ON HOCKEY PLAY-BY-PLAY

In basketball, you learned to cut back on description for TV because of the pace of the game; every pass needn't be described.

Does the same rule apply to hockey, at its lightning speed on skates? "Everybody does it different," Ken Wilson says.

"I call just about everything that happens, virtually every pass . . . probably 98 percent of them. I don't do much, 'Here come the Scouts out of their own end, now they're at the Blues' line.' That type of action.

"I would say, '. . . And the feed goes to Jones. He shoots . . . . Johnson feeds into the corner, picked up by winger, Johnson skates out of his own end, over the red lines, where he dumps the puck in!'

"For me, doing every pass is easy, but I can understand why some might find it difficult. Everybody thinks hockey is the hardest game to do. I think baseball is the hardest. I'll do a baseball game one night and a hockey game the next night, and it's like the hockey game is half of doing the baseball game."

Wilson believes that playing time in hockey is vital to successful broadcast booth time. "The key is to understand the game, to have played it. You then have a sense of what should happen, what could happen, enhancing your ability to describe action—which is essential in calling any game. But in hockey everything happens a little more quickly, and my sense of broadcasting it is that it's quite easy if you have the anticipation to react quickly and describe the action precisely."

On preparation

In the rapid shuffle and clashing of bodies on the ice, constant substitutions, bulky uniforms, and helmeted heads, player identification presents some challenges, just as in football—although the arena is more intimate than a football stadium and faces much more visible. To master player identification in hockey, learning the nuances of players' individual skating styles is essential because jersey numbers often get blocked from view.

Wilson says that he constantly is asked how he follows the players. "They come on, they go off, all the time," he said. Low attrition helps. "Once you know the players from year to year, the turnover is not great," he says. "You obviously know one team inside-out. In essence, you learn only one team every game." He suggests:

•Watch the opposing team's warm-ups, especially early in the season. "I see all the players once or twice in a 5-8 minute period, and that's usually enough to make me familiar," Wilson says. You learn numbers with names, and some player characteristics.

•Prepare an ID sheet, which is not a traditional spotter board. "I write down the players in terms of lines, rather than a 1-to-25 roster. I write the center at the top, left wing to the left, right wing to the right. And then I put below them the second-line center and wings, third-line, and fourth-line, in a stack on the sheet. That way I have the forwards organized in the lines they typically play in. I do the same with defensemen. Write the left defenseman, right defenseman, going top-to-bottom on the sheet.

"So, if I call a game in which I don't know the players really well, I'll key off the main player. If I see the center, I will know the left and ring wings. That's not always true, but at least my mind will be inclined to look for them. I use the sheet for a shift or two—about half a period—and then I put it away, because by then I'm familiar and I'm rolling. I won't look at any more paperwork again."

Finally, Wilson addressed the common issue of how much to watch the monitor vs. keeping an eye on the action. "I always watch the ice," he said. "The only time I look at the monitor is when I do a game from Madison Square Garden in New York City, because the booth is so far away that you can't always make out the jersey numbers."

"So, if there's a face-off, they are focused with the cameras and you can clearly see faces and numbers on the monitor. I take a quick glance to double-check—it's No. 28, not No. 26—and that's the only time, because I'm afraid I might miss some important action."

MARV ALBERT ON HOCKEY PLAY-BY-PLAY ON TV

Marv Albert has called hockey on both radio and TV. "After hockey games I'm exhausted, particularly after radio," he said.

However, TV requires almost as uch commentary as radio—because of the viewer's unfamiliarity with the sport. "In hockey, because people don't see the puck and don't know the players as well, and it's such a fast-moving game, I find the TV call almost as far-reaching as radio," Albert said.

"There's a little bit of difference, a subtle difference, but I find that it's a lot of talk both ways. The better announcers have to talk, because otherwise the viewer wouldn't know who the players are. Not only do you have helmets and a speedy game, but many of the players are European. So, it's a lot of chatter on TV, more so than other sports where the rule is less is more."

On radio Albert tries to capture every pass in words. "You're a victim of location," he said. "If you're high enough, you see plays develop, and you can cut out and generalize some, like on a fast break in basketball.

"When you're lower down, as we are in the Garden, sometimes I have to get involved in every pass. If I don't, all of a sudden they're in on the goal, taking a shot, and you're behind."

Albert addresses the extreme differences in the sport on TV and on radio. "Hockey is a tough listen on radio. The sport has a fanatical following and a very specialized audience. The general sports fan might attend a game or two, and you are not likely to grab them for a radio listen. The team fan, though, is going to tune in to one or the other, or both, when the team is on the road. It's very difficult for the casual fan because there's so little scoring, and it's hard to picture what's going on."

GOLF

> *"Golf is softer, more lyrical than other sports.*
> *It is a genteel sport."*—Jim Nantz

If you take the word of Nantz—a premier network golf announcer—you might want to consider yoga and English literature as a training ground. "A lot of my preparation in golf," he said, "is just relaxing and thinking about the situation."

Because the event spreads so vastly across acres of playing ground, and the key action in a tournament can take place on any given hole among 18, at any given stroke among thousands by any given player among dozens (especially in the first two rounds), the production of a golf telecast requires more complex teamwork than most sports. It is in the same realm with auto racing at a major course, with cameras and announcers at every turn and straightaway.

Roger Twibell notes, "Golf is the biggest production in television sports… miles of cable, and 15 cameras at every event."

Vin Scully, one of the multitude of smooth, low-toned voices on courses through the years, described golf announcing as "a verbal relay team…. At all times I have to be ready to cut to the 15th from the turn, or the 16th tee from the 15th green. When you do golf, you are part of a huge team."

Another veteran of many rounds, Jay Randolph, points out, "You require a tremendous amount of help from people behind the scenes in golf. A good crew is very helpful. The logistical problems are great because you're dealing with a large area and many different players. It is very important to know the players by eyesight."

Both Randolph and Nantz rely on their experience as players for expertise in describing golf. Randolph was a national junior champion at age 16, and Nantz is a low-handicap player who roomed at Houston University with an eventual PGA Tour superstar, Fred Couples. Let's delve more into their insights for golf announcing, plus the well-traveled Mr. All-Sport, Roger Twibell. Also, keep in mind as you absorb their tips that golf is unique as strictly a television sport; radio work on golf is confined to reporting scores, recapping rounds, and interviewing.

Jay Randolph:

"The fact that I was a good player was helpful because I could put myself in a player's shoes. I know what he's looking at in a shot. But because I never played the pro tour, I never got overly strong on that subject and left it up to our analysts.

"We use monitors a great deal in golf because an announcer is sitting only on one hole, but might be describing action at three holes. You analyze where you are, what you can see by the naked eye, and what you can get from the monitor. Different directors have varying styles, and each of the golfers have their own nuances.

"You really have to know the players well. I always went to the first tee and watched the first 25-30 go off, visited with them before they teed off, and got a feel for what was going on. I would walk the course and survey the holes where I was going to be stationed.

"The level of concentration—with constant talking in your ears, telling you what you're going to see and call next, more than any other sport—has to be keen. After a two- or three-hour golf show I am mentally exhausted. I love it, though, because it is very challenging. When everything is clicking, it is kind of magical."

Jim Nantz:

"It is a paradox, in that golf is the busiest broadcast, and yet it is the easiest sport for me to work. It makes the least demands for preparation. You're looking at the same guys every week. You know them all. Preparation becomes a matter of getting to the leaders each week and asking about new things. You don't have to pore over media guides every week.

"The sport is not filled with controversy.

"I just think about being a great storyteller.

"The pitch in your voice is much different than it would be for a basketball game. The greatest contrast I experience every year is going from the night of the NCAA championship basketball game on Monday to Augusta on Tuesday. It's much softer at Augusta.

[Editor's Note: Nantz and his broadcast partner, former golfing great Ken Venturi, experienced a telltale round at the Masters in 1996 that displayed their credo and style. Greg Norman blew a commanding lead in the last third of the final round, yielding the champion's green jacket to Nick Faldo. Nantz recalled, "We never used the word 'choke.' At about the 12th hole when we began to feel how the tournament was going to turn, we talked about Faldo's charge, not Norman's collapse.

"We simply told what we were seeing, reported the scores, and let the pictures do the talking—especially the close-up facial shots of Norman. I believe both the golf fans and the golfers appreciated and enjoyed the way we handled it."]

Roger Twibell:

"Broadcasting golf is not that much different than any other sport, except for the pace of the game. I keep up with golf through various magazines and newspaper articles. But I gather all my information for the telecast at the golf course. I arrive early and talk with the players, either at the practice tee or the putting green. I've established friendships and rapport with many of them through the years.

"Golfers are easy to deal with. The whole key is that if they know they can trust you, they will tell you if their wife has left them, or they're going through divorce—personal things that might affect their game—and they know you will use it in a way that explains their play without embarrassing them.

"That's the whole reason for developing relationships. It's not that I'm going to sugar-coat anything. But if the players are going to bring it to the golf course and the tournament, then it's going to get out. So I go out to the putting greens and have these conversations.

"I also talk to the caddies and ask questions about their equipment, any changes, etc. There's not a lot of stuff to write down. You basically remember it. Some days you avoid mention of any statistics, other days they are relevant. When we jump from hole to hole, I tell people how long the hole is, and what is par. Later in the tournament you have stats on how each hole has been played so far.

"To keep up with a tournament, the producer talks to me constantly, and we have spotters positioned all over the golf course. If I hear something like, 'Roberts, two-stroke lead,' I'll repeat it over the air. Then on a cue word, I'll stop, and the analyst will take over.

"Golf is a very analyst-driven sport on the air because there is plenty of time to describe what has happened and what is going to happen and still get plenty of commentary in between. You want the viewer to be informed about weather conditions because they can affect the play on any stroke or any hole, especially the wind. How a hole lays out, the pin placement on the green, position of bunkers and water—these are things you want a viewer to understand.

"The PGA and the LPGA give us an information sheet about the difficulty of each hole, on the course in general, and eventually on how each golfer fares on each hole.

"Identifying golfers is easy. You know which golfers are playing together— the starting lineup, so to speak.

"Broadcasters of golf are consultants to fans."

TENNIS

"Tennis is the most overanalyzed sport on television. Just let the viewer watch the game…let it breathe."—Bud Collins

PAT SUMMERALL ON TENNIS PLAY-BY-PLAY ON TV

Summerall, renowned for his role in pro football, was a tennis champion as a kid. At 16 he won the Florida state championship for his age group. "Working tennis is like working football—a team game in the booth with the play-by-play announcer and the analyst," he says. "Tennis is a game where you really depend on the person working with you."

For many years he worked with former professional great Tony Trabert, and they became as familiar at tandem as Summerall and Madden on NFL telecasts. "Primarily, as play-by-play man you set the scene—give the score constantly, talk about the players," Summerall says.

"That leads to the prerequisite for doing any sport—you must get to know the participants. Viewers want to know all they can about them. So you humanize them as much as you can, remaining as objective as possible."

When the action sets in, though, Summerall shuts up. He believes that in tennis, less than less is not only more, but the *only* choice. (Keep in mind that not much tennis action is broadcast on radio, so the audience is seeing the volleys and rallies.)

"Once the ball is struck on serve, it's always been my philosophy to say nothing," Summerall states firmly. "Let the analyst explain what happened. Explain under spin or top spin or a lob, what kind of serve, whatever ground strokes. You, the play-by-play announcer, will have ample time to interject human interest thoughts about the players, or relevant statistics and the like."

BUD COLLINS ON TENNIS PLAY-BY-PLAY ON TV

No sports broadcaster is more tightly linked to his sport by viewers than Bud Collins. Collins accidentally fell into his career, starting as a copy boy at the *Boston Herald* in 1956. "The lowest form of life in a sports department was covering tennis," he recalls.

"You were either on the sports editor's bad list, or the youngest guy, or the staff drunk, something like that. It had no importance whatsoever."

Because he had played tennis at Boston University, had teamed with Janet Hopps for the National Indoor Mixed Doubles championship in 1961, and had coached tennis at Brandeis University, he drew assignments for the *Herald*.

After receiving good feedback from a tournament director about Collins's enthusiasm, the sports editor called him aside and said, "What are you trying to do? There's no career covering tennis." Collins proved him wrong, starting from announcing a ragtag tournament staged by an educational TV station in Boston and ascending to the courts of the U.S. Open, Wimbledon, and every major event in the world.

On his background:
"I worked the National Doubles tournament at Longwood. I was the only

commentator, and I worked 5-6 hours a day on camera, with the luxury of time, and that's where I learned. That tournament became the U.S. Amateur, and one year Arthur Ashe won in a great five-set match over Bob Lutz. Afterwards I interviewed Arthur for 20 minutes—unheard of now.

"We were going into the black power stuff, and the Black Panthers, and when I got off the air a guy at CBS called who had seen it on Channel 13 in New York. He asked me to do the U.S. Open. That was the kickoff for me.

"When I'm asked what kind of homework I do, I answer, 'Forty years.' That's not fair, because other announcers are doing it well without that background. But I think tennis is over-talked by every announcer on the air—and I'm guilty of it, too. We forget that it's a visual medium."

On being the lead announcer:

"Tennis is relatively easy to call. You have just two players, or four. Whereas basketball, 10 people, and all I want to know is 'who has the ball?' Maybe we will never reach the ideal in television because people just started doing radio broadcasts with a picture. I'm guilty sometimes.

"A critic once wrote me that he turned down the sound when I was on. I wrote him back and said, 'That's a good idea. Turn me off and put some Mozart on and enjoy the match.' I generally turn off the sound, too, and I listen to classical music while I watch tennis.

"As the lead announcer, you have two primary functions: Make sure you know the score, and who is playing.

"The lead guy has to be more conscious of the score. When a viewer just had four stations to watch, you felt people would stay with you for a while. But with this channel-hopping all the time, the lead guy sometimes thinks he's holding you by not giving the score. All he's doing is being annoying. The score has to be paramount. You've got to reset, as they call it, a lot. Saying, "We're at 5-all, but Agassi had a great chance when he led 3-1."

"You let people know what's happening all the time in the match. They're tuning in and out on you, except for the hard-core degenerates."

On being the analyst:

"The word analyst makes me think of Dr. Freud. Maybe that's correct—I mean, with all the players getting thrown off the court, the dopes. The analyst should take the cue from the lead guy. That's always been my role, to hook onto something he's saying, just as a writer has a paragraph flow from another paragraph in a story. Maybe that's my writing training seeping through.

"Keep on track with the lead announcer. That's hard sometimes when you're working with a guy who doesn't know a lot.

"I don't want to show off. Some guys love to embarrass their partners. If a guy makes a mistake with me, I will write him a note. Donald Dell and I used to try to upstage each other, but it was an act. If you find your partner in error, dab him a note and let him correct himself. If you made the mistake, just say, 'I just misspoke,' or something similar, and correct it.

"That is a good rule for a secondary guy—never show up your partner.

"The analyst feels he has to tell you what went wrong with every stroke. Why must he respond on every point? Let it breathe for a while. The second guy does not have to act like he is paid by the word, and he does not have to give a lesson. It has become too pedantic. The viewer can see what's going wrong. Just give them a hint now and then.

"If you know the players you can say, 'Graf seems to be getting fatigued, or perhaps that knee is bothering her.' That sort of thing can be helpful.

"If you're well-grounded, go ahead and criticize. I think some people wear you down. Like Connors and McEnroe, if you reacted to every breach of propriety they made, that's all the show would consist of. So you wait until they actually strangle somebody."

On knowing the rules:

"If you know the rules you should call the officiating to task when you think it's wrong. You can do it in a reasonable way and say that you think their judgment was wrong. Again, it all depends on whether you are on solid ground. I often reread the rules. I got that from my father, who was a basketball and football official. I'd see him reading the rules and I would ask, 'What the hell are you reading the rules for, you wrote them, didn't you?' He would chuckle and say, 'Oh, you never know.'

"You must know the rules, because something is going to come up. I see announcers who thought the umpires were all wet, but didn't know the rules and got it wrong. I'm embarrassed for them.

"All sports are mismanaged. If you love the sport you will defend it from officials who damage it.

This is the author at the age of 24 in his first year as the radio voice of the KU Jayhawks. Notice that the author had a lot more hair at the start of his first stint as the Voice of the Jayhawks.

Future Hall-of-Fame runningback Gale Sayers in August of 1963. In this combination, Gale would do the running and scoring touchdowns and Hedrick would definitely be the talker. The former Bear would make the author proud by his election to both the College and Pro Football Halls-of-Fame and by his earning a master's degree at KU.

Hedrick listening to Gale describe his 99-yard TD run in 1963 against Nebraska. "He knew he would go all the way once he got a block from Steve Renko and when he got that he would be in the tall clover." John Chanin of ABC thought that the good professor should have given Sayers an "A" for that performance.

A young Tom Hedrick interviewing George "Sparky" Anderson of the Reds in 1971 at Riverfront Stadium. That was when Sparky dyed his hair, and in 1972 when the Reds won the pennant Sparky was sudden grey all over.

"It's great to be in The Show." Tom is joined by two-time MVP and Hall-of-Fame catcher Johnny Bench and co-worker Bob Waller in April of 1971 at Riverfront Stadium. Notice that Bench, who had his own TV show then, has the mike, somehow getting the microphone away from Tom.

Gary Bender, now with the Bears and WMAQ, and Hedrick doing the KU-Wisconsin football game in September of 1975 in Madison. Bender was paid his normal fee of a slap on the back and a coke at halftime. KU won the game over the Badgers, 42-14, led by Nolan Cromwell. Steve Sutherland is on the far right and engineer Tom Doyle on the left.

Ted Owens, the former KU head coach for 19 years, and Tom doing a radio interview on the KU Network in 1977. Notice the longer hair. Owens taught Tom how to eliminate the bald spots out of his hair and also took care of paying for the meals and rooms on the road for two different terms at KU.

Tom and Kevin Harlan chatting about how he loved coming to KU and getting to do football games as a freshman on KJHK (the student station). He also was thanking the professor for all the free meals that he had on Sunday nights his freshman year. Note: the other KU sportscaster did not get the same treatment.

A reunion of the directors of the KU Network in the spring of 1981. Hedrick (voice of the Chief and Reds), Gary Bender (CBS, ABC, and TNT Sports and now the voice of the Bears), Monte Moore (former voice of the Kansas City Royals and Oakland A's for 25 years), Merle Harmon (original voice of the Jayhawks who did the A's, the Brewers, the Rangers, and the Jets), and Bill Grigsby (with the A's with Harmon and has been doing Chiefs color since 1963).

He can do TV, too. Tom is doing a dress rehearsal prior to a UMKC basketball game with Arkansas State in December of 1990 with KMBC-TV's Dave Stewart. Notice that the author is doing most of the talking—or all of it—and Dave is listening.

A spring training visit with Hall-of-Fame third baseman George Brett of the Royals. Tom did at last count 868 interviews with George and never had a bad interview. Tom would start it with, "George, do you have time for three questions?" It was never just three questions.

Tom is calling a UMKC basketball game over KMBZ in Kansas City in January of 1993. On the right is Brian Purdy, who does the best imitation of the "professor," and on the left is John "Duke" Wathan who has stolen more bases (36) than any other catcher in the game. Greg Ecklin is seated on the first left.

Tom interviewing Hall-of-Fame pitcher Bob Gibson of the Cardinals. Gibby revealed in that interview that he never intentionally hit any hitter; he just threw inside a lot to keep them honest.

Tom and Kevin Harlan on a visit the KU campus in May of 1996. Harlan is now with CBS-TV and TNT covering the NFL and the NBA. Tom and Kevin shared the mike at KU in 1988 with Tom doing the football play-by-play and Kevin did the basketball play-by-play on the KU Network.

Joe Castiglione of the Red Sox and WEEI and Tom Hedrick posing for a shot for this book at Kaufman Stadium in Kansas City. Tom and Joe teach sportscasting at three of the universities in the country. Hedrick is asking Joe, "Can the Red Sox win the pennant before I die?"

Two generations of sportscasters. NBC's Bob Costas, who has won six Emmys, and Tom, who won the top sportscaster in Kansas six times and Missouri once. Bob was visiting the KU campus to guest lecture in May of 1998 because Bob heard that Tom was repeating his old stories and he wanted to add a fresh approach.

Tom is introducing Bob before his sportscasters class at 9:30 in the morning. When Costas walked into the classroom, the students gave him a standing ovation. Costas quipped, "I heard that you were a tough grader, but these kids apparently are trying to suck up to get an A. You must be a hard grader." (Photo by Wally Emerson)

Bob Costas and Tom with the future Bob Costases of the business. Left to right: Bob Fescoe, Brian Sieman, Nate Bukaty, Brian Petratta, Costas, Brock Bowling, Michael Erb, Jay Erickson, Jaime Sioo, and Professor Hedrick. All of these budding sportscasters have jobs and are doing play-by-play. (Photo by Wally Emerson)

Tom Hedrick and close friend Dick Purdy on the left doing a Baker football game in November of 1998. Purdy knew in 1952 at Baker that he wanted to be a football coach and he won 270 games and six state titles. Hedrick knew that he wanted to be a sportscaster in that same year and Tom got to do three Super Bowls, nine Cotton Bowls, the Chiefs for seven years and Major League Baseball for three years. Both got paid for what they wanted to do.

"I think taking criticism comes with the territory, too. I mean, who really cares? I have a little machine and I type into it [in his writing] and I knock people, so the critics get to say what they think about me, too. If you don't like me, well, I'm sorry...."

On getting started:
"Tennis [announcing] is the least available of any sports for new talent because of so few jobs. There are no minor leagues. It's really hard to break in. You face the 'jock-ocracy,' too. Many who have broken in should not be there. But they won something one time. So, go to the boonies. Learn your trade.

"In summary, don't become a cipher in the booth. You must give your opinion. Let your personality shine through. So much of sportscasting has become deadly dull, conforming to script. It's not supposed to be World War III. Or the NFL mentality.

"Sports is supposed to be fun."

SOCCER

"Soccer is pretty easy to understand. Go easy on statistics, and stay simple in describing a play—or else people won't understand your call at all."—Roger Twibell

Americans enamored of their football often have only nominal understanding of what people elsewhere around the world call "football," that the U.S. populace—which has created a revolution in youth participation in the sport over the last 25 years—calls "soccer." American fans' interest in pro soccer peaks only in certain urban areas with diverse populations (hence the success of Major League Soccer) and whenever the World Cup comes around and the elite players of other continents dazzle television viewers with their skills.

Twibell, a veteran of prime-time soccer assignments, focuses on simple calls of the continual action and on the personalities playing the games. "Soccer is all about creating space," he says. "I talk to coaches, and ask a lot of questions to learn and gain understanding of the game.

"It's different, and easier, covering it because the players are not wearing helmets. I identify them by characteristics like height, body build, the way a player runs, the color of their skin, hair styles—the same techniques used in other sports, really, except soccer players are easier to identify. I rarely memorize numbers. You can't always see the numbers anyway."

Also, Twibell creates a spotting board, but the method is unique. He uses a manila folder, writing the rosters of each team on separate halves of the folder. "At the top I leave some space to write how the team has performed recently," he says, (such as a game featuring Ireland when it had not scored a goal for six consecutive games.)

"I also leave space for some individual notes on players beside their numbers. At the bottom I write information on the coaches of each side. And, to be safe, I keep a roster in my hand all the time in case I forget someone."

This sport, like ice hockey, requires extra attention to the detail of pronunciation because of the preponderance of foreign teams and players. The best source is the player himself. If translation is a problem, every team has a public relations director or staff translator who speaks English.

"It is important to be prepared for the distinct differences in accents," says Twibell. "I spell the difficult names in phonetics."

On the call, Twibell's best advice is to keep commentary sparse and simple, and lean heavily on the expert commentator. "I like the analyst to come in whenever the play is in the midfield area," Twibell said. "In the early going, I describe everyone who touches the ball and give the audience a name with each number. I introduce every player twice."

Twibell only surveys the field in all the sports he calls, relying on the monitor only for replays and on plays when several players crowd around the ball and he needs to know who is in control. "I give the audience a feeling of being present in the stadium," he concludes.

TRACK AND FIELD

"In track, you build a skeleton, and you fill in the skeleton with muscle."—Charlie Jones, NBC-TV

Outside of Olympic years, the coverage of track and field on network television has dwindled to mere special events. Mostly the sport is covered in highlights on news shows.

Jones draws many major track and field assignments. Adding to his skeleton analogy, he says, " You try to make a beautiful bronze by the time the telecast is over. You way you fill in [the skeleton] is with the people and personalities and backgrounds and records."

Mr. Versatility, Roger Twibell, also had some key thoughts about calling track and field. He believes in relying on the persons who have been in the heat of the competition, either as participants or coaches. "The people in the track community are the best commentators on the sport," Twibell says. "We regular announcers are very dependent upon their knowledge because of our minimal exposure to the sport. The analyst plays a huge role.

"All I am there for is to tell you who's in the race, identify their jersey numbers, perhaps a little bit of info on them as they get into the starting blocks [or, in field events, into the starting position]…basically set the scene.

"I let the analyst jump in and dictate the race or event, say who is in the lead coming down the stretch and the likely contenders challenging from behind. Or to analyze the vault or jump or throw."

Twibell pointed out the differing nuances of sprints and long-distance events. "Distance events are very unstructured in the call," he said. "I work off the analyst. Shorter events are, bang, start, and over. There's not much time to say anything. I identify runners by lanes; the top sprinters usually occupy two or three lanes on the inside. Then you do the replays."

Finally, Twibell suggests handling the track and field broadcast with discerning care. "As an announcer, you pick your spots well and depend on your analyst, statistician, and other track experts for insights," he said. "As much as I follow all sports, I find minimal information on track and field. The sport on TV is a huge production, like golf. It's very different, but it's great fun."

CHAPTER 6
JOE CASTIGLIONE ON BASEBALL

By Joe Castiglione

Joe Castiglione steps from the radio booth of the Boston Red Sox—where he has followed the likes of Curt Gowdy, Ken Coleman, Ned Martin, and Bob Starr—into the pages of this book. Castiglione has taught courses at Northeastern University, Emerson College, and Franklin-Pierce College.

He calls the action on 162 regular-season games with sidekick Jerry Trupiano through WEEI in Boston and across a 45-station network in New England.

Castiglione advises you on getting a start in the business, preparing for games, keeping score (he keeps his own pitch count!), describing the action, developing your own style, handling opinion, and other salient points. You'll learn why it's important to know the history of the game (it takes a lifetime), to keep up with the players, coaches and managers, to know the rules, and to be conversant in many areas of life.

Castiglione makes time for involvement in community and charitable affairs, representing the ball club. Joe made it big without the big voice, by paying attention to strong preparation, use of language and descriptive powers.

Let's start with two important ingredients for calling a baseball game—*conversation*, and *consistency*.

Conversation: The key to a good broadcast is what you say between pitches. Jerry and I talk about many things in a broadcast that lasts 2¹/₂ to 3¹/₂ hours. We talk about movies, restaurants, recreational activities, hobbies, things in the news. Sometimes we're putting each other down in fun. Good repartee is vital because there is so much time between action.

Consistency: And you've got to be there every day. You must call those balls and strikes. You can't be hot one day and cold the next. You've got to be the same every day. If your team is going bad, you just hope for good games. With good pitching, you can have a good game any given day. You might see something you've never seen before. Be ready for it.

PREPARATION FOR BROADCASTING BASEBALL

The key is understanding the game. There is just not enough action during a game to sustain a broadcast. A typical game is about three hours long, and the ball is in play 10-15 minutes. You must fill the rest—when the pitcher is holding the ball, or there's a conference on the mound, or the umpire is putting a new ball in play. The action is routine, repetitive, and unworthy of analysis. So you must rely on your lifetime of background in the game's history and tradition, rules, and players to relate to the game on the field today.

Over the course of a major-league season, you have about 500 hours of dead time. To fill that much time in an interesting and entertaining way will be your greatest challenge. Whether you finished your career at the Little League or Major League level, you have a basic knowledge of the game. Draw from it and add to it. Take inventory: How much do you know? How much do you need to learn?

Except for the designated hitter, the game remains essentially as it was at the turn of the 20th Century when the pitcher's mound moved to 60 feet, 6 inches away from home plate. Thus, players today play the same game as their predecessors 100 years ago. This allows—in fact, requires—a broadcaster to draw historical perspective: The significance if Tony Gwynn hits .400, or Ken Griffey Jr. finishes his career with 4,257 hits or 756 home runs.

If those numbers don't mean anything to you, it's time to hit the books. Those and other accomplishments must be viewed in relationship to the history of the game. Many resources are available, and there is a list at the end of this chapter.

MAJOR LEAGUES: GETTING TO "THE SHOW"

One of the first questions I always receive from students or young broadcasters is how to become a major-league baseball announcer. Unfortunately, there is no set of rules. I began in Youngstown, Ohio, in the early 1970s as a television sports anchor, also broadcasting football and basketball games for local high schools and Youngstown State University. I also traveled to Pittsburgh on weekends and conducted interviews with Pirates players.

The gracious public relations director of the Pirates, Bill Guilfoile (now vice-president of the Baseball Hall of Fame in Cooperstown, N.Y.) introduced me to Bob Prince, the long-time voice of the Pirates known as "The Gunner." Prince was one of the greatest characters ever, and he was very accommodating to young announcers. I worked up the nerve to ask him for advice and he told me, "Kid, all I can tell you is either hit .300 or win 20 games. That's the way the industry is going. Otherwise, there is no formula."

My formula: Draw from your own experience, and make your own luck. No professional broadcaster got his or her job by sitting back and waiting for the right employer to call. Getting the job means more than sending out resumes and tapes. You must network—make calls, knock on doors. And go the extra mile—work as an intern, and often you might even work just for the experience for no or little pay.

Many people are willing to help an aspiring broadcaster who is willing to work hard, listen, and go out on a limb to ask for what he or she wants.

I played the game, watched it, read about it, studied it, and talked about it almost constantly. I used a fungo bat and tennis ball to stage my own games in the back yard—imaginary games involving major-league teams, always the Yankees. And I'd give the play-by-play, pretending to be Mel Allen, usually really loud. The neighbors wondered about my sanity. This helped me sow the seeds.

When I was in Youngstown, I would tape play-by-play of a real game. Fortune smiled when I recorded and saved a tape I made of a no-hitter pitched by Bob Gibson in 1971 at Three Rivers Stadium. I used the final inning of that recording as an audition tape for several years.

It led to a TV news and sports job in Cleveland. I'd go to Municipal Stadium, sit in the upper deck with the pigeons, and record the game. One of those tapes got me to the big leagues. This path certainly is not the most direct to the major-league booth, but many other broadcasters have similar stories. My career reflects the importance of true love of the game, intense desire, perseverance, and the need to be versatile and flexible.

Aspiring broadcasters have a plethora of opportunities to gain experience: Minor-league clubs, colleges, high schools, even youth leagues seek on-air talent. Cable TV has opened a multitude of opportunities. Competition for these opportunities is vast, and it heats up as you climb the ladder, especially with the abundance of retiring players who are much better qualified than before.

But if you keep working hard, develop your talent and confidence, you can get there.

KEEPING SCORE

Knowing how to score the game is a prerequisite to broadcasting a baseball game. Baseball is like a pyramid—each play is a block that builds on the one before it. You must constantly reconstruct the game as it progresses. The scorecard is your journal. Practice scoring wherever you watch baseball, from television to your cousin's Little League game.

Keep track of the pitch count, where each ball is hit, who makes the play. Record strikeouts, walks, hits, and any important information about the pitchers, such as balks, wild pitches, and hit batsmen. Scorecards provide information for reference later, too, on games that took place even weeks earlier. It's worth the shelf space to save them.

It is essential to have a scorecard for all previous games of a season if you are the club's play-by-play announcer, because there is so much to recall. I have kept the scorecard for every game I have broadcast in the major leagues, and from them I can reconstruct any game, any time.

A typical scoring system is based on the number for each position:

Pitcher is 1, catcher 2, first baseman 3, second baseman 4, third baseman 5, shortstop 6, left fielder 7, centerfielder 8, right fielder 9, and DH is designated hitter.

Scoring examples:
- A groundout short to first is 6-3.
- A double play from second to short to first is 4-6-3.
- A fly out to center is 8. A fly caught in foul territory is preceded by F, as in F3.
- Strikeouts are designated as swinging (K or K-S) or called (backward K).
- Record hits with lines forming a diamond—i.e., a line to first base for a single, to first and second for a double, etc. (Some scorers indicate where the hit went, and use a symbol to designate line drive, fly, or grounder.)
- Designate errors with an E and the number of the position making the error, such as E-6.

• When a run scores fill in the diamond. Designate who batted it in.
• Whenever a batter or runner is out, write and circle the number of the out.

RULES

Know the rules. A quick way to lose credibility is to get a rule wrong. It's better to look it up than to guess. Any unusual happenings will require an explanation. Carry a rule book at all times. Familiarize yourself with the index and the format, so you can explain something quickly, not three innings after it happens.

THE GAME

Almost every viewer or listener has played some form of baseball, softball, Whiffleball, and thinks of himself as an expert. So you have to be even more of an expert. Having played some form of ball will help your broadcasting career, providing you more variety for explanation of action and thought processes during on-field situations. Discussions of techniques, anticipation of situations such as sacrifice bunt or hit-and-run, and available options are important.

That doesn't mean you had to be a professional player to be a good broadcaster. Playing ability is not essential, understanding the game is. You can also learn it by asking, listening, and studying trends.

Your most important focus is on pitching and catching because baseball on the air is essentially a pitcher-catcher game. It's the only game where the defense controls the ball.

THE PLAYERS

Biographical information about players, past and present, abounds. Search the team media guides and any number of resources listed at the end of the chapter. They provide vital statistics for individual years and careers at all levels.

Current information also is vital, from daily and weekly newspapers and specialty publications such as *The Sporting News* (known as The Bible of Baseball*), USA Today's Baseball Weekly, Baseball America*, and others; from daily television programs; and, in today's information age, from the Internet/World Wide

Web with more sites than you ever would have time to visit (every club, the player's union, most newspapers, many magazines and TV outlets, *ad infinitum*). A broadcaster must stay contemporary. Baseball is a daily game. To understand the significance of today's game, you must know what happened yesterday, last week, all year, and in other years. Not just for your team, but for all teams. Chances are good that developments in other venues will impact your game.

Baseball is the most and best written-about sport, whether it's game stories, trade rumors, analysis, transactions, or information found only in the tiny agate type. I compile information from these sources on 5 x 8 index cards and keep a library file of them. They contain biographical and statistical, updated media guide information (such as on new players acquired during a season), and interesting facts picked up from coaches, scouts, and front office officials.

Writing each card helps my recall, which is important in presenting information in a timely fashion. The file cards take hours to complete and update. I prepare them for the first series against a team each season and update for subsequent series.

GAME DAY PREPARATION

Get an early start. Arrive 2-3 hours before the game. Talk to players and coaches, and leave time for housekeeping and organizing your broadcast. The routine includes checking lineups, injuries, roster changes, updates on players, who's hot and who's not. Develop a few good sources on each club who trust you with information.

Seek anecdotal and trivia information from anybody involved in the game. Hang around the dugout and batting cage. There you learn all kinds of information that can help you appear "all-knowing" on the air.

The time spent during pregame batting practice is the most fun part of the day—a time for exchanging tales, and more for listening than talking. Some of the most interesting stories and facts about players are picked up in informal conversations before the game.

For game prep, learn what the opposing pitchers throw, and their trends. Primarily fast ball, curve or slider?…strikeouts-to-walks ratio…results in their last five starts, etc. Talk to the pitching coaches. You need plenty of information about what a pitcher is throwing and why. For example, if a pitcher consistently throws high and inside, you need insight into whether his control is off, or he has bad blood with the other team, or he always throws up-and-in.

Look for tidbits about the manager, team owner, and other non-players, too. Marge Schott (owner of the Reds) and Joe Torre (manager of the Yankees) never set foot in the batter's box in 1996, but their stories were among the most intriguing of the season. All of this supplemental information will prove useful at some time or another and will be well worth your effort to get out there, chit-chat, and dig it up.

Batting practice also is the perfect time to record interviews. Most pregame shows follow a set format—a player segment, a manager segment. These provide a vehicle to carry more commercials, which are a necessity to cover the broadcast rights fee that ball clubs demand to carry their games. But they also are fun and insightful.

BACK UP TO THE BOOTH

As pregame winds down you move back upstairs to prepare lineups and scorecards, update stats, and review your notes to glean items pertinent to the game. Be very judicious in what you choose to use because you are inundated with information provided by the club's public relations staffs.

A highlight marker is the best method for marking important stats. Remember, the season is long. You don't have to pack all information into one broadcast.

Remaining conversation is important, and cramming every stat into each game detracts from that. Use only necessary and appropriate information.

Make note of difficult names to pronounce. Mispronouncing or mistaking a player's name undermines credibility. Learn how to say the names right. The best source is from the player directly.

HAVE A BITE TO EAT

During the pregame meal (every major-league club has a press room that serves meals) is a good time to talk to advance scouts from other clubs, reporters who cover opposing teams, and club officials. The mealtime is a nice social respite, but also can be very valuable time to fraternize with baseball people who might be willing to provide all kinds of information on players you have not seen, on trade possibilities, or other good story lines you won't hear anywhere else or read about.

Whether you are joking by the batting cage, or having soup and salad in the dining room, you are always preparing. By the time the umpire cries, "Play ball!" you should be ready.

ON THE AIR

Every broadcaster should develop a personal style. Most of us don't set out to copy anyone, but often we pick and choose subconsciously from different styles we have heard. Long-time Yankees announcer Mel Allen influenced me, but nobody else broadcasts a game exactly like Allen could.

There is no way to come close to matching his eloquence and resonance, but at least three generations of broadcasters have been influenced by his enthusiasm, his skill at painting word pictures, and his sense of drama and history. As you listen to games throughout your life, you determine what you like and what you don't in a sound. By drawing a little from one, a little from another, and then adding your own personality, you develop your style.

Even though our styles are dissimilar, those who influenced me, either by design or by osmosis from hearing them day in and day out:

1. Bob Prince, the flamboyant voice of the Pirates, with his "little kid at the ballpark" demeanor.
2. Ernie Harwell of the Tigers for his consistency, character, and trusting style.
3. Ken Coleman and Ned Martin, former Red Sox announcers, for their sense of drama and of what is successful in the unique Boston market.

There are few stars in the business today. Many clubs now carry three sets of announcers—radio, commercial TV, and cable. There are too many of us to produce stars in the Vin Scully mode. Stars are rare because of economics. The bigger one's star, the more it costs the company.

Know Your Audience

Be aware that what works in one city might not play well in another. The late Bert Wilson illustrates this point: "I don't care who wins as long as it's the Cubs." Harry Caray still carries the torch for this kind of homerism in the Windy City. But in Boston, fans consider themselves more sophisticated and knowledgeable, and homerism isn't acceptable.

We can't be afraid of critical commentary on the home team. Nobody can dispute your commentary on an error, but you can create problems by attacking the team or individual players in other ways. Controversies arise over critical comments relating to club executives, ownership, and policies. Common sense should prevail. The broadcaster must act on his conscience and integrity.

EDITOR'S NOTE:

During Castiglione's broadcasts of the Red Sox vs. the Royals at Kauffman Stadium in Kansas City during the 1997 season, we gleaned a couple of examples of the frankness in his style:

With Johnny Damon at bat for the Royals, Castiglione said to his partner, "He sure has an ugly swing, doesn't he? But it seems very effective for him, as he is one of the bright young talents the Royals are counting on for their future."

After a trade was announced in the press box that sent two outstanding pitchers from the Chicago White Sox packing right on the heels of another earlier trade, making three stars the team dumped when they were just 3 _ games out of first place in July, Castiglione observed, "Why did owner Jerry Reinsdorf spend all that money to get Albert Belle, and then let these outstanding players go? It makes you think that the players might give up because their owner has given up."

But a fact of life remains: Self-preservation is a major consideration.

Some of the regional peculiarities change as broadcasters become more homogenous and probably will dissipate. With so many games and highlights available on TV, the public demands that baseball broadcasters be reporters, first and foremost.

Homerism is less and less acceptable. Tailor your style to meet your audience's needs. But keep one thing firmly in mind:

This is baseball, not brain surgery. It is designed to be fun, so have fun whenever you can.

Be Conversational

Broadcasting baseball is a whole lot more than babbling statistics and reading from reference guides. Baseball is the most conversational of all games.

When fans go to the ballpark they chat with friends throughout the game. It's that same "ballpark feeling" you must bring to a broadcast.

The reason the game is broadcast in teams of two or three is that fans find it more enjoyable hearing two persons discussing a game, rather than to listen to a monologue, just as they do when they watch a game.

Learning when to talk and how much to say is vital. Though too much silence can dull a broadcast, unnecessary gabbing makes it annoying. Choose your information wisely and economically.

Many of my broadcasts draw more reaction to subjects discussed completely unrelated to the particular game at hand. That is part of the beauty of baseball.

It is why broadcasters should be conversational. In both radio and TV, you can do justice to the game and have light and entertaining discussion at the same time.

Although there are large blocks of time to fill, the pace varies from game to game. Players often make adjustments during a game. Broadcasters must adjust, too, to the pace of the game. One day might bring an exciting game, filled with big plays, and another game might be boring. Every day is uniquely different.

Teamwork

Good rapport is essential between announcers, directors and producers. Developing a game plan together is a must. What story lines might be appropriate? Graphics (if it's TV)? Statistics? Without pregame planning, you might find yourself reading from notes, filling time with meaningless gab.

The play-by-play announcer and the analyst must have good rapport and awareness of each other's role. They must develop a sense or system for when each will speak and about what. Comparing notes before the game prevents overlap and repetitive comments. On TV this alleviates the most common gripe among critics—announcers who talk too much.

That happens when announcers belabor the obvious, conflict with the picture, or have little to add to the telecast. That's where teamwork comes into play. A game plan helps provide interesting commentary that entertains the viewer.

TV: THE ANALYST'S MEDIUM

Radio is the play-by-play announcer's medium; he calls balls and strikes. On TV the play-by-play announcer puts captions under pictures; it is the analyst's medium.

Broadcasters work each medium from the same basic fundamentals, but the dissemination of the information varies. Whereas radio often features two professional broadcasters, most often on TV the play-by-play announcer is a professional broadcaster who works with a former player who analyzes. While the analyst provides the majority of the commentary on TV, the professional broadcaster's job is to lead into what is discussed and in that sense, provides the direction.

RADIO: PAINTING THE WORD PICTURE

On radio, create pictures. On TV, put captions under pictures. Baseball is tailor-made for radio—the slow pace, the time of year it is played as people are in transit or working in the yard. A listener doesn't need total concentration or to be tuned into the entirety of the game.

Because of that, give the score frequently. You can never give the score too often. Additionally, give the count before and after every pitch. Everything is predicated on the count, the number of outs, and the score—so give all three whenever you can. The broadcaster must review constantly, too, recapping big plays, how runs scored, and pitching changes for those tuning in and out.

You see the game for the fan, so you must be as descriptive as possible in painting the word pictures. Special focus goes to the pitcher and catcher. The average game has about 250-275 pitches thrown, and from one-fourth to one-third are put in play, so the broadcaster is essentially calling balls and strikes.

Learn to describe pitch selection and pitch location. You might not be sure about some pitches—curve, slider, sinker, splitter?—but if you've done your homework and learned the pitcher's repertoire you should have a good idea.

Also, develop a sense of the home-plate umpire's timing, rhythm, and method of calling strikes. You can provide the listener a visual picture of his strike zone. There is nothing wrong with disagreeing on an umpire's call, but avoid getting in the habit because it sounds like you are whining (homerism).

Remember: Be as descriptive as possible, even when the play is routine. Your best aid is probably the oldest axiom in baseball: Keep your eye on the ball.

Some rules of thumb:
• On a long drive that could be a home run or an out, follow the fielder. He usually will give an indication of whether it is gone.

• Avoid gimmickry in your home run call. As veteran announcer Bob Starr put it, "All the great home run calls are already taken."
• When runners are on base, follow their course while simultaneously describing where the ball is. This creates a paradox. After so much non-action, everything happens at once—movement of the ball, runners, fielders—and you must be on top of it all. If you get behind on the play you can't hide it. The crowd noise will give it away.

I remember a column written by Jack Craig, a pioneer of sportscasting critics for *The Sporting News*, in which he stated that no two ground balls to shortstop are identical, and the broadcaster should not describe them as routine. He wrote, "Was it a one-hopper or slow roller? Did the shortstop go to this right or left? Did he field it smoothly or bobble it? Throw on the run?"

It doesn't take much time or effort to describe explicitly.

Craig also had good advice for recapping a play:

"When the play ends, especially if it was a pivotal play, recapitulate it immediately. Remember, not everyone is listening with total attention and devotion. Many will catch the play in midstream and want to know what happened."

This is even more true today in the era of TV's instant replay and highlight tapes. Listeners are used to getting a look at something they missed, or getting in on it again, or, more importantly in the context of your requirement for vivid and accurate description, something they heard you describe and will see later on the local newscast, ESPN Baseball Tonight, Sports Center, or CNN-SI, or all of the above.

SETTING THE SCENE

Part of the fun of listening to a game is anticipating what might or might not happen. So set the stage whenever possible. The listener needs to know that a pitch is on the way and is swung on. Always be ready for the ball to be put in play when it leaves the pitcher's hand. You don't want to be in the middle of an anecdote or conversation with your partner when all of a sudden a line drive is screaming down the right-field line, the crowd is howling, and you are talking about a cab ride to the ballpark.

Timing is a byword for a broadcaster. Practice and review tapes of your broadcasts to develop a sense of how much to talk and when. Observe the habits of other broadcasters on radio and TV. Note their use of statistics, anecdotes, and even silence to enhance the call of the game. Timing is as important to a broadcaster as it is to a hitter or a comedian.

You needn't fill every available second of the broadcast, but too much dead time isn't good either. If you find yourself at a loss for words, some hints: Set the defense, outfielders shaded, infield double-play depth, crowding the line, etc.

Review the weather conditions. Much action is affected by the wind and the elements in general.

Maintain your concentration. It may seem nothing important is happening, but remain poised for action and drama. It doesn't happen often, but when it does—be ready.

WEARABILITY

The games and the season are long. Baseball arrives daily, and the broadcaster is a constant. Because you are there every day, it is important to be well-liked by your listener. I like the term wearability—a broadcaster's ability to withstand the long game, the long season, and wear well on the listener. If you are hot one day, and then have three off days, you'll soon be demoted to the minors or out of a job altogether.

Go easy on gimmicks, and have no concern about making a big splash. It's much more important to wear well over the long haul. And you will if you know the game thoroughly, prepare every day, and report accurately.

Part of being well-liked and accepted by the audience is being human. You can take yourself too seriously. On occasion laugh at yourself. Admit to your mistakes with a smile and move on. The game should remain fun for the broadcaster and the audience.

SUGGESTED RESOURCES

Access the following for statistics, rules, team information, player histories, etc. Have access to all of them during a broadcast, with two or three in a very convenient place. Some can serve as 20-pound paperweights during the off-season.

The Official Rule Book, published by *The Sporting News*
The Baseball Encyclopedia
Total Baseball
American League *Red Book*
National League *Green Book*
The Sports Style Guide and Reference Manual

CHAPTER 7
INTERVIEWING TECHNIQUES

"You have to be a creative listener…and avoid over-talking."
—Roy Firestone, ESPN

Sports broadcasters neglect interviewing techniques more than any other facet of their work. That is odd, in that sports fans crave hearing from their heroes and heroines in this "up close and personal" era.

Interviews spice up television lead-ins to event coverage. Sound bites expand radio and TV reporting, so that listeners to scoreboard shows or 6 & 10 TV news can hear an explanation or perspective from the coach, manager, or key player.

So, given the proliferation of interviews, from far-ranging one-on-ones to quick-hits of 6-to-15 seconds, why are so many interviews of the "how-did-you-feel?" variety, interspersed with unoriginal questions (or, worse yet, statements instead of questions—"you had to feel good about that one") and dull, repetitive responses? Why do we find a dearth of interviews that draw out the personality, extract original thoughts, lend insight into a personality or poignancy to an athlete's or a team's situation?

Several factors account for this. One is the nature of the beast: the strongest appeal in sports broadcasting is play-by-play. Virtually everyone who enters the field yearns to describe the action.

Another factor is time. Whereas a print journalist might line up interviews of up to an hour to dig up information and quotes for a feature article, a broadcaster would find that futile. It would complicate the editing process to cull the interview down to the allotted few minutes on the air. Further, time is severely limited for all of the media in a post-game situation—even the networks, which usually are cutting to another event or rushing back to regular programming.

Howard Cosell's strength points up another general weakness of broadcasters in interview situations, that of timidity. Athletes can be intimidating when confronted with questions they don't like. Or, the broadcaster might be uncomfortable with broaching a subject that is personal or controversial or simply in the discomfort that follows a loss.

Cosell proved himself to be far from timid—and it paid off for him. Decades before the brash, young lions like Jim Rome raised athletes' ire with pointed questions, Cosell took the "tell it like it is" journalism approach to an art form. He asked the tough question, got the original answer. His one-on-ones with Muhammad Ali, nee Cassius Clay, are legendary in the business. Cosell cut to the quick of Ali's refusal to report for induction into the military.

Bob Costas is so skilled at interviewing that NBC-TV initiated the late-late-night program *Later…* with Costas as the host, going one-on-one with entertainers, politicians, authors and assorted other public figures. Costas conducted an interview for the ages with Indiana basketball coach Bob Knight, who is known for chewing up media people and spitting them out. Costas probed Knight on the way he tears down his players and then builds them back up, referring to Knight in the questioning as "a bully." Costas also asked him why he was so tough on the media. Instead of going on the attack, Knight answered the hard questions calmly and directly.

"Because I have had such diverse experience with the interview show, I think I have a better ear," Costas says. "I'm always thinking of the next question."

Finally that brings us to a weakness of sportscasters that contributes to sloppy interviewing: listening skills. Tom Cheatham, formerly producer of the Kansas City Chiefs and Royals radio networks, bluntly points out, "Most play-by-play announcers are poor interviewers. It's because they don't really listen while they are interviewing."

Former player and manager John Wathan, although experienced on both television and radio, admits, "Interviewing is the toughest part of the job for me. Especially the post-game interview. And especially after the Royals have lost. I struggle with what to ask and phrasing of the questions."

Roy Firestone made a signature mark on the industry with his interviewing skills on ESPN's *Up Close*. He says, "You have to be a creative listener…you have to follow up [on responses]."

Interviewing not only provides content to expand event coverage or a news report, but also serves as the lifeblood of all broadcasting—preparation. Jack Buck of the St. Louis Cardinals tells how his three 5-minute interviews before every baseball game help augment his play-by-play, giving him insights into a manager's strategic thinking and how a team or player is performing. Likewise, Lindsey Nelson, who handled radio for the Mets for many years, habitually conducted a 15-minute interview with the opposing team's manager before the first game of every series to learn all he could about the Mets' current opponent.

"I can't emphasize enough to any young interviewer to have as much information as possible on the subject," Firestone says.

The good interviewers, then, underscore the same values as the good play-by-play or color announcers. They do their homework, listen carefully, play off of what they hear, and never shy away from the tough, pointed question that gets to the heart of the matter.

As a broadcaster you have one advantage over print in that most of what you capture on audio or video tape is usable. That is, the subject generally knows that he or she is an interview subject and therefore responds knowing that what they say might be aired. Exceptions are spontaneous outbursts, but often in those instances the subject's salty language takes care of your material selection. In some situations, if a scenario is newsworthy, any obstructive profanity might be edited out and the material used anyway. If you want the subject to speak "off the record," make that clear and turn off the tape.

For contrast, consider the thoughts of two among the best interview talents in the business:
• Firestone, renowned for his lengthy, in-depth, question-and-answer sessions on ESPN, such as a classic conversation with pitcher Dwight Gooden.
• Leslie Visser, also with ESPN after many years at CBS-TV, whose assignments include in-game sideline or courtside interludes and pregame lead-ins for event coverage.

ROY FIRESTONE

"I believe in preparing...knowing as much as I possibly can..."

One of the hallmarks of Firestone's popular interview sessions is his seemingly bottomless pit of knowledge about his guest. That base of information not only sets up the tracks for the interview, but also gives him the confidence that puts him at ease as he broaches all subjects.

"I also find that the in-depth preparation shortens the interview," Firestone says. "That is, instead of having to ask the subject to explain what happened, I can just state the circumstances leading up to a point and then direct a specific question that gets right down to the nitty-gritty. Sometimes an athlete might not have total or accurate recall of an incident. I read as much as I possibly can about the person before I interview them."

Another Firestone strength is his ability to put a subject at ease and then to evoke natural responses—laughter, when it's appropriate, rather than canned or forced . . . and, quite often, pathos and quiet, poignant moments of reflection on life, health, family. In those cases, Firestone also knows when to pull back and let the picture help tell the story—the look on the subject's face.

"I like the phrase human dignity. They appreciate that."

"I like to give people dignity," he says. "These people have feelings. They have families. I'll use a phrase like, 'I think you will agree,' or, 'Would you agree?' in leading into a tough area of questioning. I want to get the subject to side with me, give me a little bit of footing so that I'm not assailing." [Commentary on his interview with Gooden, coming up, illustrates how this puts his subjects at ease.]

"You do not want to be hitting somebody over the head. Especially with more and more athletes getting themselves into trouble or controversy. It's embarrassing for people to be held up in the light. I'd rather have something revealed to me than feel compelled to 'give it up,' as they say."

On his famous interview with Dwight Gooden:

One of Firestone's more memorable one-on-one interviews brought candid, emotional responses from Dwight "Doc" Gooden after he had revived his career following drug and alcohol rehabilitation. Firestone recounted the situation:

"I don't believe in over-preparation, but I do read as much as I can. I had read both books about Doc Gooden. The last one, *High and Tight,* was about Doc and Darryl Strawberry and the 1986 Mets. By the time of the interview I had crammed like it was a midterm exam. I had all of the information in front of me. I don't write out each question, but I have a chart of 4-5 key words to keep me on course."

Even with all the preparation, Firestone received a curveball from a guy known for his fastball strikeout pitch. Gooden granted him just 15 minutes for the interview.

"I was prepared," Firestone says, "but not for that. So I had to get down to the nitty-gritty quickly. Whether you want to ease into a subject or get quickly to heavy issues depends on how much time you have. [With Gooden] I couldn't dilly-dally around. It sometimes puts people off if you get right into it, and I generally don't like to do that."

Fortunately, Gooden did not respond in an irked manner, giving straight-forward answers without flinching. Firestone contrasted this tight situation with another subject of controversy, pro football owner Art Modell after he had stunned Cleveland by moving the Browns to Baltimore.

"I had one hour and 45 minutes, so I could take my sweet time getting into the tough questions," Firestone says. "He was extremely open and willing to talk about all the issues."

On his interview with Brian Blades:

Another tough interview lay before Firestone just days before he talked for this book project. He queried pro football player Brian Blades. "This is a man who was convicted of manslaughter, and a judge overturned the jury's guilty verdict," Firestone says.

"It's not easy to talk about killing somebody very dear and close to him. So I said to him, 'I'm not holding you up to ridicule. I'm looking to discuss some issues, and some of it will be hard and I hope you will bear with me. I want to be respectful of your human dignity.'

"I like to use that phrase. I think the interview subjects appreciate that. I don't believe in villifying people needlessly. That doesn't mean I'm weak or un-willing to be tough with somebody. But I think you have to allow a person a sense of dignity to come through. Because if you don't, more often than not they will react with hostility or discomfort, and it makes for an uncomfortable exchange."

On broaching the subject with Blades of the killing of his cousin, Firestone adds, "When you are coming up with the big, big tough question like, 'Did you pull the trigger?' or 'Were you intoxicated?' you have to preface it with, 'Listen, there's a lot of speculation, and I'm just going to ask you…?' From a legal standpoint, he couldn't answer that. But I had to ask it."

By breaching the dignity rule of thumb, Firestone explains, you risk alien-ating the subject and obtaining less information. "I have found that most athletes give out less information these days, and I would rather have something revealed to me than to feel compelled to give it up myself."

> *"It's one thing to be in the spotlight. It's another to
> be held under a microscope."*

On creative listening:
"You have to hear the answers and be creative enough to establish that you're going to break some new ground," Firestone says. "The whole idea of interviewing is to find out information. That comes in the form of a response. You must follow up on answers."

Over-talking is probably the greatest sin in interviewing. Nothing is more annoying to a listener than to hear the interviewer ramble through a preamble to the question, showing off how insightful he is rather than getting the insights from the subject.

"Conduct the interview in the fewest words possible," Firestone suggests strongly. "Be efficient with words. Exercise brevity, clarity in painting a picture. Keep it tight. Keep it short. Keep it simple, so that everyone can understand it."

That points up another sin—complexity, in the form of convoluted or ambiguous questions. Or worse, the dreaded non-question question ("Two big hits tonight, you had to feel great . . . .").

Talking too much, by the way, also can inhibit you *before* you go on the air. Firestone said, "I like to put the subject at ease, make them comfortable before we go on, but I do not want to have them talked out beforehand."

Firestone brings to light an example of bad reaction that he witnessed during the Olympics in 1996. "A guy was interviewing sprinter Michael Johnson," he says. "He was talking about the 400-meter race. The interviewer said, 'Michael, tell me about the race,' and Michael said, 'It's history. It's not something I'll talk about.'

"The guy was stunned. He just stood there. He didn't know where to go with it. That was a natural. 'What you're telling me is that once you finish a race you forget bout it and focus only on the future?' There's a whole lot of questions to be asked here. That was a good opportunity for this interviewer to follow up, and he didn't.

"You have to listen to what someone says. Many times there are hidden agendas in the way people phrase things."

Firestone gives as an example an unexpected answer he received from former Los Angeles Dodgers pitcher Hideo Nomo in an interview through an interpreter. "I asked him if he felt he had been treated fairly by the press in Japan, and he said, 'No, (pause) not yet.' Well, you can move right on to the next question. Or, as I did, you can think, 'Wait a minute, does that mean he feels it is going to happen—them being fair to him?'

"You have to listen to an answer and be creative enough to establish that you are going to break new ground. The whole concept of interviewing is to find out information, given to you in a response—and you have to follow up."

He concludes, "The two most important ingredients for success are practice and preparation. You prepare over and over again, and you practice over and over again. The by-product of that, over a long period of time, will be grace. You'll becom graceful in the way you do things, because you become comfortable with yourself. You know you have your material down pat."

On reviewing the tapes:
After an interview is concluded, Firestone reviews tapes. Here is what he looks for:
• "Did I get something out that the audience held interest in? Did I break new ground? Did I get something from this individual that defines his or her passions, focus, drive for excellence, or something that reveals the human side?
• "If I do all that and get it stated in an articulate or profound way, or a way that makes you laugh, or moves you, then I have succeeded."
• "Also, I look for whether I have been fair to this person. Have my lines of questioning been to the point? Did I develop good chemistry between me and the guest? If I did those things, I feel that I have done a good job."
• Firestone's passion for his work comes through distinctly to a viewer, and he stresses the need for that passion to any aspiring broadcast journalist: "It's a mean, tough business. It's exhilarating and fascinating, but harsh. It's a business of ratings, of cosmetics, and one that requires a tough hide."
• "The only way to supercede those qualities is to develop a strong passion for the work. Really believe in what you are doing and represent yourself with that passion for your subjects. Do that, and if you are willing to take some knocks, you can succeed in this business."

LESLIE VISSER

"Conduct an interview like a conversation...and try to make a memory."

Leslie was a pioneer, of sorts. She was one of the first prominent on-air personalities to move from the print world and one of the first females to break barriers. She worked for the *Boston Globe* from 1975-84 before becoming a sideline reporter for CBS and later joining ESPN.

She takes a double-dip into the world of sports broadcasting because she is married to network announcer Dick Stockton. They met when each was covering the 1975 World Series.

Before her interview for this book Visser worked a pregame intro assignment on the Kansas City Chiefs in which she interviewed head coach Marty Schottenheimer and five players. Beforehand she spent three days writing notes that she reviewed before each subject entered the interview room the day before their game against their most-reviled rival, the Raiders.

However, although thoroughly prepared and set with a line of questioning for each subject, during the interviews she rarely glanced at those notes.

She explains, "I try never to look down at my notes. It works best if I don't even bring a note pad. Having covered sports for more than 20 years helps, and then I simply attempt to have a conversation."

Sound scary—an interview with no notes? Preparation, remember? As you have noted in every phase of sportscasting, solid preparation breeds confidence. In interviewing, having a theme or track in mind with a few questions to lead with gets you rolling, and then good listening will carry you from there.

Visser said that the first priority is finding common ground with the person to be interviewed. That comes with some ice-breaking chit-chat before the interview, perhaps even revealing the line of questioning, or at least some part of it.

"You want to make some kind of connection, establish rapport with your subject," Visser says. "Everyone structures the interview. But the players are savvy to that. You will be surprised, though, how sometimes the easy questions or introductory questions really take off and go somewhere if you are willing to follow the pitch."

Some of that rapport comes with the experience level. Either you have come to know many of the subjects you interview, or they at least know of your long-standing reputation and take a certain measure of respect and trust into the interview from that.

"Credibility is about longevity," Visser says. "You wouldn't be around that long if you didn't know what you were doing, and the athlete knows that. When I started at CBS in the mid-'80s I never pretended to know something that I didn't. I only asked questions about something I had observed. I had a passion for sports and developed a good working relationship with the athletes.

"You never want to put yourself in a position where you are more learned or a better observer than everyone else."

By, leaning on those observations, drawing on the rapport, and listening carefully, Visser takes the interview wherever the subject leads it. "I follow their answer," she says. "You must be willing to do that. Sometimes you don't get satisfaction from their answers, so you have to go at it another way. Also, you learn to recognize when an individual has said what he is going to say and will say no more."

Visser suggested that a good learning tool is to watch good interview shows. "The best interviewers," she says, "like Dick Cavett, Johnny Carson, Larry King—they are terrific at hearing and understanding the essense of what a person is saying, not just the facts but also the content."

The gender issue carries enough baggage for any woman in the business; Visser also has to deal with the innuendo about her marriage to an established broadcaster, Stockton. "It has helped," she says. In terms of getting or holding a job, she is evaluated on her own merit. The help comes in the form of how they assist one another in improving on their craft.

"We understand the demands of the job. There is a lot of travel. We love that," she says. "Sometimes we get assigned to the same game, so we save ABC, Fox, or ESPN the cost of a hotel room."

Citing an example of her interview technique in action, Leslie recalls a give-and-take with Bob Knight in which she refused to be intimidated. "I've known him about 15 years, and I used to be terrified of him," she confesses. "I told him that in the first 6-7 meetings I had with him. I would ask a question and hope that I crafted it well and didn't stumble, and then got out of his way.

"Then at the NCAA tournament [1996] I worked a game with Indiana against Temple. I asked Knight why his team was so effective against the Temple matchup zone defense, and he gave me one of those curt answers, 'We scored more points than they did,' or something like that. I couldn't help it, I don't know what came over me, but I cut him off with a 'yeah, yeah, yeah,' because I just didn't want to hear it.

"Then I came back with another more technical question. I've been around Bob Knight enough to have a good working relationship with him, and I have enormous respect for him. That's because 90 percent of what he does is right, and then on occasion he bullies people. Then you can call him on it.

"Really I am comfortable interviewing anybody."

SUMMARY

To be an effective interviewer:

1. Research the interview subject, from reading articles and talking to other journalists and team officials about them.
2. Put the guest at ease. If you are nervous, the guest will be nervous, too.
3. Take no more than 20 seconds to introduce the subject, pronouncing the name clearly and correctly and stating correct biographical information such as title, position, etc.
4. List the first three intended questions, with the third one carrying the kicker—the main point to address.
5. Speak in conversational style and tone.
6. Rephrase a question that the subject did not answer fully or directly, giving him another crack at it.
7. Listen creatively, the Achilles heel of most interviews.
8. Loosen up the guest if he is tight, using soft questions.
9. Take control of the interview when the subject rambles.
10. Avoid cliches and saying uh, oh yeah, and you know.
11. Pause effectively.
12. Arrive well ahead of the interview, making certain to remain in charge.
13. Conclude the interview effectively, especially if it is timed—starting the wrapup with a final question.
14. Repeat the name of the subject during the interview (on TV the name flashes on the screen frequently), and close by stating who was just interviewed.
15. Tape the interview and review it with a checklist for effectiveness.

When Brian McRae (now with the New York Mets) was playing major-league baseball for the Kansas City Royals he took classes in broadcast journalism at the University of Kansas and worked as an intern on radio in the off-season.

He remembers, that as a player he experienced three basic types of reporters who approached him for radio or television interviews. Here are McRae's categories and his comments about them:

The Drifter. "They have no plan or purpose. They just drift from one player to another, stick their microphone in the group or start the camera, and get anything they can. Usually they don't even ask a question. Whatever they get is pure luck."

The Game-Plan Reporter. "These are the beat writers, or the local radio and television people, who know exactly who they want to talk to and why—what angle they are searching for. Their questions have purpose, and they usually get good material. The players like to cooperate with those types."

The Watergate Snoop. "In every major-league clubhouse there is the one reporter who is looking for the big, sensational story—the so-called Watergate scoop—and you had better watch out for that person."

CHAPTER 8
JOCKS IN THE BOOTH

"...I love the game....people like hearing that from an ex-athlete."
—former pitcher Steve Busby

"I don't think you can do color in a sport if you have not played it.
You have to understand the mechanics of the game."
—former football player Paul Maguire

Red Grange probably started the phenomenon. Dizzy Dean and Paul Christman elevated it to art form, with Pee Wee Reese hot on Dizzy's trail. Coach Ara Parseghian became a staple on television broadcasts after he left the sideline.

As a result, "jock schlock" permeates today's air waves on TV and radio. Former players and coaches inundate the broadcast of every event with insights and tale-telling. Often the insights are incisive, enhancing the fan's understanding and enjoyment of the inner workings of the game or event. Often the tales are tall—funny, heart-rending, or, again, insightful in turning the performers into real human beings.

Theory balanced with real life: That is what the expert former-athlete/coach color commentator adds to the play-by-play of the action. In some few cases the ex-jock becomes the play-by-play voice. Bob Uecker comes immediately to mind behind the radio microphone of the Milwaukee Brewers and on national telecasts (as well as in satirically fine humor with the fictional Cleveland Indians in the hit movie, *Major League*).

Grange, a legend as "The Galloping Ghost" at Illinois and in pro football,

173

introduced the concept with his commentary on Chicago Bears football. But the voices indelibly imprinted in the minds of listeners and viewers across the nation as pioneers are Dean and Christman.

Ol' Diz took some heat from the likes of English teachers for slaughtering the language in his down-home style ("he *slud* into second" and his rampant use of "ain't", but he was beloved for his endearing personality and humor. And he was no buffoon: His commentary held strong credibility.

I can recall a classic Dizzy Dean moment when he pointed out that a certain pitcher had no control this day because he was working from the wrong side of the rubber. Dean said that if the pitcher would move over on the rubber he would start throwing strikes. Sure enough, the pitcher made that adjustment, and started throwing strikes. Dean relied on the smooth professionalism of veteran Buddy Blattner to balance the broadcast and keep it flowing on an even keel.

If, somehow, you can find vintage tapes of the pioneer color analysts, it will provide a very enjoyable learning experience.

Pee Wee Reese and Joe Garagiola made distinctly strong impressions in baseball broadcasts with grace, humor, and keen knowledge. Garagiola paired with Harry Caray on St. Louis Cardinals baseball, and they formed one of the most famous tandems ever in terms of the entertainment aspect of broadcasting. Each exuded robust enthusiasm, flair, and humor that reached right to the heart and soul of every fan.

In football, as a former all-everything Hall of Fame performer at Missouri and in the NFL, Christman brought not only outstanding credentials but the same solid footing of knowledge to the task opposite the play-by-play by Gowdy on ABC's first college football experiments in the late '50s.

Many of these jockcasters have become legends, such as Frank Gifford on Monday Night Football; Pat Summerall and John Madden (TV) and Hank Stram (radio) on other NFL football; Uecker and Tim McCarver in baseball (what is it with former catchers? Jeff Torborg, Joe Torre, Buck Martinez, John Wathan, Ray Fosse, Bob Rodgers, among many, have been color commentators); Bud Collins in tennis; Ken Venturi and Gary McCord in golf; Terry Donahue and Lee Corso in modern-day college football; Dick Button and Scott Hamilton in figure skating. Len Dawson and Nick Buoniconti have been hosts of the longest-running cable TV show in history, HBO's *Inside the NFL*, joined in recent years by Cris Collinsworth, Jimmy Johnson, and others.

That is the challenge that you face, and the whole point of this chapter: To work seamlessly, coherently, and in concert with your game analyst. Throughout the play-by-play sections you heard the greats talk of the challenge and methods of working with their color counterparts, and how it differs greatly between radio and TV. In hearing from several of the former athletes/coaches who ply the trade, you gain insight into how they work and what they bring to the table.

DICK VITALE

Vitale is a former basketball coach at the high school, college and professional levels. He converted his love and passion for the game into probably the most renowned energy-burst on television—certainly one of, if not *the* most recognizable. (Dick Vitale impersonations abound, and contests are even held around the country that bring his clones out of the woodwork!) His method of commentary on college hoops is legendary.

Yet, as unique as Vitale is with his coined phrases, exuberance that borders on screaming, and exclamation-point running commentary, he named the same first basic tenet of performing as a former-athlete/coach in the booth: "I just tried always to be myself."

And people who know him off-camera confirm that you get the same Vitale-ity that he splashes across the screen. "When it comes to getting into the basketball arena, I've always been this way before I ever got into broadcasting. I was labeled 'Mr. Enthusiasm' by my friends.

"Once I get into an arena I remember that I'm spoiled because I'm going to Lawrence and Allen Fieldhouse, to Bloomington, Indiana, to Cameron Indoor Stadium at Duke, to the Dean Dome in Chapel Hill, North Carolina—to the greatest environment of them all. If I can't get excited and enthused when I walk into those places, there's something wrong with me."

Vitale says he carried the same passion to every game, at every level, when he coached. He loves the atmosphere and the competition (he's also an accomplished tennis player).

"I tried to transfer from the locker room of my coaching days that same attitude to the broadcast booth," Vitale says. "I don't consider myself truly a sportscaster like the guys I work with—Mike Patrick, Brad Nessler, Brent Musberger, Roger Twibell, Gary Bender, John Sanders, Bob Ley, Jim Simpson. I'm an analyst. I try to entertain, to have fun."

Vitale said he took a cue from John Madden, his counterpart (though not as animated and colorful in his language) on pro football. "He's having fun and making it simple," Vitale says. "I can feel his passion coming through the screen. That's how I have attacked my job, and not allowed critics to get the best of me.

"I respect everyone for their unique way of doing games. My style is totally different, but if I tried to be a low-key guy I would be kidding viewers. That's not me. You've got to be yourself, and build from there."

Other thoughts on the basics of his work:
• "I pride myself on preparation—long-term, and short-term."
• "I watch the floor about 60 percent of the time, the monitor about 40 percent. It is important for me to know what the people are seeing at home. And replays are vital."
• "I am honest and say that a kid is having a bad day shooting and why, and that he'll bounce back. I love people, so I don't want to hurt anybody. But you have to be honest and objective about what you see on the tube."
• "I don't worry about politics...I just go do my job. If you develop a name, a reputation in the business, that's helps along the way."

▲▲▲

STEVE BUSBY

Like several former athletes—most notably Herb Score in baseball—Busby's pitching career with the Kansas City Royals ended prematurely with an injury. He pitched two no-hitters and won 20 games one season before his arm went bad when he was still in his 20s. During rehabilitation he decided to test the broadcast field.

Royals announcer Buddy Blattner invited Busby into the booth. He found a flair and eventually accumulated numerous credits in radio and television, among them both play-by-play and color for the Texas Rangers and Royals from 1983-96, eight years with CBS Radio, and a stint with *Baseball Night in America* for both ABC and NBC television.

Busby relies more on the personalities and traits of the players at the core of his broadcast than research in statistics. "My preparation depends on being around the players a lot," he said. "I want to capture the mood of the players and the team. I am not a big numbers guy. Baseball is an individual game. So it's important to know about the individuals and the matchups."

Thus, working with a partner like Busby, an important component would be setting him up, cueing him to draw out the information and insight he has gathered from the clubhouse, the batting cage, the hotel on the road.

"I explore the matchups of pitchers against hitters, catchers and pitchers against runners," Busby says. "Also, I like know things that can influence a game, such as a runner with a hamstring history or a pitcher with a tired arm."

Several former participants in the game drew a parallel between preparing to play and to broadcast. "It's still competition—strength against weaknesses," Busby says. "It's similar to getting ready to pitch a game, but not in the same depth. But I ask myself how much I can add to the broadcast and the enjoyment of the game."

Criticizing players is a sticky wicket for a former player. Busby accents the positive, yet strives for balance. "I don't think of myself as a teammate of anyone on the field," he says. "That removes the onus of being fair and unfair. You can overdo being critical. You don't have to dwell on a negative point to get it across."

Although he grew up in the Los Angeles area listening primarily to Vin Scully on the Dodgers—"I'm sure there's a little of him in me somewhere"—Busby loves to let "a little Dizzy Dean creep in there...to have fun, enjoy the game as a little kid."

To the aspiring former athlete with an eye on the booth, Busby suggests two things: first, study the good play-by-play announcers to learn the techniques and learn to read aloud effectively. He practiced by reading newspaper articles alone. "There is no substitute for picking up the morning paper and speaking into a microphone," he says. "Then listen to it. You can change the entire meaning of a story by intonations—so did it come across like you, and the author, intended it to?"

"I put in my two cents' worth teaching baseball and letting my feelings show. I love the game, and I show it. Sometimes I give a passionate description of a play because I love the game so much. I think people appreciate hearing that from an ex-athlete."

TERRY DONAHUE

One year Donahue was coaching in a bowl game for UCLA, the next he was offering color analysis of bowl games for CBS-TV. The adjustment was considerable. "When I coached I could look up at the scoreboard and know if we won or lost the game," he says. "As an analyst you look up at the scoreboard and you're kind of lost about whether you did a good job during the broadcast or not"

Donahue passed an audition before taking the air. He believes he caught a break working with smooth veteran Jim Nantz on the Fiesta Bowl and Sun Bowl assignments the first time out of the chute. "We didn't have hand signals," Donahue said of his debut work. "There were natural breaks when it was time to make an observation. I got a feeling for Jim's rhythm and what he wanted to accomplish during the broadcast."

The biggest adjustment? Easy. The same one that makes all newcomers to TV squirm—a director talking in his ear while he is talking on the air. Otherwise, Donahue said, "I had a natural reaction to describe the play again rather than analyze or critique it by making some observation or comment."

In terms of critique, again the coaching instincts kicked in. "My nature is not to be super critical. But I'm not afraid to say what I see or say what I think. You have an obligation as a color analyst to point out that someone made a mistake. But it is easier to second-guess from the booth than to be out there making those instantaneous decisions in a 25-second span under all that pressure."

Coaching also prepared Donahue for handling critics. "A coach is very prepared to deal with that in the booth because he deals with it on a regular basis on the field," he said. "Take constructive criticism and react to it. If critics point out a weakness in my performance, I'll work on it as hard as anyone in the industry to improve. At the same time I'm not going to be sensitive, because it's hard to please everybody. You work hard, be prepared, know your subject matter, and please the people you work for."

Musing about how he misses the close association with players, Donahue readily recognizes the Number 1 difference in his role in the booth from his former role on the sideline: "You don't win or lose the game up here."

KEN HARRELSON

He always marched to his own beat as a player long ago. Known lovingly as "The Hawk," Harrelson hit for power and played with flair. He provoked Kansas City A's owner Charles O. Finley, who unloaded Harrelson to the Boston Red Sox and he helped them into the World Series. Later, he gave professional golf a brief fling, and eventually he became general manager of the Chicago White Sox.

Harrelson found a home in the TV booth with the White Sox, and his varied background as both player and management served him well. He and partner Tom Paciorek are an unusual pair, in that they both were players; most booths feature one or two "real" broadcasters and a former player/coach. Harrelson and Paciorek created an unusual niche with their humor, storytelling, and blatant "homerism" that runs counter to the norm. Nobody can ever call them dull.

But Harrelson doesn't just show up and wing it. "Broadcasting is just like playing," he says. "You have to come to the park ready every day. I've seen a lot of broadcasters in 20 years in the business who had a lot of talent, but they took things for granted and let things slide. Thus their performance went down. And there is always somebody in the wings ready to take their place."

He says he relies on scouts as his main source because players, coaches, and managers give "slanted" viewpoints.

The toughest adjustment for him was criticizing. "You want to be objective, but you can't. My perspective is sentimental to a player. The broadcaster sometimes doesn't give the fan enough credit for knowing what's going on.

"I want to bring the imagination of the viewer into play. That's probably my biggest thing—my trademark, if you will." His main ally in that approach: "Silence is sometimes the best communicator."

Harrelson sums up what former players or coaches must bring to the booth in order to serve their purpose: "Energy...[in] delivering what they know. Delivery is everything. You've got to be a little bit of an actor—projecting the voice, using inflections. The analyst should work with people who know the business and have them critique tapes."

MIKE GOTTFRIED

This former head college football coach (most notably Kansas and Pittsburgh), found disobeying his mother as the hardest part of broadcasting. "That earpiece, somebody talking in my ear while I was on the air, that was the toughest adjustment," he says. "My mom taught me to be quiet and listen when other people are talking.

"So when I'd hear that, I'd stop in the middle of a sentence. In my first assignment, Texas A&M and Hawaii, on the third play an A&M back ran through the line of scrimmage and the director says in my ear, 'Tell the American people why that play worked.'

"I said, 'Okay.'

"He said, 'You can't say okay. You just said okay to 60 million people.'

"I said, 'All right.'

"And that's how my day went. Eventually I learned to listen to them and still keep talking. There's a lot going on during a broadcast, and you just have to keep thinking ahead and not get totally caught up in the game."

He took solid advice from Andrea Kirby. "She told me, 'One point—and make it a headline.' I stick to making one point on a play."

On the onus that all the ex's deal with—criticizing coaches and players: "There's a way of explaining what they're doing. If a play doesn't work it doesn't mean it failed. There's a reason, and I want to give it. If there's a mistake I'll say that. Understanding coaching, I know they put a lot of effort and preparation into the game. I explain that it's not as easy as it looks."

TOMMY JOHN

Here's living proof that all baseball analysts aren't catchers. The rest are left-handed pitchers! (Herb Score, Jim Kaat, Jerry Reuss, Paul Splittorff, Ken Brett, Al Hrabosky, et al.)

Known for his miraculous comeback from reconstructive surgery on his pitching elbow (left)—so renowned that the procedure, almost routine these days, is referred to as "Tommy John surgery"—John is a remarkable case study in the booth, too. He worked hard to overcome a speech impediment; he stammered when he was interviewed during his playing days.

John approached announcing with the same zeal as pitching a game. "I read all the newspapers I can get my hands on," he said. "I listen to local TV and talk radio."

In an unusual twist, he takes a different approach to information gathering. "I don't hang out at the batting cage," John says. "I talk to the managers and pitching coaches, sometimes the hitting coaches. But I don't like to bother players during their work time. I'll talk to them in the clubhouse."

Because he was a pitcher, and a very good one, John realizes that he can become too technical for a listener or viewer. "If you talk about the way to throw a curveball, people don't care about that stuff. My wife tells me to do more human interest, to show that ballplayers are human beings."

To that end, John credits former catcher Tim McCarver with the best tip: "He said that when we're on the air, we're out in a bar [with the listener/viewer] having a beer, watching a ball game, and just having a baseball conversation." Remember Goudy's "baseball conversations" in Chapter 1.

John is careful not to emulate McCarver, though, or any other of his peers. "You can't think, 'Gee, I want to be like Tim or Jim Kaat.' You take some from a lot of different announcers, pick up bits and pieces, listen to various techniques." You've heard this before, too (remember "Go to Boise?"): "What I should have done, and my wife tried to tell me, was get a job at a radio station, even if it's as a disc jockey. Do as much on-air and on-camera work as possible, watch and listen, and then go have fun."

The failing of many of the former participants is that they understand their topic fully, but show no understanding whatsoever about the ins and outs of broadcasting. That's where the play-by-play or host announcer kicks in, leading the way and drawing out the best that the analyst has to offer.

John reveals a keen comprehension of that interactive nature of the broadcast team. "I hate to hear an analyst say things just to be saying something," he says. "Sometimes the play is obvious. My partner is in if there's nothing for me to add. That was the hardest thing for me to learn—when to speak, and then get in and back out, because sometimes a story needs explaining."

John points out good plays and bad plays, recognizing the inherent difficulty of handling the same team every day. "By and large it isn't your job to hammer people," he says. "If you're network it's probably a little easier to do that. I believe in giving people a positive outlook."

As an example with his own team: "The Twins bottomed out around the All-Star game [1996], and then started playing better. I said, 'This team may be a player or two away from being a competitive club.'"

JIM KAAT

Like Tommy John, "Kitty" enjoyed a long and illustrious career, from the Twins early to the Cardinals late, and translated the experience into expert commentary. Some of it didn't come naturally. "I had trouble getting used to watching every pitch," he says. "As a player you can look down or to the side in dead time. In the broadcast booth everything happens so fast, and you have to be watching at all times." He also had to get used to talking frankly about what occurs on the field, and then mingling with the players after the fact. Kaat says, "These are my friends. The only thing I'm really critical of, though, is lack of effort. If a player makes a mistake and I point it out, it's not like I'm tearing him down personally. I make myself available for any player to ask me about something I've said, but usually they don't. I spend a lot of time with players, coaches, and managers for preparation. You'd be surprised at the interesting things you hear at the batting cage." He follows the same line on umpiring. "I know their reputations for the strike zone, and I get a read on them in the first inning," Kaat says. "I'll point out when they're wrong on close plays, but if it takes three or four replays to figure out what happened I point that out, too." Kaat's approach follows the standard line of thinking—"I do the how-and-why, my play-by-play partner does the who-and-what."

Joe Garagiola also gave Kaat a fundamental axiom that has served him well: "I was fortunate to have been involved in public speaking activities as a player. During the 1983 World Series, Joe told me to just use my natural voice and tell people what I know, because they know I played the game."

I had an experience with Kaat on that topic at a time when Kaat was fretting about it. The scenario unfolded at the College World Series when Kaat worked as my sidekick in Omaha, Neb., on ESPN radio.

Kaat called me late one night in a bit of a frenzy. Tim McCarver had told him that he was too laid-back in his style. I asked him if he wanted to do play-by-play or color, discerning between the differences in energy and style in those distinctive roles. He said color. I told him that McCarver was wrong.

I thought Kaat was just right. We listened to a game together, and I didn't even have to take a note for six innings, he was so right on. Another lesson from our pairing in 1984:

On a Sunday night, LSU and Miami played six innings and the score was 10-8. The broadcast already was three hours long. Kaat turned to me and said, "Professor, I'm out of notes."

I replied, "So am I."

Panicky, Kaat asked, "What are we going to do."

I said, "We're going to tell stories...have a Q-and-A on baseball."

We filled the last $1\frac{1}{2}$ hours of the broadcast that way, with me leading Kaat, my expert commentator with questions, and sharing tales from our respective experiences as broadcaster and player.

PAUL MAGUIRE

Blunt in his assessment of how a color commentator cannot perform effectively without having participated in the game he or she is calling, this former football player says, "Playing the game enables me to know the keys to what teams are doing on offense and defense. When you talk over a replay you have to tell the viewers why the play works—not what they just saw.

"And you do it without ever saying, 'Back when I played or coached,' because they don't care."

Maguire and his team in the booth work with fewer replays and stage more conversational patter among them than most. He goes the positive route on plays that could draw criticism. "I would rather say that a guy made a great block than a guy got his rear end knocked off. It's more important that a player made a great move, that he got behind the opponent, than that the opponent got faked out of his jock strap. It's more natural for me to do it that way because I played the game so long."

Although his playing experience drew him into the booth, McGuire went at it just as he advises students today: "Sit up in the stadium with a tape recorder and record some play-by-play. Practice in front of a mirror."

He faults former coaches or players who "talk just to say something," rather than jumping in only when they have something important to add. "Say only things that are important to the game," he says, "and on replays tell viewers why a play works. Don't tell them what they just saw."

Thin skin won't hack it, Maguire said. "Just like as a player," he says. "I've seen so many players worry about what's written or said about them. I feel sorry for them for letting themselves get so caught up in it. Most people who write and say the stuff have never been there anyway."

BOB UECKER

With more than a quarter-century as play-by-play voice of the Milwaukee Brewers among his many credits, Bob Uecker often is referred to as "Mr. Baseball." He also has handled virtually every major network television baseball assignment.

Uecker's range extends far beyond the baseball regimen. During the late '60s, after a mediocre baseball career as a catcher, he followed the lead of another of the same lot, Joe Garagiola, but with a more dry, sublime approach to wit and humor. On the banquet circuit, Uecker developed his routine and blossomed into a full-fledged entertainer.

He appeared numerous times on NBC's *Tonight Show* with Johnny Carson and Jay Leno, and other talk shows, and he starred in a network sitcom called "Mr. Belvedere." His Miller Lite commercials became a cult favorite, with Uecker sitting alone in the worst seat in the house at ball games, playing off the phrase, "Here we are in the cheap seats." Likewise, Uecker's bit role as the announcer in the movies *Major League* and *Major League II* had viewers saying, "J-u-sss-t a bit outside."

Uecker's approach to the Brewers broadcasts, however, does not follow a comedic track. He loves the game of baseball, and he sprinkles his announcing with dry humor in the vein of Skip Caray in Atlanta, but he treats the game with respect and reverence. He credits announcers Merle Harmon and Tom Collins, his partner in the Milwaukee booth, will aiding his transition from field to booth.

"You think you know the game as a player," Uecker says, "but you have to know it as a broadcaster, too. It's a big learning process, developing a rhythm, a style, and flow. Some announcers still resent former ballplayers coming into the booth and knowing it all. Plus, I was more critical of myself because I grew up in Milwaukee, and I wondered...feared that people might be laughing at me, and not because I was funny but because I was bad."

He lends some insights into the differences in the daily coverage of the same team and the spot assignment on national television. "When you are with the same club day in and day out, you prepare based on the little nuances and happenings that occur with your team," he says. "You become familiar with opponents that you see two to four days in a row, and several times a year.

"On a TV assignment where you haven't seen the team or players all year, you have to dig into local and national newspapers, talk to many sources, and absorb all the knowledge you can about the players." He says that the larger audience requires a broader appeal than the colloquial presence of a club's daily announcer.

"But basically, even though you have all the technical people around—directors, producers, camera operators, you still have the same duty: Report the game."

He notes the differences in performing as play-by-play on the Brewers, and a TV assignment on which he is a color commentator, requiring a different preparation and set of information. "I've always thought that the color man has a tougher job than play-by-play, because you basically are repeating what the announcer has just told everybody. So you have to be choosy with what you use. Some things get punched up on the monitor that bear repeating.

Uecker emphasizes two points:
• "One of my pet peeves is an announcer not giving the score enough." He says he uses no timer or signals, but he has developed a habit of repeating the score frequently. "My mentors taught me you can't give the score too often," he says. "I think you can tell which team is winning from the play-by-play announcer's voice and enthusiasm. But it's amazing how often a listener will go away, come back, and somebody has hit a home run or scored, so you have to give the score several times every inning."
• He is careful with his number 1 trademark: humor. "I will not have fun at the expense of ballplayers," he says. "I use humor on myself, or I look out into the stands and point out something funny. Now, if a player does something on the field that everyone sees, you can't deny that and have to point it out. But I never have been one to make fun of players."

In some cases, to the "pure" broadcaster, these color commentators seem to be the bane of their existence. They get good work and good pay without going through the rigors that the purist usually must endure, from school to beating the bushes to getting the big break. The ex-athlete / coach gets work simply because of his or her accomplishments, sometimes even when the voice or other nuances of good broadcasting are not up to snuff.

There are exceptions. Irv Brown was a basketball referee for 25 years in the Big Eight Conference, and he admits, "That's a fair assessment that [my reputation] helped me . . . . I met a lot of people while officiating games, and I think it led to my break." But he worked hard at developing a style to supplement his wide-ranging knowledge of sports, and it led to 16 years of talk radio in the Denver market.

"My English is horrible," Brown says. "I don't know anyone else who talks like me. But I work hard at it. I read a lot, talk to many people. Somebody's always going to test me, so I have to do my homework. For me, hockey is hardest. I really have to bear down because we have a Stanley Cup champion [in Denver]."

Former big-league pitcher Paul Splittorff spent several years in small-market radio, listening to tapes, and gathering advice from coaches before becoming a radio and TV analyst for his former team, the Royals. Ditto, pitcher Jim Kaat, who eventually worked ESPN coverage of the College World Series with me.

Learn to live with them because they are only going to proliferate, not go away. The color analyst is here to stay, and in many cases color analysts only serve to make you even better and more important to the flow of the broadcast.

CHAPTER 9
WOMEN AND MINORITIES

Part I: Women

"I see many women making great strides, and we cannot pinhole sportscasting in any different manner. I see some good, strong women on the air."—Terry Shockley, owner of a TV/radio conglomerate

A relatively new standard exists in sports broadcasting. It is just that, too—a separate standard, which, unfortunately, is a stark reality. The door to the studio (primarily television) has swung wide open to women, yet they continue to be scrutinized by different standards than men.

A flood of women on the air started in the '80s, and by the mid-'90s it was a tidal wave. Hear the Fabulous Sports Babe by day, see the ESPN lineup (Linda Cohn, Robin Roberts) by night. See a woman anchor on your local sports cast, join a woman at the backdrop of a network event interviewing the coaches.

Sportscasting for many, many years was the Good Ol' Boy Network (GOB). Sports were for men—played by men, watched by men, discussed in bars and barbershops by men. And, men would describe the games to you and tell you the scores on the news.

Phyllis George changed that.

She became Miss America first. Then, as the '70s unfolded as an age of protest and revolution, to include the women's-rights movement, she became the first woman to broadcast sports on a major network. Some woman somewhere else might well have been the original pioneer, perhaps on a local TV station; but Phyllis George was the first to appear before all of America, live and in living color.

Phyllis George, Miss America 1972, burst onto the national network sports scene as a studio host and at featured events, becoming more of a novelty than a polished sportscaster, although her reviews were awful. Eventually, she made her mark on a national non-sports morning news show and as wife of the governor of Kentucky, where she produced her own TV program.

Even after her, the first wave of women in sportscasting consisted mostly of former athletes, providing color commentary on their sports, such as Nancy Lieberman in basketball, Donna DeVerona in swimming, Billie Jean King in tennis, Carol Mann in golf, among others.

Two trends altered the frontier drastically: 1) A huge increase in the number of women participating in athletics, from grade school through college and into professional leagues, and 2) a large upturn in the numbers of women attending sports events or watching on TV. The number of women in the NFL fan base, for example, is closing rapidly on 50 percent, according to a survey released in 1997.

Slowly, eventually, the emergence of schooled journalists with honed on-air skills brought changes to the landscape of women sportscasters, too. Gayle Gardner at ESPN and Leslie Visser at CBS (and later ESPN) blazed a path for "real" journalists, "real" broadcasters, known not for their prowess on a field or court, rather for their skills in front of a microphone, or on mike in front of a coach or player.

Suzy Kolber is one who jumped in behind the trailblazers. "When I was at TBJ-TV in Miami, I worked on a series on women in sports, and I recorded Gayle Gardner's goodbye at ESPN," Kolber said. "She was very impressive. She was the first to be looked at as a hard-core sports woman in broadcasting."

Another of those, Linda Cohn at ESPN, observed, "When I started in the '80s as a freelancer at News-12 on Long Island, they had openings in sports but would never give me the opportunity. News reporting or anchor, yes, but sports, no. That was 10 years ago. Things have changed for the positive, as I and others have become kind of entrenched."

Several women sportscasters insist that their involvement in athletics aided their career path—Robin Roberts is adamant about it—but many have cut to the chase without ever having scored a goal, hit, or pitched.

"I don't think having played the sport means anything. You don't have to get hit by a truck to know what it feels like," says Suzyn Waldman, who sprang from a show business career into radio sports reporting on the Yankees and Knicks for talk-radio giant WFAN in New York City. She never played baseball or basketball.

A quarter of a century, later opportunities abound for women in the industry, still mostly on TV, but widespread from network to local anchors, from sidelines and courtside, and in many positions off the air (producer, writer, director, public relations, marketing). Not only are women welcome, they are in demand. In light of equal opportunity employment laws and quotients, the hiring of a woman is as paramount in broadcasting as any other business.

In sports, that hire is a treasure, because that specialization is a rarity. Women deliver news and weather all over the TV map, but there aren't an abundance of women like Karen Kornacki, a highly-rated sports reporter and weekend/backup anchor in the Kansas City market who works on the KCTV staff with football legend Len Dawson, the primary anchor.

Of the dozen or so sports talents on TV and another couple of dozen on radio in the Kansas City market, Kornacki is the only woman. The only other women to surface as "personalities" in sportscasting there during the last 20 years were Chiefs' wives, Jennifer Montana and Cynthia Phillips.

Al Jaffe, the primary talent scout at ESPN, says, "The timing is right for women and the market is wide open to them. I encourage them to pursue play-by-play more as well. The women anchors here have proven themselves to our audience."

Proven themselves translates to on-camera broadcast skills, appealing personality—wearability and credibility, as we have termed it throughout the book—and also the depth of their insight and knowledge of sports across the spectrum.

Linda Cohn sysd, "Accuracy is the key. It puts us ahead when the Joe Schmoe on the couch says, 'She knows her stuff...she knows what she's talking about.' And we do."

Waldman had no sports background when she started covering New York professional teams, but she built her credibility with thorough knowledge.

Visser was an NFL beat writer for nearly a decade in Boston before converting to TV. "I was alone back then," she recalls. "Now you see women at every major event, covering sports at the highest level."

Still . . . .

Even though the law prevents anyone from saying it out loud in the interview or hiring process, women know they must deal with two things that men do not: Physical appearance and pregnancy. There also are matters of credibility and the lockerroom. First things first.

"It's not half the battle—it's more than half the battle in this business, to look good."—Linda Cohn, ESPN

Looking Good

In setting the precedent, Phyllis George inadvertently set up the prototype against which all women in the business are measured, at least in television (not many women engage in radio sports): Good looking, and then, oh yeah, she knows her stuff, too.

That's an unfortunate double standard, but very real in the broadcast world, so you must recognize that it is going in. If you are a female entering this business with a desire to go on camera, you face a blatant double standard. Check it out. Who do you see out there today?

Revisiting: Visser. Roberts. Waldman. Cohn. They all know their stuff.

Visser was an accomplished print journalist with *The Boston Globe* from 1975 until she switched to CBS-TV in 1984 and eventually slid to ESPN. "Back then, when I was a covering the NFL, people thought I was from Mars," she says of her early years.

Roberts grew up on sports, played college basketball, crammed knowledge of all sports, and polished her broadcast skills as sports director and disc jockey on a radio station in Mississippi for $5.50 an hour.

Waldman reported for a decade on talk radio before she became the first woman in a network baseball play-by-play booth for ABC on *The Baseball Network*. Hers is an amazing story of determination and self-development.

Yet, when each of these accomplished women sportscasters appear on TV, what is noticed first? Her exceptional knowledge of the games she describes and reports on? Her interviewing skills? Her trained delivery style and personality?

None of the above. Quickie quiz: If any of them were bald, would you notice or care? Absolutely. You'd laugh and switch channels. Yet, bring on all the Joe Garagiola or Dick Vitale that time permits.

For women, looks come first. Almost without exception.

What Suzy Kolber of ESPN (and Fox Sports before that) told us in Chapter

1 bears repeating:"…We're judged on a different standard cosmetically.…You have to be an unbelievable personality to get on the air if you're not at least somewhat attractive."

Roberts observes, "There is more pressure on a woman to look more attractive than men. With all due respect, I work with male colleagues who aren't the best looking people in the world…maybe a little overweight…but no one seems to care if a man is perhaps bald or a little paunchy. But they would care if it was a woman. If a woman is a little too heavy or not pretty, she probably won't have a job."

Kobler concurrs, "There's a lot more leniency in terms of who they'll put on the air if you're a man. We've seen that with men, the sky's the limit. With women, few exceptions are made."

"The Fabulous Sports Babe," Nancy Donnellan, is an exception to the rule. Personality moved her along, not cosmetics. But she made her reputation in talk radio with schtick and rapport in the Seattle market long before signing on with ESPN radio, which also appeared on ESPN2 as she broadcast live. Donnellan works solely in talk, not 6 & 10 reporting or anchor situations.

Will this ever change? Some would like to think it has. Station owner Terry Shockley says, "Cosmetic appeal is important for both males and females. People on television can't care enough about personal appearance. It's one of the most important staples of their career."

Andrea Kirby is an on-air announcer for ESPN. Additionally, she recruits and coaches talent. She says good looks "are absolutely important." Not just for women, though.

"The best thing you can do, man or woman, is spend a lot of money on a good haircut and clothes," she says. "Dress, hair, teeth—have them the best they can be. The problem is that most people can't see themselves properly. I'll tell people, 'You don't know me, but I'm going to give you some really good advice.' I'll say they really need to cut their hair or get some clothes that look really expensive. Most people are appreciative of that, but there are some who won't tell you those things because they're afraid it will offend you."

Cohn says that women must get used to a way of life in which the standard differs between genders. "A guy's hair can be out of place, his tie crooked, eyebrows jutting out over his eyes," she says. "But if anything on a woman is out of place, or out of sorts like long earrings, it is distracting.

She also points out an irony in the double standard: "The criticism [of looks] is definitely harsher on a woman. What's funny is, women viewers are more critical of women sportscasters…sometimes you get more bashing from a woman."

Dan Patrick works with many exceptional female on-air talents, and his thinking runs along the line of the universality of television demands, which start with ability, not looks. "I don't think we have to be models to do this," he says.

"I don't think ESPN said, 'Let's find the best-looking people we can.' It used to be a lot like that. We had to cross all barriers there with sex and race, to satisfy everybody. But I believe we hire on talent. Looks can help you…being too good-looking won't hurt you…but it still comes down to this: You can be empty upstairs and be good looking and not get a job. So I would be more concerned with working on my talent than I would my hair style."

Roberts likewise paints a bigger picture for women, although conceding that good looks probably are unnecessarily necessary. She concludes: "I long for the days when I can go back to radio, because I was informing people. I feel like I am scrutinized when I am on television. It's not a woman thing, though. I have to face the facts—that's what people do when you're on TV. I wear makeup on the air and I dress appropriately. I look at it as, we are on television—so look right. That's how all of society is about women and looks, not just about sportscasters."

▲▲▲

Motherhood

Where in a few instances the issue of appearance might slide across gender lines, the matter of pregnancy certainly does not. It's generally a matter of assumption that men are fathers, or will be, and life goes on without skipping a beat, let alone nine months of beats. With women, the question always looms whether she will allow motherhood to "interfere" with her career.

Cohn provides an excellent model on this front germane to women. The matter of children, present or future, doesn't even come up in conversations with men in the business.

Cohn broke new ground when she handled ESPN's *SportsCenter* while pregnant with her second child. (Joan Lunden and Kathie Lee Gifford continued their daily network roles through pregnancy, too, but in non-sports programming.) Cohn was carrying when she granted this interview. "I guess I feel like a pioneer," she says. "Although, that sounds like such an old term. I don't want it translated that way.

"The point is, there's no reason to stop doing what you love [while pregnant]. Why stop my career just because I want to expand the family?"

She described the experience as "kind of cool...feeling a lot of movement right on the *SportsCenter* set. I think my unborn child is a major sports fan, because there is a lot of kicking going on. That's kind of nice, and it puts things in perspective.

"Here we are, always under the gun on *SportsCenter*, and, yes, we are having a good time—don't get me wrong, that sincerity that people say they love about *SportsCenter* is real, we are having fun up there—but just to feel that baby kicking is a piece of 'real' life."

The men she worked with not only didn't show any resentment about her situation, but actually blended it into the work. "Sometimes the pregnancy issue came up during highlights," she says. "It was a running joke with my tag-team colleagues."

Cohn spoke of the challenges and difficulties facing women in sports broadcasting as they deal with maintaining balance between career and children.

"I won't lie," she says, "if my doctor said tomorrow, 'Linda, you're under too much stress,' I'd be home. Fortunately, there are only some times when this job is stressful. We're in sports, it's great. You keep it light and have a good time. If I was home and not doing this, I'd probably still be watching games and probably be more stressed out because my real emotions would come out. So work may be the more relaxed place for me."

On motherhood and career paths: "It is a challenge splitting yourself. You want to split yourself into 5,000 different directions. Every free moment I have with my daughter, my first child, I make it magical. I make it special, and I never take it for granted. That helps, and it helps that I'm in a profession that I love.

"It's more than an outlet, it's really important to me. That helps give me a balanced life that is very satisfying."

"If there is one thing to remember, Linda, it is accuracy. If you are accurate, everything else will come to you. Make sure you are accurate."
—Advice that Cohn received from Ted Shaker, former
head of CBS Sports (and now CNN-SI)

Credibility

Another of the major hurdles that women must clear with at least some segment of viewers and listeners is credibility. What can *she* possibly know about sports? That might seem rather amazing, given the climate of the day—gender equity prevailing on the high school and college scenes, driven by Federal legislation requiring equal opportunities; the advent of women's pro basketball leagues, and more and more marketing of sports to females.

Cohn relates,. "If I was a guy I guess I would be skeptical, too, until I saw me do what I do," she said. She simply kicks into the gear that Shaker referred to. "All a woman can do is become knowledgeable, let her real personality come out, and then most men with a brain will say, 'Hey, she really knows what she's talking about. OK, she deserves to be there.'"

That's seems logical. Yet, in a progressive society approaching a new millenium, Karen Kornacki in Kansas City believes in her heart of hearts that some viewers long for her to fall flat on her face because she's a woman in a man's chair. In her case, the man is a revered, local-hero man, Len Dawson.

Kornacki tells of one incident that illustrates the plight. Dawson stumbled over the name Raul Mondesi of the Dodgers. Royals player Bob Hamelin sat next to him as a guest celebrity anchor. When Dawson got tongue-tied, they laughed. Kornacki says, "If I had messed up the name, the phone would have been ringing off the wall. I really have to do my homework and be extra sharp. I have to be accurate all the time. That's the difference between being a woman and being a male and former athlete. I have extensive knowledge of sports, and I've always had to do my homework diligently to maintain credibility because I'm a woman."

Dawson maintains automatic credibility even though basically he is a figurehead sports director who reads staff-written copy. The station builds on his name as a longtime former Chiefs quarterback who is enshrined in the Pro Football Hall of Fame, the color commentator on the Chiefs radio network, and co-host of the longest-running program on cable television, HBO's *Inside the NFL*. He can do little wrong in his viewers' eyes, and they don't care about his appearance or his voice (neither of which is lacking, but the point is that it wouldn't matter if they were).

"There is a certain segment out there that is hoping I will fail," Kornacki says. "I want to prove them wrong, and I will by knowing what I'm talking about."

Kolber said that, in her mail, viewers often mention her knowledge of subject matter and not just her looks. "You're always judged on a different level. For every one mistake I'm allowed, the man would be allowed three, because everybody assumes he knows sports better as a guy, and why would a woman know?"

She, like several of her peers, played organized sports. "Why would women not love the game just as much, or know just as much?" she asks rhetorically.

Roberts speaks strongly on what she implies is a necessity to have a hands-on-the-ball sports background. "I had credibility in knowing sports, because people would read about me in the papers—having a double-double or triple-double," says Roberts, who played basketball at Southeastern Louisiana. "That really, really helped me. I don't have horror stories or negative letters. I was very fortunate to be known around town for my sports knowledge. People never questioned me on the air."

Waldman represents a totally opposite example. "I'm not performing open-heart surgery here," Roberts contends passionately. "You can't teach someone how to talk sports. I don't care whether you're a dog, cat, man or woman, you just can't teach it. I always read the sports page, got *Sports Illustrated.* I'm not like most of my colleagues. They like to turn the sound down on a game on TV and do the play-by-play. I prefer to be out there playing instead of talking about it. You learn from being out there playing. My conversational style on the air is very laid back, and my partners can tell that I've played sports."

Kobler was a college softball player. Her experience bred her for the business and gives her an edge, she believes. "I can't remember a time when I didn't love sports. I loved watching, and competing. As a reporter I always had an edge in terms of what the athlete is going through, what it's like to be in a slump. That especially helps a woman, because it's apparent when she does an interview that the athlete knows she has an understanding."

Cohn played, too—backup goalie on a boy's hockey team in high school. Her love of sports was bolstered at home. "My dad...how many times have you heard that? Boy or girl, your dad gets you started in sports. Growing up, in junior high and high school, my friends would be out on a Friday night, and I'm sitting on the couch with my dad watching the Knicks or Rangers. I fell in love with sports that way. My dad gets a real kick out of what I do, because he always wanted to be what I am."

Continuing on the question of credibility, Cohn says, "You're not going to please everybody. It took me a while to realize that. I could be a perfect sports-caster, and there are people out there who just don't want to hear sports from a woman. OK, I understand that now. I didn't for a while because I thought I was doing a good job and but, but, but...it doesn't matter. That's the way life is, the way sports fans are."

She is not just man-fan bashing, either. She includes herself in the critical crowd. "I'm the first to criticize, woman or man—it doesn't matter who's up there—if they're not doing a good job, it's embarrassing."

But especially, she says she has a tendency to "frown on women who are not working at their craft and showing improvement, because that reflects badly on all of us who really work hard to get to this level, and to win over skeptics."

How can thinking still run so Dark Ages? You can analyze it all you want and to no avail. The women of the air suggest the same ways to build credibility that you learned without gender reference earlier in this book: work ethic, knowledge of the craft, knowledge of the subject, *et al.*

Cohn observed, "I've seen a little change, and I think this building (ESPN) had a lot to do with it, because people like me and Gayle Gardner and Robin Roberts proved themselves and climbed the ranks. It's not like some woman wins Miss America and then is part of *NFL Today*. That wasn't good."

Once again, recall "go to Boise...Poughkeepsie." Look at some of these beaten paths of Long Island and Mississippi, where credibility was nurtured ...

Cohn grew up in the city. Make that, *THE* city. Her advice to aspiring women sportscasters—volunteer, and move.

"If you're looking for a glamorous job, this is not it. For many years until recently we did our own makeup," Cohn says. "I suggest getting involved in all the radio and TV you can while you're in school. I volunteered to do things.

"Early in my career I was making terrible money, and I volunteered to cover the New York Islanders on a Long Island radio station that carried their games. They paid for my gas. That's where I got experience in the lockerroom, doing interviews, on-the-spot reporting. And it's where I found my next job...someone was impressed with my work and hired me. Luck is a big part of this business, but you know what? You can make your own luck, too."

She did so with culture shock, moving from the fast-paced New York en-vironment to the different kind of bustle, and points of interest, of Seattle.

"To make it to this point, most of us have gone through the 'local' route,"

Cohn says. "It was really weird to be around people who think of sports as a last priority. Seattle is a really big sports town, crazy about the Huskies and Seahawks and Mariners, but it was hard for me to fathom [that it wasn't like New York].

"It was very frustrating, but an important part of the building blocks is going through that local route. Local TV helped me hone my skills and prepare for the worst. Handling a sportscast when the technical people might not be up to par...this happened to me—I'm introducing a highlight of a Knicks-Pacers playoff game, and suddenly an Isiah Thomas clip from like 1988 comes up, and I'm saying, 'Obviously this is not the highlight.' That prepares you."

Exposure to different emphases also boosted Cohn's experience base. "Growing up in New York, college sports never was that big. Especially football. In Seattle, I'm into that Pac-10 situation—the festivities, fanfare, Rose Bowl—all that stuff was priceless. I never would have gotten that exposure if I did the typical, ignorant New Yorker thing and said, 'New York's the greatest, I'm going to stay here all my life and the heck with everything else.'

"Also, I saw a part of the country I probably wouldn't have. Seattle and the Pacific Northwest is so gorgeous, and it took something great like ESPN to drag me back to the East Coast."

Kolber and Roberts delved into another area regarding credibility: Learning the ropes inside the studio and behind the camera, as well as the on-air skills.

Kolber says, "I suggest to anybody trying to break into the business to know as much as possible about what everybody else's jobs are. That always helped me. I was my own producer, assignment editor, I set up the stories, did the reporting, and then wrote and edited them. Even though I wasn't the one on the air, I learned those skills, and now in the field it helps everybody who works with me because I know the importance of getting the right shot or asking the right question.

"And just in terms of respect, too. Especially for a woman, people will see that she doesn't just want to be on camera, that she's been willing to do the behind-the-scenes stuff, too."

Roberts was willing to play country music to broaden her scope. " I worked at a local radio station as news director at first, and I hated it. I didn't like going to city council meetings and the like. So I quickly changed to become sports director. I had to deejay country music on weekends in exchange for being sports director Monday through Friday. Later I landed a job in Mississippi at

$5.50 an hour, 35 hours a week, and anchoring sports on weekends. I handled play-by-play for high-school football, basketball, you name it, I did it. It was great training for me."

The message rings clearly: Do all you can, anything they will let you do.

"...We developed some scar tissue."—Visser

The Dressing Room

There is one more mountain to climb in the gender issue. The dressing room.

The first glaring headlines on women invading the men's facilities stunned America back in the early '70s when two *Sports Illustrated* reporters stepped in boldly—Melissa Ludtke and Stephanie Salter—and were kicked out. They took their cases to court, and the rules changed soon thereafter.

Michael McKenzie remembers how a woman reporter from his staff at *The Tuscaloosa News* was physically restrained from going into legendary (and highly-traditional) coach Bear Bryant's dressing room after an Alabama game. About 10 years later, McKenzie, then with *The Kansas City Star and Times,* stood with other men reporters side-by-side with Visser outside the University of Houston dressing quarters following a Cotton Bowl in the mid-'80s after Houston Coach Bill Yeoman had Visser escorted out of his team's locker room.

Visser tells a story that typified the situation. "It was pretty rugged. I was the first woman to cover the NFL as a beat writer back in 1976. The players' wives thought the reason I did that was to meet their husbands. There were no provisions for equality."

She worked the Patriots' game against the Steelers one year at Three Rivers Stadium in Pittsburgh. "They had no access for me. I had to stand in the parking lot and wait for the athletes to come out to their bus and cars. I'm waiting and waiting, and Terry Bradshaw came along. I'm there with my note pad and pen, and I asked him a question.

"Before I could finish he grabbed my pen and gave me his autograph on the note pad. I said, 'No, I'm a reporter, you goof.' That got his attention and he answered my question. Now I work with Terry and know him very well, and I never let him live it down. He said that it was just so weird to see a woman sportswriter.

"I have to say we took some hits. We developed some scar tissue.."

The dilemma of equal access for reporters of both genders led to the common practice of closed dressing rooms and the escorting of coaches and players to an interview area so men and women could have equal access after events. Most professional leagues have open dressing rooms, pioneered by the NBA.

Cohn comments, "If there was a way to bring everything we need to us, if athletes would work with us more cooperatively…but they don't, so we have to go in there."

Her strongest advice, when the occasion calls for covering a men's dressing room: "Just go in, get the interviews you need, and get the heck out. That's always worked for me: Be professional, and you'll be fine. Nowadays most of the guys [athletes] are much more enlightened, and that helps."

▲▲▲

Despite the double standards and stacked deck, more and more women enter the field, mostly in television. The strongest advice for women on that career track is to be aware of the conditions and slow-to-change climate, but also realize that work ethic, fundamental knowledge and reporting ability, and healthy attitude make the opportunity boundless.

A chip on the shoulder will not move you along. As Shockley points out, "A great opportunity exists for women who want to be sportscasters, but they must stop being so sensitive about being a woman. Just go be a good sportscaster, get the job done—just as a woman has to in an executive position in any business."

The final word on gender issues comes down to Visser's concise remark, "The key for a woman in this business is knowledge…that is what will distinguish her."

Roberts says she strives to talk to a broad-based audience in knowledgeable terms. "I've always felt comfortable with the way I've done things, and I haven't really thought about anything else. I never have tried to win over the [male] audience."

Cohn summarizes the gender issue with a realistic but optimistic assessment: "We've come a long way, but still there is a long way to go. The situation has improved because there's more competition. Many more women want to be sportscasters."

Kolber nailed it, with: "As a woman, you definitely have to rise to a different level."

▲▲▲

SUZYN WALDMAN

For a sterling success profile of a woman in sports broadcasting, turn to Suzyn Waldman—an example of the results of fortitude, positive attitude, dogged determination, refined talent, and work, work, work:

• The only woman on a major-league broadcasting crew.
• One of the few color analysts who is not a former player.
• A sportscaster who learned on-the-job, rather than from specialized schooling, spinning off of her life-long love of baseball.

She took the heat from men who didn't like her accent or her presence—players, club officials, and other reporters—and pressed on. Here is her amazing story, from *Man of La Mancha* to Madison Square Garden, and her thoughts for women pursuing this career, starting with, "...it's a business where you are not wanted...the most difficult profession....[but] never let them tell you no."

Waldman is a former actress/dancer who championed the woman's cause in the booth many ways. She broke new ground with three breakthrough appearances in 1995 on *The Baseball Network*. She had covered the Yankees (and the NBA Knicks) eight years for WFAN, an all-sports station where she started her career by doing updates every 15 minutes from the first day it went on the air, July 1, 1987.

A year later, she began covering the Knicks and Yankees regularly. In 1996, WPIX-TV in New York signed Waldman to 13 Yankees telecasts with former Yankee great Bobby Murcer. Then in 1997, Suzyn became a color analyst on 25 Yankees games on the Madison Square Garden cable network, in a rotation with former star players Jim Kaat, Ken Singleton, and Bobby Murcer.

Susan speaks of her fascinating career transition from the theater stage to the broadcast microphone (she still sings the National Anthem at events), of male peers who shun her, and of the professional plight women must overcome. She overcame much more.

Just after learning of her hiring on WPIX-11, she learned, too, that she had breast cancer. She underwent surgery a few weeks before spring training. But she would not forego the season. "I wasn't going to give up," she told *Sports Illustrated.* "I worked too hard for that shot on television. They were going to have to cart me away. I was going to have to die for me not to be on the air."

Waldman worked half the season while undergoing chemotherapy, injecting herself daily to sustain white blood cell count. The Yankees helped out by storing her medicine at the stadium, on team airplanes, and in press boxes. She experienced ongoing nausea, and often had the shakes. "There wasn't a day in six months when I wasn't worried about throwing up or passing out," she says.

After the Yankees won the World Series, only then did she submit to the next treatment, radiation therapy. Her medical reports came back clean as a new season dawned. Team owner George Steinbrenner, who at first resisted her presence and refused to grant her interviews, cited her for "great courage...Suzyn is fearless" and supported her hiring onto the MSG network rotating crew.

"It's a dream come true," Waldman said.

On the ABC experience:

"I'd like to do it again and do it correctly. There was more hoopla than I expected, and we didn't want it to be a sideshow or publicity stunt. I didn't make any major mistakes, I didn't swear on the air, so all in all it was pretty good."

(Editor's note: Many media columnists across the country panned her performance, something she was used to from theater critics, but when she played back the tape she cried for two hours. She said she remembered that basketball coach Rick Pitino once told her that anybody who says they learn from losing is lying, and that she didn't see any value in the down side of that experience.)

On being a non-player:

I'm not sure that means anything. I've been watching baseball since I was 3 1/2, a very long time. I've been in the business 11 years. I'm not doing open-heart surgery, I'm watching games that I love and putting my feelings into talking about them. That's very important. We have gotten away from the humanity of this game. People relate to the players, and when it becomes all analysis and statistics, they might as well have robots out there playing, or turn on your Nintendo. The feeling is not there that we had growing up. Maybe I can help restore that.

On handling fans:

"Just have the courage of your convictions. One thing I have found in New York, it's not me being a woman, it's sports fans talking to each other, and that's the beauty of the sport and the medium. I love talking to callers and bringing them something they can't read in the papers."

On preparation:

"I talk to players, watch a game, and dissect it. I get to know everybody involved. Especially I make friends with scouts. They are always willing to talk baseball. You can't read a book and learn this. Prep is different for the call-in show and the game broadcasts, of course. For the games I learn tendencies of players I haven't seen. I talk to the pitchers and pitching coach. My network has been good to me over the years. I might seem over-prepared, but it works for me."

On taping:

"I tape myself all the time, but I don't listen or watch for a while—a couple of weeks. I look mostly to see if I'm telling the truth. I listen without shutting it off and check out, one, if I'm interesting; two, whether I talked too fast, which I have a tendency to do when I'm excited; three, if I've made any grammatical errors."

On being criticized:

"I've never learned how to handle it. It hurts every single time I read criticism, and I can't understand it. I've learned not to read it. People love to tell you bad things. If I read it, it is to see if anything rings true. Sometimes they say it in a way that is not very pleasing, and it is bothersome."

On being critical:

"I always have been critical where it's appropriate. My style didn't change when I started doing their telecasts. I see no reason to sugarcoat. Viewers and listeners know what is going on, and they are not dumb."

On using your voice:

"My vocal training was mostly singing, how to use the vocal cords, how to avoid putting strain on your voice, how to pace yourself. The best thing to do is listen to yourself on a tape recorder. If you can listen, then you are your best critic. Avoid concern about your accent or your pitch. Just be who you are and learn to communicate well. The voice doesn't matter much in this day and age."

On getting started in the business:

"If I have to tell you how to get into it, then you do not belong here. I travel with a group of nine reporters [for newspapers] who haven't talked to me in nine years. There is a price to pay, and it's a very big one. You cannot let anyone tell you that you can't do it. There has to be other women out there who can do what I did. I'm sure that Robin Roberts or any number of others could if someone would give them the chance.

The burnout rate for women is very big. When we were growing up, sportscasting wasn't the thing [for women] to do. My grandpa took me to Fenway Park in Boston, and my mother knew things, and the nuns in school knew more than any 50 men could ever know. I didn't know I wasn't supposed to know until I tried to do it for a living."

Waldman said in her interview with *Sports Illustrated* that "sticking it out" is the most important factor in women making it in this field. "If anybody says no, don't believe them," she said. "If you think you can do it, don't let anyone laugh at you. There shouldn't be some six-year-old girl out there thinking she can't be an announcer because 'women can't do that.' So never let them tell you no."

PART II: MINORITIES

Bryant Gumbel, before he opted for a long stint as co-host of NBC's prestigious *The Today Show*, left distinguished and indelible mark on sports broadcasting as the first African-American on-air talent with "star" quality at the national network level.

Remember the GOB Network mentioned earlier? In truth, it was the GOWB. White was in. Especially on television, minorities were not part of the sports broadcasting consciousness (or broadcasting in general, other than *Amos and Andy* until Gumbel came along; and, like women, black broadcasters started arriving from journalism schools, rather than just football fields and basketball courts.

In early years of the TV sports boom what we remember is Bill Russell commenting on basketball, and later Harvard graduate James Brown, who took things up a notch. Pro football brought us Irv Cross and Ahmad Rashad. More recently, John Saunders at ESPN and Fred Hickman at CNN gave polished definition to the anchor's role on nightly sportscasts.

And somewhere along the way, local markets got the drift. Diversity of race and gender took a seat in those anchor's chairs.

You will hear from a few who developed their careers along different paths.

A good starting point is with someone you already have met in this chapter: Robin Roberts. She represents a quintessential model: a black, female, former-athlete, journalism-schooled, national-network, on-air sportscaster.

"I never see color," Roberts insists. Remember, she also didn't see cosmetics as a women's issue, but rather a general matter of professionalism? Is her head in the sand?

"Often I was the only black child in school or in my neighborhood [in Louisiana]. My sister, Sally Ann Roberts, who is a news anchor in New Orleans, remembers seeing the first black woman on television in Philadelphia. That inspired her to become a news anchor. I didn't see gender or race.

"But not seeing a black woman sportscaster never stopped me."

Roberts, tells black, Hispanic, Asian or others in racial minority to brace for the competitiveness. Her unwavering ambition is far from blind. Indeed she does indicate an awareness of two distinct trends that those aspirants must buck:

As with women, the minority will face more scrutiny than the average white male. "You must have thick skin," Roberts says. "Realize that you have to be better than your co-workers. But try to make that a positive. Don't look for handouts. It will not be easy, but stay committed. If this is something you truly want, you can make it happen."

She recommends mentors—latching onto somebody successful in the business, follow their model, ask questions, cram knowledge of the ins and outs of the industry. "You might have to sacrifice, as I did by being a disc jockey of country music. Accept that. You can't be bitter about it. Anything worth having is worth working for."

Male counterparts echo some of Roberts' sentiments and advice. William Jackson traversed a trail from Detroit to Birmingham, Alabama, to the set of KCTV in Kansas City as its primary sports anchor. When he was a kid, Fran Charles tagged along with a neighbor in St. Louis with network ties, Jay Randolph, and the inspiration carried him to Stanford and Columbia and eventually to some of the loftiest heights of his profession. Jason Jackson (no relation to William) dashed to ESPN by age 23.

The one thing Jason Jackson had that others before him did not was role models. Such as Fran Charles.

"Jay Randolph obviously was a model for me," Charles said. "I grew up across the street from him, and he would take me and his son, my good friend Jennings III, to the NBC affiliate where he worked. I was 10, and I remember walking into his office and thinking, 'Wow!' I was overwhelmed that this is what that man did for a living, and it stayed with me as something I might want to do. As I grew older, I loved sports and I loved to write, and the seed was planted in my mind about becoming a sportscaster."

He selected two prestigious university schools of communication on opposite coasts to hone his interests—Stanford ('90) in Palo Alto, Calif., and Columbia in New York City—working with the student radio and TV stations. He opted for grad school over "go to Boise." Charles says, "I felt comfortable with my knowledge after Stanford, but the practical skills and writing weren't in place yet.

"Rather than go to a tiny market where they are more interested in getting the product on the air, I thought it would benefit me more to spend a year [Columbia] to learn how to write. That's pretty much all they do there, print and broadcast. I worked alongside people who covered stories for affiliates in New York City."

He combined that with what he learned in the formative years from observing his neighbor, Jay Randolph. "It was great that I could connect the man with a face and a voice," Charles says. "I could see him work the local angle on the NBC station, or cover an event for NBC or ESPN. When I first got started, I copied the guys I liked."

As role models, John Saunders—"steady, smooth, no gimmicks—here's what happened, described in a colorful fashion"—and Bob Costas were the patterns by which Charles wove his style.

It lifted him to Sunbeam Communications, which owns a TV station in Miami and WHDH in Boston where Charles works. "I told Joe Cheatwood, the vice president of Sunbeam, "I'm not going to be a clown, do back flips, pour water over my head, or have people smashing pies in my face. That's not me. I lay it out right in front of you, so there will be no confusion. What you see is what you get."

With that approach, Charles said that his race has had no bearing on his career, in his opinion. Instead, he said, encouragement from peers, internships, mentors, and work ethic have helped him rise through the profession quickly.

"One of my mentors is Eva Erlick at KDSK in St. Louis, who really opened my eyes to how well I could do in this business. I'm kind of an aberration—introduced to it early, I could afford to work internships for free to get college credit.

"I think you don't see many minorities in the business because often when kids can afford to go to college and they do well in college, you turn around and tell them that they must go work in Des Moines, Iowa, for $12,000 a year. Most kids say you can forget that—I'm going to major in something that will make me $25,000 or $35,000 a year."

William Jackson knows that drill.

"You must pay your dues," he says. "I spent a lot of years when I didn't make any money, and I was robbing Peter to pay Paul. That's part of the business."

Jackson worked an internship in 1981 in Detroit. "Ray Lane and Charlie Neal, who cover the NBA for CNN, set the tone for me at Channel 2 in Detroit," Jackson said. "They gave me the confidence that I could do it anywhere, and that started the process of paying my dues."

He worked four years in Flint, Michigan, six in Pensacola, Florida, three in Birmingham, Alabama, and moved to the major market in 1995. Before he started the march, he ran into the issue of color. "An instructor at the University of Michigan told me, 'You don't want to do this, you'll never make it.' And he said that if I insisted then I should intern at the local radio station, because television wouldn't let me.

"Well, I have always been one who, if you tell me I can't, knows in my heart that I can and I will. I use that as ammunition. That professor inspired me, and I am serious about my career. I did it on my own."

At the outset he heard similar messages, that a black man would not get an opportunity on television. "Once you get there and they see you as a sportscaster, color doesn't matter," Jackson said. "I like viewers to be watching William Jackson, not watching the black sportscaster, and like me for what I do. That's when you have arrived. When you go on the air, viewers formulate opinions. But when it's all said and done, I want them to appreciate my work, not that *black guy's* work. So far that has gone well."

He believes that viewers in the markets he worked have taken to his excited, up tempo style. "At first I tried to be Joe Sportscaster, sound a certain way—the just-right inflection. It wasn't natural."

Whether it was race-related or not, Jackson isn't certain, but he says that he did encounter closed doors. "I got many doors slammed in my face," he said. "I tell people in the business now, there are many doors slamming. But all you need is for one door to open to make it. So, be prepared so that when that door swings open you can take full advantage of it. Once you get your foot in that door and do the right things, more doors will open for you."

He, too, mentions the alligator-skin syndrome so important to development of all sportscasters. "After a few years you learn what it takes to stay in the business," Jackson said. "But get somebody in your corner patting you on the back in the beginning, because you must develop thick skin. If somebody loves me, there's another who hates me. I get good letters, and nasty letters. It cuts both ways.

"If you prepare yourself and get the foundation right, then you develop the confidence to branch out and do things distinctively, different from the norm."

His strongest advice, minority or not, is to "get internships, write for the school and local papers and/or stations, and just hang out…and never worry about getting paid, because some of your best experiences ever, you don't get paid for. Just stick with it. Sooner or later someone will pick you up. I didn't move up as quickly as I wanted to, but I made it, and I'm loving it."

Conversely, Jason Jackson experienced a meteoric rise to ESPN, an example of how times have changed. He decided at age 17 to become sports broadcaster. "Mainly that was because of ESPN and *SportsCenter*," he said. Six years later he was on its set.

"To be here is beyond amazing. All I have to do is not mess it up and stay for a while."

Oddly, even though he is from the newest generation, Jackson named Marty Brennaman on Reds baseball and Bob Costas on network as his primary role models. "As an African-American, you're always looking for that African-American on the air to relate to and deal with the things they do everyday," Jackson said. "In the '70s, '80s, and early '90s there weren't many African-Americans on the air. So I just sought out who I thought was the best."

He loved Brennaman. "That's just someone I wanted to be. I wanted that gig, to sit there with Joe [Nuxhall] and talk about the Reds all day. For television, Costas was far and beyond. Without a doubt he was the pinnacle during the '80s, so I looked to him and said, 'This is what I need to do.' As time moved on, Mike Tirico was a young guy to relate to, and then Robin Roberts came along, and things have gotten better."

"There's an advantage for African-Americans now because networks and stations realized they created an injustice in the past," he said. "They hadn't even dealt with the issue of color."

Jackson describes a concept that he believes will assist any minority person attempting to become a sports broadcaster, and, really, any potential broadcaster. "The word I've created for this, the position where you have to put yourself, is *digestible*," Jackson said. "What I mean is Idaho, Florida, Texas, and New Mexico all have to 'get' what you're doing.

"Many times it is important to an African-American to remain in that mold, so the mainstream may not 'get' what he is doing with his presentation. But the African-American community understands you and brings you in. If you can become digestible, and bring everybody inside, then you've created an atmosphere that makes you marketable to everybody, everywhere."

Jackson's theory on becoming digestible: "I don't like pepper, but it adds flavor to every meal. "So I dash a little bit here and there. So, if you give a little of what makes you comfortable, and a little of what makes the audience you're presenting to comfortable, then you've done an amazing job of balancing who you are and what you're suppose to be as a national sports reporter and anchor."

His main disadvantage, he says, does not lie in color, but in his age. "I have to be better because I'm 23," he said. "That's my major issue. I've spent a lot of time reading, and that's a way to make sure I have the crucial knowledge necessary to hang with Chris Berman, Dan Patrick, Keith Olbermann. These guys were alive when a lot of major things happened, and they were at many events. So I research everything I can get my hands on, use every bit of information available to be accurate. I create an amazing umbrella of credibility, ranging across all sports."

Jason Jackson represents what can happen rapidly in today's environment of minority hiring. With the right blend of talent and background, the climate is such in the industry that the 13-year trail of a William Jackson can be shortened extensively, as illustrated by Fran Charles and Jason Jackson.

"Everybody [in TV] is hurrying to create an atmosphere that is representative of the community that they broadcast to," Jason Jackson said in summarizing the state of minority hiring. "Good or bad, that's happening. So for all the disadvantages that minorities have to go through, let's take advantage of the advantages. I don't know how long that's going to last, so hurry up."

If women and minorities have an inside track in the hiring policies for sportscasters today, so be it. As you have seen, they have trails to blaze that men, especially white men, never set a foot on because it is not pertinent; they long have held not just the inside track, but until the last three decades, the entire track.

Still, there is not a sports director, producer, or talent scout alive who does not demand the same ingredients, regardless of whom he or she hires. You have had these common traits crammed into your consciousness for several chapters, and whether, as Robin Roberts put it, you are a cat, dog, man, or woman, and we will add white, black, brown or purple, you must get them down pat: Prepare, practice, do it, study what you did, do it again, prepare some more, do it again, ad infinitum.

Keep in mind that Federal law prevents anybody from distinguishing you by gender or race, and, if anything, is favorable to women and racial minorities (EOE mandates), so if you get the foundation in place, make the sacrifices, pound the pavement, play the politics, you'll see the only color that matters—the little red light of your dreams flash on before your very eyes: "ON AIR."

Oh, and when it does, have a ball....

CHAPTER 10
TALKIN' SPORTS

"Most of the time you hope they disagree with you, because that's more entertaining."—Greg Brinda, talk radio host on WKNR in Cleveland

Here's an easy pop quiz that could dishearten you, if one particular niche of sports broadcasting tickles your fancy—Talk Radio.

Q: As a talk radio host, which phrase does not fit in the following group?
1. Controversy.
2. Opinion.
3. College degree/journalism background.
4. Sports nut.
5. Dynamic personality.
6. Gift of gab.

The answer, 3, is rooted in a basic fundamental of life: to have an *opinion*, you don't have to *know* anything. And, sadly, there you have Talk Radio in far too many cases. Not in every case, as you are about to see. And some leaders in the field emphasize your education and other fundamentals, in keeping with the main themes of this book.

But what a jolt. If you have Talk Radio in mind as a goal, and you enter the market armed with the classic background—formal schooling, internship experience, a deep and abiding fundamental love and knowledge of sports, and a knockabout resume that is stamped, "Paid Dues," you find out you should have gone to barber school.

As you read on, you'll learn the fascinating success story of a sensational sports talk host who didn't finish high school and was a hot dog vendor.

But before you give up the chase, take heart in the success of "real" broadcasters, too. The emergence of seemingly anybody and everybody behind a microphone babbling about sports with callers just makes the job scene more crowded and competitive, not exclusive.

Sports talk sprang up as early as the 1960s. Pete Franklin deserves much credit for sowing the seeds in an industry field that now grows like weeds. Franklin put together a specialty format using sports personalities and topics in a major market, Cleveland. He did for sports talk what politico Rush Limbaugh and shock-jock Howard Stern did for talk radio in general, some two decades later. Franklin, who now thrives on KSO in San Francisco, drew the pattern from which today's glut of sports talk hosts cut their niche, whether they realize it or not.

"A long time ago I worked with a guy named Joe Pyne who was an insult king on radio," Franklin relates. "Once in a while I would talk about sports, and I'd have a sports personality on the show, and I enjoyed that more than anything else. So I introduced sports talk shows for various stations where I worked, and then hit Cleveland in the mid-'60s with a full-blown sports talk show.

"It became the first sports talk show on a major-market station to acquire the most important thing—numbers [listener ratings]. Without numbers, you die."

But sports talk, and talk radio in general, really burgeoned by a quirk of fate when a major revolution took place on the other half of the radio dial, where the longer waves exist—FM. When stereo completely changed the listening habits of music lovers, gluing them to FM, the AM band started filling up with what is loosely called "info" radio.

That translates to what radio has done since the beginning, when Marconi figured out how to transmit voice across air frequencies: Talk. A certain listenership wants to know what's going on in the world as they drive to and from work, or have a radio in the background at work or at home all day.

Rare is the AM station that only plays music. Now, AM thrives on news, weather, interviews, and opinion.

Only now, the listener talks back. And the listener and hosts go at it, exchanging opinions and barbs. Sports talk in most formats means that anything goes on any subject. Some are specialized—mostly in the form of pregame and/or postgame rap around the local sports teams, to discuss how they did.

There, the armchair quarterback and backyard manager have a field day with the studio host.

A smattering of sports talk sprang up hither and yon after Franklin, until we got all-sports stations, like WFAN in New York City that operate 24 hours a day around sports talk, emulating what ESPN brought to television as the '80s dawned.

Ron Barr probably was the next most notable individual trailblazer after Franklin because he put together a national network in 1988, *Sports By-Line USA.* He strikes a balance between information, preparation, and opinion.

Somewhere in there amongst the opinionated waxing on hot sports topics, shock and schlock crept in. Sports talkers went where Howard Stern and Don Imus built their reputations in New York City—tromping on subjects with irreverence and vulgarity. Franklin says, "Immediately upon enjoying great success, I discovered something rather essential. I could do a normal talk show and insult someone and get you really excited and really ticked off about politics or something, where you would hate my guts forever.

"In sports I found I could do the same thing, which I invariably still do to this day because I'm very opinionated. I've discovered it doesn't make any difference because it's like two guys going into a bar and arguing about the Giants and Dodgers, or whatever rivalry it might be. They argue vigorously, they'll bet their last 10 bucks, and really get annoyed at each other. But the next day they're back drinking a glass of beer again because there is a camaraderie that shares one thing in common—sports."

So, across the chart, that two-guys-in-a-bar syndrome bolsters sports-talk radio, feeding the boisterous super-fan base, and it's why a former barber in Dallas on a 24-hour, all-sports station known as *The Ticket*, a hot dog vendor in Chicago, and a former basketball referee in Denver enjoy huge success, regardless of their total lack of formal background or training in broadcasting.

Thus, a good jumping-on point for a discussion of radio sports talk as a profession is opinion. But, in many cases, the same fundamental skills and work ethic come into play as in other areas of sportscasting, as you will see with yeomen like Franklin, Barr, Greg Brinda, and Lee "Hacksaw" Hamilton . There also is a large crossover from print as sportswriters and columnists well-known in their market take to the air to extend their reach.

Further, you will learn that while production schtick and gimmickry can enhance a show's presentation, such as with popular, rat-a-tat quipster Johnny

Renshaw on *One on One Sports* out of Chicago, you also can go a long way on strong interviewing, reporting, and speaking skills, too.

Even so, if you can't deliver and/or field the opinion, you probably are headed down a dead-end road.

Irv Brown, the former college basketball official (he has worked a Final Four) who made good enough in Denver talk radio on KHOW that he's stuck for 18 years, said: "You have to have some controversy if you are going to have a good talk show."

Mike North, the dropout hot dog guy who literally bought his way onto the air with no experience or credentials, says: "I don't try to be controversial, but if you are honest, then you are controversial. When you give your opinion, people won't always agree, so it's automatically controversial."

Greg Brinda, big in Cleveland, puts it this way: "You have to make a statement. You cannot be wishy-washy in doing a talk show. You must have a definite idea of what you want to say in a very declarative way. Once you give your point of view, then listeners either must agree or disagree."

At the heart of this strong base of opinion and controversy is the willingness to be critical. The listener needs no prompting for that. At the slightest provocation—an error, a dropped pass, a manager's decision to use or not use a pinch hitter or to relieve or not relieve a pitcher—the average listener, *i.e.,* fan, is all over it. Not just slightly, either. Vociferously. Often viciously.

Callers usually have free rein in a sports-talk format to call for a coach's or quarterback's head, and that's commonplace throughout the workaday world after a bad loss or during a losing skid. But, given the anonymity that talk-radio affords ("on Line 2, Fred from Idaho"), listeners often slam away at players and coaches/managers regarding their intelligence and personality, throwing around phrases like "idiot" and "jerk." They are like 007 James Bond-type secret agents.

Some hosts invite that. Others cut it off. Some join in. Opinions flow back and forth freely, frankly, charged with emotions that ride on the edge until someone or another strikes a wrong nerve ending. You'll hear name-calling, shouting matches, exchanges of insults. Don Fortune, a TV anchorman turned radio sports talk host at KMBZ with more than 30 years in the Kansas City market, observes, "I don't like people insulting the guests or the other callers. When you speak or write you have a certain responsibility to be fair. Too many broadcasters aren't being held accountable."

Ron Barr says, "They are misusing the power of the radio." Stay tuned for more on that from him later.

However it is executed, the game plan is to stimulate calls. Talk radio isn't like basketball, played most effectively inside-out; it thrives only when calls come in droves.

As the phone lines light up, as opinions collide and temperaments flare, the host is likely to be drawn into the crossfire, too. Right at the fore of radio sports talk, then, is to paraphrase: If you can't stand the heat…stay away from the mike.

Greg Brinda says, "Everyone has an opinion and point of view, and in this business you have to realize that not everybody likes you. If you don't realize that, then you are in the wrong business."

The Hacksaw himself, Lee Hamilton, addresses that issue. He is not shy about addressing issues (how do you think he got the nickname?) on his nationally-distributed program out of San Diego's 50,000-watt XTRA, where he also carries credibility as the voice of the Chargers. "Do I say things just for the shock value? No. But I say things that obviously rile people and rally them to the telephone.

"My theory as a talk-show host is to have information, to express opinions on that information, and then get someone to call and react to my opinion on that information."

Brinda's approach in Cleveland, where the groundwork has been laid longer than any other market, is to deal with the nasty callers off the air. "We don't handle our critics on the air. I take offense to cheap shots or things that are inaccurate. Sometimes I'll have a private conversation with those people."

Fortune allows that "sometimes it depends on the mood you're in…I don't want to insult anybody. But some callers tell me I'm too nice sometimes. It's a difficult call to make."

Callers aren't the only ones taking pot shots at radio personalities. Spawned by a regular feature in the sports section of *USA Today,* radio-TV columnists have sprung up on sports pages around the country to critique the presentation of local and national programming and announcers. Brace yourself for what the pioneer, Franklin, beholds in that journalistic sector:

"They're trash."

Okay, Pete, tell us what you *really* think.

"I've had criticism all my life. There's always somebody who hates me. First of all, people who write for a living are grossly underpaid, and they loathe those of us in the broadcast business. Most of these writers want to be in broadcasting, or to be on the boob tube. They want to be an on-air personality with people asking for their autograph. Nobody asks a sportswriter for an autograph, or a radio-TV critic. These are people who can't cut it. You don't pay attention to the midgets."

If anybody brings up on his show what a columnist or critic has written, Franklin runs with it. "I attack them viciously, especially if they are very well-known, and I mean that with all, deep sincerity. The key is not spending a great deal of time worrying about the critics. Deal with them like what they really are—trash."

Even a guy nicknamed for a sharply-honed, steely, jagged-edge cutting instrument, Hamilton, isn't that strong. "It depends on what's been written," Hacksaw says. "If it's a fair critique, OK, I have no problem with that. If it's cheap shots and contained negative stories week-to-week, then I'm going after the guy. As long as they are fair, if they want to critique something I did, fine.

"Somewhere along the way something has to be positive, too. If they are not going to write something positive about you, too, then they have no credibility and I'm not going to waste my time on them."

Hamilton chuckles at the moniker he acquired for his outspoken opinions that cut to the chase, and, often, to the quick. "What you hear on the air is what you get off the air. I don't do things for effect. I am who I am. I've been critical of sports management and of players. I deal with issues as they come up, but I'll say this—you might not like what I say today, but I guarantee that if you keep a scorecard on all the things I've said, you'd find 10 positives to every one negative. I think I'm fair."

Brown says he ignores critics, whether they are callers or columnists, because "you're not going to turn them around anyway," and North points out, "If we make a mistake on radio, someone is going to call us on it...we have to answer to it. Column guys don't retract. That's the difference between radio and newspaper guys."

Franklin refers a Sammy Davis Jr. standard in expressing his stance. "He [Sammy Davis] sang, 'I Gotta Be Me.' There are no two human beings alike. Mel Allen is Mel Allen, Red Barber was Red Barber. I'm Pete Franklin. The great radio personalities in the early days had a schtick or punch line—something unique to them in their delivery, their style, their voice. God gives each and every one of us that.

"So there is no need ever to emulate someone else, except perhaps on a broad scale. The key to success is to be yourself, work to please yourself, and you build up great self-esteem, which is not to be confused with a false degree of conceit."

At the same time that the advice on being yourself weaves a thread into this area of broadcasting, just as it does through every on-air position out there, talk radio, because it isn't visual, relies strongly on personality and entertainment value. "You have to keep people listening to you," Brinda notes. "The competition is strong in this day and age of talk radio. It's not like when there was one show in any given market, if at all. Now there might be three or four going head to head. You have to be unique, entertaining, and give people out there a reason to listen to you."

"...The hot-dog street guy image worked. It's been one of those miracle, rags-to-riches stories that would happen only in America."
—Mike North, talk show host in Chicago

Mike North's phenomenal, almost unbelievable success story paints a picture of "it's just me, folks, come and get it" as well as anybody's. Mostly that's because it identifies a uniqueness of talk radio's niche—direct contact with the fan, which brings out the fan in the host more than in any other sportscasting role.

North is Mike Fan. That's where he came from. That's where he stays. That's where he delivers from...the hot dog stand, when you come right down to it. His roots, his essence. "I appeal to the blue-collar folks," he says. "I went to high school just two years, then got my G.E.D. in the military, and worked different jobs until I was 37. Then this job cropped up."

Well, not precisely. He first planted, sowed, watered, and grew the crop. "I'd listen to other radio guys and think, 'I know I can do better.'

He found a way to prove it. North had a reputation on the street, where he sold hot dogs, of conducting sports patter with customers as they chowed down. He thought that the same rap would work on radio. But he started on TV, leasing time at $300 an hour.

"I created the *NFL Handicap Show* on Saturday night, only during the football season." North sold advertising at $50 for 30 seconds, $100 for a minute, and he enjoyed a two-year run. "I sold $1000 in advertising each week, making $700 for myself. I heard about a radio station looking for a talk host. I went up against 200 [applicants], and they liked my stuff and gave me a one-month trial. After six months, they gave me a contract and a new deal, because they found out that the hot-dog street guy image worked."

The hot-dog guy image he referred to stems from a simple formula of directness combined with information and no false pretenses. "I'm honest, first and foremost," North says. "I pride myself for being a tough interviewer. I've asked the tough question ever since I went on the air, and that's how I made my mark. I thought this [Chicago] was a soft media town, and I guess my style seems harsh to some [interview subjects]. A lot of these athletes are corporate types anymore."

Honesty, to North, correlates to no back-stabbing, plus balance and fairness. "If I do run on a guy, and then he comes on air with me, I'll do it to his face." He does his thing on *The Score*, WSCR, in Chicago.

A constant balance to strike in sports talk radio is preparation vs. spontaneity. Most programs are caller-driven, yet the host bears some responsibility in setting up the show by focusing on specific events or performances that are the talk of the town.

Take a look at how some of our subjects handle prep:

North, who has four hours daily on the air: "We let our listeners steer the show. I don't write down what we're going to talk about. We go by the phone lines. I always have two emergency topics ready."

He offers an example of an early summer day when the lines were dead, so he asked a simple question wrapped around the two Chicago baseball teams: "If the Cubs and Sox were out of it, what two teams would you root for?" That lit up the lines and stimulated a give-and-take. "Always keep a couple of emergency topics on hand," North says.

"We don't have a plan or time schedule. I talk about what the callers want to talk about. [Examples on the day we talked to him: Dennis Rodman, Shaq O'Neal, and the White Sox series.] One topic will light a fire, and then calls will pour in about it."

To prepare for the spontaneous combustion of callers, North watches a game—any Chicago team that's playing—and Sports Center and local news. He reads the two Chicago papers and *USA Today*. "I want a local and a national perspective," he says.

Another thing he does is diversify the conversation, weaving in and out of topics directly sports related to other areas of life. "I read the front page, the gossip column, all of the paper, because I don't just talk about sports," he says. "My philosophy is that if you talk about just sports, you do something that's been done 1,000 times before. If you walk into a bar with your buddies, you'll talk sports for about 20 minutes, and then you'll talk about politics or a couple of hot-looking ladies who walk in. That's what I do, mix it up."

Hamilton runs hard, 12 hours a day, in prepping for his four-hour talk show that is syndicated coast-to-coast. "I work from 9 to 9, and the show is on from 4 to 8 p.m.," he says. "My show is different from many others—more of an information-driven show that I produce myself. I book my own guests, and I pay attention to what's going on."

At his disposal are three 24-hour sports wire services and a computer hooked up to the Internet, on which he scans through out-of-town newspapers. "I spend a large chunk of the day gathering information," Hamilton says. "A talk show host networks with people all over the place. I talk to hosts in other markets about what rumors they have heard, or the background of a hot story in their area. It's very time consuming."

He books three guests for each show and lines up topics. "I don't do a lot of in-depth reading because of the time it takes," he says. "But I scan a ton of stuff—10 or 12 newspapers' sports sections on the Internet. You need a lot of information as a talk show host, so develop a system to get enough of that information without getting overwhelmed. I've heard horror stories of how some people in this business got addicted to the computer and Internet. Plan for the time to chase interviews, tape interviews, go through wire copy, browse newspapers."

Greg Brinda says ditto, basically. ESPN and CNN sports, three local and one national newspaper, arrive at the station about 2½ hours before show time with a general idea of topics to pursue on the air. "I lay out three main topics, and have some hooks to get them going," he says. "I meet with the producer to talk about subjects and who we want to talk to, and then we line up guests."

Pete Franklin points out the oxymoronic nature of the talk show—planned spontaneity. "Preparation is very misunderstood by most people," he says. "You can't pull something off totally extemporaneous. You don't know what the next caller is going to say...what will come up in the next 30 seconds or two minutes. So the method I've used all my life requires no preparation."

Hmmm. Another oxymoron—non-preparatory work.

Let's translate. Franklin is talking about his normal life style, which prepares him for the on-air duty of talking. "I'm always reading 8 million books and newspapers from all over the country, talking to people everywhere, because I'm interested and eager to know what the right tackle of the Steelers is doing, what the new prospect at UCLA looks like, and so forth.

"You have to be mentally ill like I am in order to be successful at this," he says, laughing. "My attitude is that there is no work attached to it. Once you're talking about sports, it's a lot of fun, not work. I suggest to people who think they might want to do this to absorb as much knowledge as humanly possible without working at it. If you have to work at it, you won't last a lifetime, and it's definitely a lifetime thing, day in and day out, month in and month out, year in and year out."

Whereas many talk shows touch on national developments, but focus on local teams and their current activity, Hamilton prepares for breadth of topics because his show goes across affiliates nationwide. "We do such a very different talk show than most places," he says. "Primarily that's because it's national, and we spend a great deal of time on all NFL teams, all baseball teams, the NBA, the NHL, colleges.

"And, because we hit so many hot buttons, it's not a problem to go out into the marketplace and get phone calls. Everyone wants to talk about their favorite team. Everybody has an opinion about what's going on. We cover the whole waterfront."

The word *producer* came up. All but Hamilton agree that a strong producer is essential to a successful talk show. The producer generally schedules interviews, lines up background for the interviews, keeps voluminous files and research material handy for finding answers to callers' questions or to lend support to a point of view, and screens calls.

Sometimes listeners are amazed at how, say, Ron Barr, who is in San Francisco, can come up with detailed information about the offensive line of, say, the Philadelphia Eagles on the other side of the atlas. Kudos to his producer for that. Some talk-show hosts have their brains jam-packed with minutiae, but they can't know everything, yet a strong producer can make it seem like they do.

Instantly, too, it would seem; that is a function of clever screening and ordering of calls, so that information can be tracked down while the caller is on hold. (Callers have an amazing tolerance for hanging on for many minutes, maybe even an hour, especially on national shows because it's so hard to get through the busy signals. Besides, usually they're calling on a toll-free number, and they can hear the show piped through the phone line as it airs while they wait.)

Producers also signal the times for cutting away to commercials and news/weather/traffic reports. The host often relies on the producer for pacing, too. "Caller is down" is a common phrase the host hears in his headset as he wraps up a thought or response about a caller's topic.

Our subjects concur that callers should be limited to short spans on the air, generally. "We limit the calls to no more than 2-2 $\frac{1}{2}$ minutes," Brinda says. "After that, it becomes redundant. Not many callers need more than that, and most don't need more than a minute or minute-and-a-half.

"We don't let the same people call back the same day, and we try not to let them on during the same week, but that's hard. When we have a frequent caller, we limit even more."

Suzyn Waldman, featured guest in the previous chapter who works on all-sports, round-the-clock WFAN in New York, says, "I make sure the same people don't get on. If the same people are calling, then you are talking about the wrong things and maybe you should change what you're doing."

Are you ready to start? Sure you are. What's the big whoop, right? Everybody talks, right? If a barber can do it, a hot dog salesman . . . .

But know this: No matter how good a talker you are, if you don't know what you're talking about, you're a big puff of dead air. If you are ill-prepared, ditto. Wanting to be a star, egomaniacally focused on your own opinions and thoughts, rather than being conversational and on par with the caller, double ditto.

Plus, toughen your skin. Talk radio is not very popular, frankly, with the athletes and coaches and managers, because so much of opinion and controversy centers on the negative.

Finally, if you come with all style and no substance, listeners go elsewhere...or to sleep. There's room for trademarks. Nancy Donnellan, "The Fabulous Sports Babe," has her moniker, her gender, and her Geek of the Week Feature working for her at ESPN, where she landed after charming visitors to her call-in sports in Seattle. (She gets away with something men never could, calling people "honey" and "sweetheart.")

Johnny Renshaw has his ad-lib rhymes and "drops," as they're called—musical bits or sound bites from movies or interviews that are dropped into a segment, and he goes up-beat, full-stream on a zillion different topics, seemingly in one, five-minute breath.

Up and down the dial you can find Papa John, The Regular Guys, The Sports Princess, and any number of catch-phrase types.

Entertainment value drives the industry, but it can run mighty thin mighty quick, making a listener both weary and wary. The giants of the talk waves you have heard from take it up several notches, and they tread the same paths common to all other sportscasting roles.

"Accept the challenge," Hamilton says. "Don't be afraid to work. Go sample everything you can in media in the marketplace. Knock down every door you can to get internships. You might not like what you're doing, but the experience factor helps you get in the front door somewhere. Select good college courses, sample everything available."

Brinda stresses, "Become knowledgeable in the field you want to work. If it's talk show host, then you really have to know your sports, know how to listen, and know how to have a good conversation. Develop a style that you can't really write on paper. Use personality in your delivery. Then start banging on doors."

And for the love of Hacksaw, love your non-work. "You have to have an avid love for all sports and be willing to go anywhere, do anything, work for peanuts for a long time, pay your dues. You must have an enormous amount of perserverance.

"My perspective is that if you do something you love, your four-letter word becomes p-l-a-y, not w-o-r-k. That four-letter word [work] is the dirtiest word in the English language. If you approach this as something you're going to p-l-a-y at, if there's a key, that's it."

"I think the reason we have been around a long time is because of the credibility of what we do night in, night out."—Ron Barr

RON BARR

For a microcosm classic example of premium talk sports on radio, Ron Barr's *Sports Byline USA,* airing weekday nights from 7-10 p.m. Pacific Time, sets the standard. On Oct. 24, 1988, he launched the program with 13 stations signed up. Entering its 10th year, the call-in and interview show blasts across the largest sports network of radio stations in the world, plus the World Wide Web. Barr worked in local radio and television in San Francisco when a friend approached him to host a start-up concept of sports talk on radio called *The Evening Sports Magazine.* "I always knew I could interview people, and, since that was the concept of the magazine approach, it was perfect, even though I had never done sports talk before," Barr says.

At the outset of his own program when he spun off from those roots, he told persons he hired to the production team, "I don't care if you fail, I care if you don't try," Barr said. "I've never been afraid to fail.

"When I hire somebody to my company, I hire them without looking at resumes. I just sit down and talk to them."

Because that's what he does every night—sits down with hundreds upon thousands of listeners and talks to them. Never over them, never above them, never at them. "You can't talk down to your audience. Talk down to them, and you have lost them. They have to trust you, and that's where your preparation for this job comes into play."

Following are some random thoughts and advice on the ins and outs of talking sports with Barr:

"You have to be very careful about taking a topic and making it controversial by the style you use to deliver it," he says. "I hear talk show hosts across the country say things that I know have no basis or foundation, and it's wrong...they are misusing the power of the radio."

Barr places heavy emphasis on research to back up opinionated or reported story lines. "Too many times, somebody will hear something or watch something on television and accept it," he says, referring both to listeners and to program hosts. "Because we have turned into a society that won't go find out for ourselves about things we have accepted as gospel, the rumor or report can become a very dangerous weapon."

His tack is to 'fess up that he isn't in the know, and then do everything possible to be in the know. "I keep in mind every night that if I don't know about something, I say I don't know," Barr says. "Then I find out the information I need. If the item is controversial, get the facts as best you can, but don't find yourself caught up in the mass hysteria of everybody else."

With his broadcasts circling the globe, Barr pays close attention to his guest list, offering a wide variety every week. He'll average a name guest every hour, and sometimes doubles up. The guests, more than his opinions, link him closely to the audience. By example, he remembers a night that Duke Snider, the former Dodger outfield Hall of Famer, was a guest. "A man called and said, 'You know,

Ron, I waited 35 years to talk to Duke Snider, and tonight you're giving me that chance of a lifetime.' I thought to myself, 'That's really what this is all about—giving an opportunity to fans to make a connection with their heroes," Barr says. "Also to be able to interact so that we can have an exchange of ideas.

"It's unlike normal talk radio, where the subject would possibly limit the participation, where a lot of people might be intimidated, talking about religion or sex or politics. Sports is where there are no wrong answers. Somebody can call up and say the Chicago Bulls are the greatest team ever in the NBA, and somebody else can call up and say, no, it was the Lakers or Celtics. Nobody is wrong.

"That's what makes sports talk unique [distinguishing it] from other forms of talk radio."

Barr relies heavily on a team of producers and research staff, combed into his own personal accumulation of experiences and data. "My producers do a good job of giving me biographical background on the athletes we have on, and I scan it. I don't think you have to read a book. I will tune into a ball game at the exact point that a key element is going on. I will read a passage or thumb through a book quickly for 10-15 minutes and pick out a couple of things of interest, and then I can quote from them or refer to it in an interview.

"That's always been part of my makeup. I don't sit around and watch sports on the weekend and let it dominate my life, because I think we give the broader perspective. The only way that can happen is by having a perspective outside of sports alone."

The hallmark of Barr's broadcasts is his enthusiasm, delivered with sustained high energy. No stunts, no gimmickry. "You have to be both journalist and entertainer," he says. "You can be informative, but if you can't entertain with the information, then people are not going to listen. If you happen to be an entertainer, but can't back it up with credibility, then you are not going to have a long shelf life."

CHAPTER 11
THE 6&10 TV SPORTS/SPORTSCENTER

"You combine elements of show-biz with journalism....wrap the...medicine in some sugar."—Bob Ley, ESPN

TV SPORTS: ESPN

You want to go to sports broadcasting heaven? Go to Bristol, Connecticut

When ESPN first aired in 1979, everybody laughed behind its back. It was a joke. Now it's a legend as a trendsetter, a staple, and a bonafide "inside" source. (So-and-so is going to replace so-and-so in a coaching vacancy, or such-and-such trade is in the making. ESPN said so.)

ESPN also has become, for many aspiring sportscasters, the zenith of the industry. Many value ESPN as the top in this trade—absolutely so in the news-room. Later, you will hear from several sports anchors at local affiliates on their unique offerings and impact, which is still vital to the sports fan. However, the key word here is *local*.

Because of its sheer size, ESPN provides the keenest insights into how to deliver sports news in the most comprehensive package—from gathering (film-ing, viewing, editing, and writing) to delivery from the anchor's seat. Plus, they do it round the clock, not just twice or thrice nightly. It offers the best models, the most-coveted internships, and a superb point of light for the aspirant who would report from the scene or anchor in the studio in a traditional TV news format.

In time, ESPN moved out of strictly news and analsis into the glut of ma-jor-event telecasts and proffered play-by-play opportunities, too. There's noth-ing else out there like the ESPN melting pot of talent—on and off the air. (The organization also includes ESPNEWS and ESPN Radio.)

ESPN has far more scope. But it also refined an important aspect of TV sports: it had E as a body part from the get-go. Do you even remember (or care?) what ESPN stands for? Entertainment and Sports Programming Network.

Forgot about the E, didn't you? Today, ESPN, to the average viewer, means sports.

But it took root as 24-hour programming, and it grabbed at straws, putting on obscure event after obscure event, not always sports. The entertainment aspect spread into its sports delivery, too.

ESPN established standards for news format, in-depth interview format, team-by-team reporting, features, you name it.

There, former and current newspaper reporters blossom as on-camera, expert reporters. And traditional broadcasters have played with the craft out on the edge, refined their schtick to an art, and entertained us to the hilt—while still delivering the goods, *all* the goods, far more goods than anybody ever delivered before, including some goods we didn't even know existed.

ESPN delivers the goods with pizzazz and personality plus. It's where Chris Berman and Roy Firestone were born.

SportsCenter hatched on ESPN. Today, it still commands killer ratings among the proliferation of copycats like *CNN-SI,* Fox Sports, etc.

It's where Bob Ley pioneered late-night anchor work in innovative ways, and where the Dan-and-Keith dog-and-pony bit resculptured the standard for nightly newscasts, mixing biting fun-and-pun repartee with incisive reporting and highlight-reel narrative that everyone wanted to emulate.

According to Ley, "We wrapped the hard facts—the medicine—in some sugar, which is good pictures, funny comments, song parodies, bizarre cutaways of fans with dog bones going through their heads. Bottom line, people had to want to watch us."

The nightly *SportsCenter* provides a glorified evening newscast. It brought that hungry American sports public a far larger serving than any local newscast could. Instead of three or four minutes with an *hors d'oeuvre* of highlights, the fan could feast on one solid hour of highlights and reports on all sports, all teams, at all hours.

The monster grew many heads and, almost two decades later, now stands as a monument to everything that is good about nighttime, news-time sports reporting. The only thing sports-related with a longer life on cable TV is HBO's *Inside the NFL.*

Because most young broadcasters start out wanting to be on the air, we zero in on three of the most prominent ESPN talents: Bob Ley, Dan Patrick, and Chris Berman, along with snippets of others.

"They asked us, and allowed us, to keep reaching until we got it right, so we kept reaching...people behind the scenes, too."—Berman

Berman was a local personality in the region where ESPN began, and he was hired partly for that identity. He introduced methods that some critics labeled cornball, but viewers took to him in a big way. You have to believe it was because he was just a big, funny guy, having fun.

This guy obviously knew his material, knew sports, and could deliver it in a way that kept a fan satiated, but enjoying a chuckle, too. "My whole TV style developed because I had an hour," he says. "If you talk to people for an hour, you have to know your stuff. You could act up in a $3\frac{1}{2}$-minute sportscast and get away with it. If you're doing an hour, you'd better be who you are and incorporate TV skills with it."

Part of the freedom to develop came from that scope we talked about. "We had so much to do—24 hours—they [management] couldn't watch every word that was said. I did overnight for almost three years. I've seen everything—stuff fall over in the studio and crash, everything. My first two years were like dog years...like 14 years."

What you see now is the glamour. As with all the super-talents Berman paid the dues to get there. "I used to announce darts, and now I do major-league baseball," he says. "Having been here 16 years, having seen it grow from 70 employees to some 1,400, having gone from hoping that people got cable to ESPN2....it's been exciting all the way along."

A salient point that Berman offers is that, yes, ESPN is unique, but you make your own path wherever you are. "There are many other unique situations, and in this business anyone with enthusiasm, intelligence, creativity, and spunk can develop a niche in any market. Some people are good to a certain degree and might not be good enough or up for the big markets. But this business is so much fun. You could be the sports guy in Providence, or anywhere, for your whole life and have a pretty good life.

"Anyone who gets in it to make the big money or become a big star will do neither. Anyone who gets in it and understands that those things are possible, and files that away, and works hard at the other things might reach that."

Berman holds to what he calls "old-world values." Hard work, preparation, loyalty. He may never leave ESPN. "I like it that people think of ESPN and think of me," he said. "I represent what we represented back then—the old-world values of this place. I know what we were. You don't take things for granted. I'd like to play my entire career with one team if I can."

Bob Ley has a style that fit viewers like a comfortable pair of shoes—a paradoxical combination of dressy shoes and slippers.

He stood at the fore of the *SportsCenter* evolution that impacted on local sports newscasts across the country the way the national newspaper *USA Today* influenced the look and feel of local daily publications. "It was very tough," he said. "The subject matter is so pedestrian at times. If you want to talk about Art Modell's finances [as owner of the Cleveland Browns/Baltimore Ravens], most fans would be interested by it…it's a good print story. How do you distill a conversation I just had with Bob Griese for 20 minutes down to two sentences that won't make you change the channel?"

TV transcends journalism. Remember the E . . . .

"The transcript could read like a great *Wall Street Journal* article," Ley says, "but if the show doesn't rate well or adequately, we have failed. Our job is to keep the audience, inform them, and in so informing them, entertain them from time to time. It's a very delicate balance."

"There's no net in live TV."—Dan Patrick

As we move through the essential elements of the nightly-news sportscast, two basics flow constantly at the core as the lifeblood to support the entertainment value—pictures and words, in synchronicity. Every sports director, every anchor, every producer and director dwelled on the strong need to develop ability to "see" what you're going to "say." The root word of TV is vision, and we all know the axiomatic worth-a-thousand-words bit. In this facet of the business, it's to live by.

The need takes the craft of writing to a different level.

"You have to think visually at the same time you are writing," Ley said. "You have two tracks in your brain going. I know I have some great facts we've learned about Modell and the Browns and his finances; how do I wrap that together in a story with pictures?"

A common theme, to be sure, and common within the theme is the need for personalizing the written word.

Julie Smith, who ascended to producer of motor sports events for ESPN2, once was a writer for Berman. But not in the strictest sense, she said. She would watch game action for him, write play-by-play highlights, and turn them over to him for scripting. Berman wanted facts only, legible and fluent, and then he would script to the highlights in his own style.

That is the way of most. ESPN has a full staff of writers, yet the on-air personalities often insist on the final word—their word. Or, they ad-lib from the prepared script after rehearsing it.

Dan Patrick and Keith Olbermann were masters at that. Glib, dry humor, sarcasm, puns, and terrific chemistry between them took *SportsCenter* to a new dimension. "I would say 65-70 percent of the 11 o'clock show is ad-lib," Patrick said. "What we read on camera is scripted for the most part, although not if the games are just ending."

The night before Patrick spoke to us, a tragedy involving several deaths occurred at a soccer match in Guatemala while *SportsCenter* was on the air. "Often you're ad-libbing on things you haven't seen before," Patrick says.

"A lot of highlights that Keith and I see, we're seeing for the first time. So that's where knowledge and preparation comes in. You have to have something to fall back on. You trust your instincts. There's no net in live TV."

Like Berman, Patrick and Olbermann always appears to be having a good time. "If you don't want to have fun at this, then don't show up for work," Patrick says. "It's the overall attitude at ESPN." Oddly, that was hard for him to get used to. He moved over from CNN. "I was really afraid to show a personality. CNN is the world's most important network, and that was really overbearing, heavy to carry. When I got to ESPN, it was Keith who said, 'You should show your personality the way you are off the air.' I heeded that, and we're both the same on and off the air."

Berman sheds light on that subject another way: "Look at it as a cross between you're having a good time and your job depends on what you deliver. This approach developed here, not by them saying to do whatever you want, like throw a pie in your face. The nicknames and all that stuff [his trademarks] were accidental, not done to become a personality, but to fill the hour."

Patrick says, "You also have to deliver the information. Sometimes we get that order out of whack and put entertainment first. Keith and I constantly have to remind ourselves, information first and then entertainment. If you can combine both, you're offering something a little bit different to the viewer."

The main point to be absorbed here is that ESPN doesn't hire clowns or stand-up comics.

Al Jaffe is a vice president at ESPN for production recruitment and talent negotiations, the person primarily in charge of finding new talent. Known in the industry as "The Kingmaker," he says that in his constant search, "We look for credible people who have a lot of knowledge of four major sports and who communicate effectively in an entertaining, informative, compelling manner."

In an interview in *The Kansas City Star*, Jaffe said that an anchor's potential "starts and flows from sports knowledge....[but] not just people who know sports and every stat, but who have a feel for other things and can make references to music or politics or other areas."

He also stressed that he does not look for carbon copies. "Local sportscasters have a tendency to try to be like Keith or Charley [Steiner]. We look for distinctive style...not cookie-cutter people."

Finally, how does it all come together, this flood of information? When you tune in to ESPN's *SportsCenter*, you don't see a couple of talking heads who dashed into the studio 30 minutes before air time and started reading.

The anchors attend news meetings with production personnel a full nine hours before air time. Together, they design the story budget, plan the show, select video clips that accompany the stories (...accompanied by explanatory "shot sheets"...), and write the scripts.

This process is ongoing right up to the time the red light blinks on, and even continues on late-breaking items (such as late-finishing baseball games) as the show unfolds. Although with their injection of humor and personality—the glib anchors lend a spontaneous flavor to the telecasts—believe Dan Patrick when he says, "We never wing it."

Walk with Patrick through his typical day:

"Do you want me to start with changing my daughter's diapers?" he says, demonstrating that he is, indeed, whimsical off the air. "I'm usually up around 9:30 and watch my three young children until around 2:30. I get into work about 3:15. I start checking wire services and look at the New York newspapers and *USA Today*. We have the benefit of a great research department that provides articles from around the country on whatever big games are going on—further information to help with stories so you go into battle fully armed.

"We start writing early, Keith and I, about 5 o'clock, and hope to be finished about 9 or 9:30. After that we look at highlights, watch games, and then go on at 11, do the hour show, go home and start it all over again the next day."

The give-and-take between the partners takes place behind the scenes, too. Patrick said that he and Olbermann constantly went "back-and-forth on how does this sound? Too little? Too much? Good? Bad? You build rapport and trust. I see him more than I see my wife."

And for a closing shot, Patrick offers some of the most blunt advice doled out by any of our subjects to prospective sportscasters:

"I would encourage them not to get into the business, because too many people aren't willing to pay the dues to get this far. Like everybody else, I wanted to be the next Brent Musberger, Bryant Gumbel, Bob Costas, but I failed to see where they started, how long it took them to get where they are. It's so easy to say, 'I want to do that,' but do you want to go make $10,000 a year in Poughkeepsie where you have to shoot your own video, do a stand-up, your own interviews, put in too much time, don't see your family enough— really sacrifice?

"If you are in this to be on TV, in it for the money, don't get in it at all, because you will be unhappy." (Editor's note: Olbermann left ESPN in 1997 to join MSNBC as host of his own news/interview show.)

Part Two of this chapter moves to the local level to which Patrick referred, although not to the entry level. Plenty has been said on that topic, so the purpose here is to see what the local markets offer uniquely, and to underscore that many basics remain in place regardless of whether the scene is local, national, large or small, pro or amateur. A viewer is a viewer is a viewer.

Know that viewer inside-out, and give whatever is sought. Which most often is right in that viewer's back yard.

"Always lead local, and go from there."
—Frank Boal, sports director, WDAF-TV in Kansas City

TV SPORTS: LOCAL

ESPN, CNN-SI and other similar news-and-highlight formats grow in popularity increasingly with time, they remain national in scope.

So the local TV sports news, however brief during the span of a 30-minute or one-hour newscast, always has one trump card: up-to-the-minute, inside information and interviews with the local teams—especially in a pro or highly-rated college team market.

You must deal with the complexities of production, writing, and delivery, but above everything else on the checklist: on local TV give the viewers all that you can squeeze in about their favorite teams in the immediate area.

• Give them the score.
• Give them the highlight footage.
• Give them personal interviews.

Then worry about the national scene. A fan wants to know national scores in a pro market, because they relatively affect his hometown team. The NFL has a broad-based following. Michael Jordan, likewise. Golf fans track the national tournaments, race fans the national circuit, and of course the major events of all sports hold a universal appeal.

But if you go local, you can't go wrong. Fans will wear out their remote control jumping around to local stations to see highlight footage and snippets of interviews with their local team heroes and goats.

That's why on the subject of writing/scripting the 6 & 10 sportscasts, TV sports directors sound like a broken record: local, local, local…film, film, film.

Mike Bush, who spent five years in Kansas City and has been in St. Louis since 1986, says, "If you are a local station—and aren't we all?—then lead with the best local story…99 percent of the time…."

Frank Boal at WDAF-TV in Kansas City offers a great example. At the time he was interviewed, golfer Tom Watson had recently won the Memorial Day weekend PGA event and was about to stage his annual local charity event, a huge fundraiser featuring top-name participants that draw heavy local media coverage, both live and for newscasts.

"We always feature the local angle," Boal explains. "Whenever Tom Watson wins or challenges in a golf tournament, that's a main story. So, the Sunday night after he won the Memorial, leading with him was a no-brainer, an easy pick. Tonight at 6 o'clock we led with the Watson package, since the Children's Mercy Classic is tomorrow."

Continuing on the theme, Boal says, "Kansas City is a pro market. We'll lead with Chiefs and Royals most of the time during their seasons, and we'll almost always lead with local over national. Our rule of thumb is to cover the Chiefs, the Royals, the Wizards [Major League Soccer], the Comets [indoor soccer], the Blades [minor-league hockey], Kansas, Missouri, Kansas State, and UMKC first—all the local teams—and then the big national story. And on the colleges, we go with them in the order of their rankings."

Many factors come into play. Baseball dominates the summer months until the NFL camps open, but Boal says during 1997, "With so few people in the stands, I wonder sometimes whether we should stay with the Royals as the lead. It's not as easy at it looks. A rival station will always lead with the Chiefs because they carry their games. I know that on our local version of *Sports Machine* during football season [Sunday night preceding George Michaels' nationally-syndicated *Sports Machine*] I will always lead with the Chiefs."

Boal also dealt with large local stories on the Royals—their impending sale, and the wrangling over whether to move to the National League—during the heart of football season. Prioritizing stories is a constant juggling act, based on knowledge of your audience, plus, sometimes, what the competition is doing. (Don't let anyone kid you—these people monitor what the others are doing at 6 & 10.)

Bush follows a similar routine on the other side of the state. He says he makes exceptions to the local axiom on exclusive, breaking news stories about an important non-local athlete or team, or "a major story that affects all fans, such as when Michael Jordan came back from retirement, out of baseball and back to hoops."

Local markets have far less staff than the legions at ESPN or CNN, but writing is no less important as a major component of news reports. In fact, possibly more so, because of time constraints. The looseness of a two-person, ad-libbing telecast is not affordable when sports is such a small portion of a half-hour newscast.

Keep in mind that some people build a career behind the scenes as staff writers. ESPN employs several, as you learned. We told you of the example of Len Dawson in Kansas City, who reads from a teleprompter the words scripted by his producer. Bush was that writer for five years.

Dick Schaap, author many books and a radio-TV editorial commentator and reporter, wrote for the *Joe Namath Show* and others at ABC early in his career to earn his own shot on the air.

`"I always have written my own scripts," Bush says. "I feel very uncomfortable reading other people's scripts. I write 99 percent of them, and I have a difficult time reading the ones I don't write."

William Jackson of KCTV in Kansas City says that his confidence "really took off" when he wrote for the Ann Arbor, Michigan, newspaper during his senior year at the University of Michigan. Then, when he interned at a major affiliate in Detroit, the sports staff let him write their scripts. "They didn't change it, read it the way I wrote it, and that helped my confidence soar, too," he says. "For a young guy that was a big accomplishment.

"That's the key to the business, too—communicating so people can understand without using another 10 seconds to figure out what you said. In that 10 seconds they might miss the whole story, and you lose them. Concise and simple are very important."

Fran Charles of WHDH-TV in Boston, featured in our chapter on women and minorities, said that he studied a lot of theory at Stanford and regrets not having delved more into writing. "One thing I hear about our business is that it lacks good writers. If you know how to write you will take care of yourself. I tell students to work on that to make it as sharp as can be, and they have to do it through practice."

Hand-in-hand with writing on the local level is fully understanding the market. Is it dominated by pro or college or high schools? No matter how well you write a newscast, if the stories aren't what the viewer wants most, you have failed. And because TV adheres strictly to ratings, you will have clear communication from your viewers about whether you have met their needs.

Give them local, and give them what they crave. In the my community, the Kansas City area, the television stations from nearby Lawrence, Topeka, and St. Joseph, plus five stations in Kansas City, cannot give enough Chiefs information from mid-July until the team is either in or out of the playoffs. That same viewing area also has a feeding frenzy off of national-power KU Jayhawk basketball.

Stations in smaller, more remote areas might hit the high schools more heavily and up front, putting the universal interest in football or baseball in a secondary or tertiary spot. William Jackson offers insight into that from his market move from Birmingham, Alabama, to Kansas City. "Alabama and Auburn football are huge in Birmingham, and not pro sports, except auto racing," he said. "I did cover Michael Jordan [in minor-league baseball there].

But it was an adjustment to cover the pro athletes on a daily basis. In a way, college football in Birmingham is like pro sports because it's like a religion to their fans."

The same can hold true for rabid fans of a local high school or amateur team, or minor-league pro team, etc., says Jackson, who also worked in different types of markets in Flint, Michigan, and Pensacola, Florida.

To further delineate the processes of preparing and delivering evening newscasts, we talked to nightly and weekend anchors, some of whom double as reporters, from two major markets—Kansas City and St. Louis—but the fundamentals and principles that they apply to their tasks applies across the board. The scope of reportage is as broad in small markets, flooded with high schools and perhaps small college or junior college sports instead of pro teams. Pro fans are rampant in any market, because of the host of sports events offered on television. They love Michael as much in Lark Lake as in Chicago.

"Sports is supposed to be fun. You become a journalist...do people stories."—Mike Bush, sports director, KSD-TV in St. Louis

We covered preparation and planning heavily earlier in this book but for refresher, keep in mind that TV newscasts require strong advance planning. Bush and Boal point out that it is fairly routine.

"Each day is virtually set, unless a huge story breaks," Boal said, citing such examples as the selling of the Royals right smack in the heat of the Chiefs' hot start in 1997. Sundays offer more time; so good features often are slated there. "This industry is pretty well regulated and tightly-scheduled."

Bush's take: "We start several days ahead on stories, starting with a Monday meeting to look at the entire week. We cover all the local bases. A reporter goes to Rams practice, for example, and finds out that quarterback Chris Miller is not playing Sunday because of a concussion. We then set up an interview with the head coach and with Miller, and build it through the day's telecasts." Bush arrives at the station early in the afternoon, and he supervises the building of the news shows.

The prep that goes into story selection includes knowledge of the demographics. Bush points out, "The 5 o'clock viewing audience is mainly female. We have great female demographics, so we do more feature stories at 5. At 6 more men are home, so we do more hard-core stories and give lots of highlights."

Remember what we said about knowing your audience? Another facet of that is comprehension of the different nuances of dinner-hour and late-night reports, and even in the two dinner-hour segments—one is drive-time, one is just-got-home time.

"Five o'clock is female-driven," Boal says. "Our ratings services tell us that, so we do a lot of features for that audience. At 10 we are highlight-driven. We think pictures and local first, and then highlights of the pro leagues that are in season, and maybe end with a Chiefs or Royals feature. We might pick up a Michael Jordan feature, for instance, during the NBA playoffs."

Bush echos, "Our five o'clock audience has great female demographics, so we do more features. At six, more men are home, so we go to more hard-core sports and give lots of highlights."

Likewise, William Jackson, in competition with Boal for those viewers. "We hone in on the women at 5 o'clock—homemakers and mothers—with light-hearted pieces. You can never lose when you deal with kids and put them on the air."

Boal voices a universal opinion among his peers—that sports is more important to viewers than most news directors allow. His station, a Fox Network affiliate, runs two local, one-hour newscasts from 9-11 p.m., giving him extended coverage possibilities, plus the *Sports Machine* lead-in to George Michael's nationally-syndicated program as expanded coverage on Sunday nights.

Critics can prevent a dilemma in some cases, especially where local publications have a television reporter who reviews programming. Most announcers say they take it with a grain of salt, put to use anything that is helpful, and discard the rest, understanding that everybody doesn't like the same style and that all judgments of your work are subjective.

"I was very thin-skinned when I first started," Bush says. "Maybe some were right who didn't like my work, but I finally realized that is only their opinion. Like it's my opinion that the Cardinals need a second baseman. We're all entitled to those opinions. I don't always agree with the critics.

"The important thing is how management responds to them. There are some critics that management reveres. Fortunately, mine have been very supportive, and strong adverse criticism hasn't happened to me. But I'm told that at the national level Rudy Martzke of *USA Today* is one of the most powerful critics in radio-TV, and that some management types take him as gospel. I find that incredibly hard to believe. It's just one man's opinion, and, besides, how many people really read radio-TV columns in *USA Today* except us?"

The general rule of thumb is to be responsive to and appreciative of feedback, but keep abreast of your audience's wants and needs and work so hard they can't complain about content.

"I've never had a problem with critics," Boal says, noting that The Kansas City Star has three, sometimes four sources for commentary on TV—two specifically for sports—in addition to regular columnists who take aim once in a while. "I would never mention them on the air, and I always would consider the source. Is it someone I really respect? If so, and they were telling the truth, I'd act on it. If it's someone just coming off the wall and criticizing, I'd ignore it."

One area that Bush dealt with early in his career that drew hot and cold reviews was his penchant for humor. "I was a 'funnyman' with a lot of sarcastic comments about Kansas City teams," he says in a frank revelation that is important to knowing your audience, and yourself.

"I changed over the years. I was 24 years old, brash, and thought I was hot stuff [in KC]. I tried to be cute and smart. I thought my opinion mattered, and it really didn't. Over time you realize what is important in life and my style changed. I looked around and saw those who had been around a long time treating the games, players, and coaches as the most important thing. I matured, both as a broadcaster and person, and rather than becoming a clown on TV, I became a reporter. Clowns don't usually last too long."

William Jackson isn't clownish, but he uses an unusual delivery that sets his act apart, based largely in heavy inflection that jolts into his rapid-fire description of video action. A slam-dunk example: "HE takes the ball and JAMS it in there for two…"

"I started by trying to be Joe Sportscaster, sitting up straight, proper inflection," he says. "It wasn't natural. I kept hearing, 'Be yourself, no matter what it is,' and so I started being excited, like I was at games. If you go to Allen Fieldhouse and watch the KU Jayhawks, Jacque Vaughn makes the steal, he has Raef LaFrentz on the wing and you know he's going to slam it—you don't just sit there quietly. You build up to it, and the climactic point is when LaFrentz BANGS it in. So the point of impact is what I emphasize. I want the viewer to feel like they are at the game."

The opposite side of the spectrum in the same market is Len Dawson, holding forth now for a quarter-century on both HBO *Inside the NFL* and at KMBC-TV as anchor after his playing days as an eventual Hall of Fame quarterback. He is calm and quiet.

"I believe in being myself and being consistent," he says. "I am not one to brag about having an exclusive, and I'm not controversial. [He is on radio as color analyst of Chiefs games.] I think you last longer that way. It comes down to whether the viewers like you or not. The best compliment I get is from people who say that I am the same off camera as on. Be yourself, and remember that it's not brain surgery."

What about the doling out criticism through editorial commentary? Most anchors find a label for an editorial segment and make certain the viewer knows what it is—TV's equivalent of the newspaper columnist. Bush follows the more general rule. "I'm not big on commentary," he says. "I make maybe 15 a year. And I didn't make any until I was in the market about five years."

That's an important consideration, especially for someone new to an area. Viewers can easily wonder, "Who does this outsider think he is, anyway?" Bush says, "I think you should establish a rapport with fans so they trust you before you make commentaries. Mostly I consider myself a newscaster."

After 11 years in the St. Louis market, Bush believes that people trust his opinion. "I'm not afraid to state my opinion. So when a team is not playing well, you try to get to the bottom of it. But I never blast anyone. However, if I see the Cardinals or Rams are not spending enough money on key personnel, it's important to point that out. Not just to be a Monday morning quarterback, but to make suggestions.

"As a fan—and I am a fan first and foremost—people depend on me for insights. But generally, both on professional and college levels, players are amazing athletes. You can tell their stories in a journalistic manner and you will last a lot longer."

Dawson echoes the sentiment. "It's like being a pro quarterback." If you are getting your butt whipped, then you'd better have some fun along the way."

That brings us to the feature story. Many anchors or sports directors moved into their chairs after reporting in the field, putting together features and live-report standups at events, and serving as fill-in or weekend anchors. Leif Lisec in Kansas City is held in high regard in that role at KCTV.

He describes a specific piece he produced as a good example. It featured Royals outfielder Tom Goodwin, one of the fastest players in baseball. "He is exciting to watch, and a great interview." So Lisec combined the elements in a narrated video piece.

"We took him to first base and asked him to demonstrate his lead and talk about what he looks for with the pitcher, whether he has the green light, and things to let the fans know something about the art of base stealing. We take the fan inside the game and inside the head of the players.

"Then we combined video of game action, plus several we had on file of his steals. A good photographer makes the feature, because he will understand the story and how to shoot it. We shot this one like I was playing first base and Goodwin was leading off."

Lisec typically shoots, edits, and writes the feature. He points out how the process involves stringing natural sounds throughout along with music and other sound bites.

His mention of the photographer leads to a concluding point about what goes on the air: teamwork is vital. From producer to anchor, from director to reporter, from researcher to intern, the work ethic and togetherness—or lack of it—shows in every detail of every piece. Taylor Wilson, a sports director at KSNT in Topeka, Kansas, recalled a nightmarish situation where he worked at a station in Roswell, New Mexico.

"We never communicated, there was a lot of yelling and screaming, it was very uncomfortable," he says. "It happens a lot that we don't communicate well in this business and we lose stuff, every day. You need full cooperation all the time, and clear communication."

Recall from Chapter 1 on fundamentals that personal appearance comes into play heavily on television. Jim Kobbe, a weekend sports anchor at KCHW-TV in Wichita says that he can sort out the radio type from the TV type within minutes "…just by looking at them." He notes that a potential TV personality exhibits a certain demeanor—smile, hair, teeth, weight—things that the radio-bound are not concerned with.

Men have some advantages over women in that regard, in that men will not be scrutinized as closely for two reasons: One is that appearance standards are higher for women, and the second reason is that viewers most often assume that men know more about sports.

GEORGE MICHAEL

To explore all of the machinations of the evening sports newscast we went one-on-one with a nationally-known figure whose local telecasts fill the week in the Washington, D.C. market on WRC-TV, George Michael. He also appears across the country on his syndicated *George Michael's Sports Machine* that started in 1984, offering up-to-the-minute highlight clips and feature stories.

The Q & A with Michael holds particular punch in his closing advice to aspiring sportscasters at all levels, as he emphatically stresses some the familiar theme of dedication.

Are you an entertainer or a journalist?

"Absolutely both. Number 1, you give the information. But in TV, you want the viewer enjoying what you are saying, so it's fine to add whatever color you can. Personality separates us in the business. It may have been pure journalism in the days of Huntley and Brinkley, but that is not true in the '90s."

What are your thoughts on writing?

"I have probably the most gifted writer in the business in Pat Lackman. She won several national and local Emmys. I always told her to write in a way she would want to hear it and could understand it, not the way it is written in *The Sporting News*. In the old days of TV, less than 10 percent of the viewers cared about sports. Well, the person who doesn't care about sports still cares about what you are saying. Therefore, what you present must be written in a way to be understood and enjoyed by people who are not living and dying with what the Orioles or any other team did.

"You have got to make them care about it."

Talk about the writing vs. purely broadcasting.

"I had no writing background, nor any appreciation for writing. Someone told me way back that what you really are is an air salesman. So I didn't practice writing, I practiced getting people to care about what I was saying—selling what I was doing."

Your enthusiasm suggests how much you love your work.

"I feel a little guilty sometimes getting paid, because if I weren't I'd be watching these events anyway. I look forward to going to work, and I get paid to do what I love—that's a blessing. I've always enjoyed it. Could I get burned out? I can understand that happening, having just done six years of hockey with the Islanders. But I can't imagine ever getting burned out on TV sports."

What tips would you offer a young announcer preparing to do your 11 o'clock show tonight?

"No. 1, be very clear in what you're saying.

"No. 2, KISS—keep it simple, stupid. Simple, because some viewers are not well-informed. Avoid getting complex. Make sure everyone can understand. You can't assume everyone knows what you're talking about.

"No. 3, think of the camera—or the microphone, if you're in radio—as your friend. You are talking to your friend.

"No. 4, and most important, be natural. No phony voice. Realize what you are and do it. If it's good enough, fine. If not, then get into another side of the business."

How did radio help you?

"Without having done radio I don't know if I could do what I do now. It teaches you to ad lib. Often I never get to see the highlights before we air, so I must ad lib.

"However, I do my homework. If you stop doing homework—that's when you think you're so good you don't have to work anymore—you're in trouble. You won't be good. I read and read and read. I never feel like I know enough. Homework is absolutely essential."

How much do your read, and how much video do you watch?

"I read *The New York Times*, *The Chicago Tribune*, *The St. Louis Post-Dispatch*, *The Kansas City Star*, and our three local [Washington/Baltimore] newspapers. Reading to me is everything. If you don't make enough time to read, you're not going to know what's going on.

"On any given weekend I'm watching events or video from noon to midnight. On weekdays I start at about 2 p.m. We have 11 different people watching events on a monitor at times."

Do you use interns to monitor highlights?

"I watch the best games myself. I chart and write notes on all major events, and try to keep an eye on everything somewhat. Some broadcasters take it for granted that they can use interns, but if you don't see the most important story you've got, it will be hard to make it good on the air. Others often won't see things you think are important. Charting and writing are important keys to your success."

Outline your top 3-4 stories tonight (in August 97).

"The top story will be Redskins receiver Michael Westbrook, who beat up a teammate, Stephen Davis. How we handle it is a cross between what is journalistically correct and what is ethically correct.

"The number 2 story will be the Dallas Cowboys, America's team, destroying a dormitory. They trashed the dorm on the college campus where they hold training camp.

"Then we will go to the Orioles and Royals baseball because they have a doubleheader. The Orioles are our local baseball team, and they are trying to reach their all-time high mark over .500.

"We will do the White Sox, and then we have a couple of local guys boxing tonight. We'll have seven different stories. I get more time than most—a minimum of five minutes on the 11 o'clock, and a minimum of 10-12 minutes on the 6 o'clock."

Talk about style, and who influenced you.

"I love Jack Buck. He gave me time when I was young and listened to my tape. Because of that I listen to anyone's tape who asks. Jack told me, 'Be yourself. If you're good enough you'll have a job, if you're not good enough you'll be selling air time somewhere.' That's what I tell them.

"I used to worship Harry Caray, but he changed. I thought Buck was very good, and I liked a lot of disc jockeys who were very enthusiastic. I have lived by Jack's advice."

Give two tips for young sportscasters.

"You have to be so dedicated, want it so bad—more than a football player wants to become a starter…more than anything else. You're practicing every day, all the time, even when you're driving around. When everyone else is going out to party, you're going to practice. You're going to read one more story about Vince Lombardi or Brett Favre or whoever. Everybody else is going out to have a good time, and you're going to study…make a tape and listen to the playback, video or audio, makes no difference.

"So that's the No. 1 thing, above all: Want it so bad that nothing else matters…absolute blind dedication.

"No. 2, be willing to go wherever you must for that first job, no matter what the money is because the money doesn't count. Get yourself on the air and get the practice of doing it every single day. Nothing prepares you more than repetition.

"The reason I don't ever worry about losing my job is that no matter how old I may get I'm not going to let anybody work harder than I do. When everyone else was going out to get bombed during their junior and senior year of college, I was in a radio station practicing over and over and over, until I got it good enough to take a tape to Jack Buck and not be embarrassed.

"I'll repeat No. 1, because you can't hear it enough: Want to so bad you can't see anything else, because most of us aren't born with the natural gift. If you weren't born with it, you have to work hard at it. Most people aren't willing to dedicate themselves so much that they will not fail.

"By the way, I got a lot of what I've said from Vince Lombardi."

TEST CASE: WHAT WOULD YOU DO?

During the Washington Redskins preseason training camp of 1997 Michael Westbrook mauled his teammate, Stephen Davis, on the sideline as a practice was taking place. Television cameras, including those from George Michael's station and one competitor, captured the brutal assault. The story made national headlines, and highlight videos appeared on several sources.

Michael elected not to use the footage; he only reported what took place.

He termed his decision "a cross between what is journalistically correct, and what is morally correct."

"We were very careful in handling the story," Michael explains. "We are admitted to Redskins practices. I asked the coach (Norv Turner) for permission to get in, either me or someone representing me from the station. I told him that we would not use anything he did not want on the air. I told him, 'We won't mess you up.'

"So, this fight happens on the sideline where Westbrook basically beat up—that's the right term for it—Davis. He bloodied Davis and knocked him out. We and most of the stations there had video. Do you run it, or not run it?"

George Michael verbally reported the story, and did not run video. Here's why, as he detailed it on the day the event occurred:

"We need to be at practice, and we're invited in under special conditions. We want to observe and figure thing out for ourselves about the team—who's doing well and who's not.

"The coaches for most teams would not allow us in. Norv Turner said to all of us after the Westbrook incident, 'Folks, I don't want to see this on the air. You should not really be here to begin with, so I don't want to see this.'

"So, out of respect for him we won't use the video. Some people will criticize that. We gave our word four years ago, and he's let us into practice all that time. We said that we would not embarrass them. This is the first time he has asked us not to use anything, even though there have been other fights and altercations, although nothing like the Westbrook beating.

"We will not use the video of that fight. I will use the comments of the players and I certainly will use quotes from Norv, and the viewers will know there was a nasty fight.

"I'm in an awkward situation. Channel 9 told the Redskins to go to hell. They said it was no different than a mugging in the alley, and they're using it. They led off with in on the 6 o'clock news. Therefore, it puts me in a position to ask myself, 'Did I compromise myself?'

"I don't think so, because I don't belong there in the first place. We're not using it. And I'm sure I'm going to get criticized tomorrow."

A SAMPLE TV SPORTSCAST SCRIPT FROM GEORGE MICHAEL, ED-ITED FOR LENGTH:
(SCRIPTS ALWAYS APPEAR IN UPPER CASE, DISPLAYED ON THE MONITOR IN LARGE TYPE.)
(MICHAEL OC) JUSTIN LEONARD'S PERFORMANCE THIS WEEK-END AT THE BRIGHT OPEN HIGHLIGHTS JUST HOW MUCH YOUNG TALENT THERE IS ON THE PGA TOUR…THE 25-YEAR-OLD LEONARD, WHO, LIKE TIGER WOODS IS A FORMER U.S.

AMATEUR CHAMPION, CAME FROM 5 STROKES BACK IN THE FI-
NAL ROUND TO BECOME THE THIRD STRAIGHT AMERICAN
GOLFER TO WIN THE BRITISH OPEN...LEONARD TAKES HOME
$420-THOUSAND DOLLARS AND TOLD HIS COACH BACK HOME
HE MIGHT SPLURGE AND MOVE UP TO BUSINESS FOR HIS
FLIGHT BACK TO DALLAS TOMORROW. LET'S GO TO TROON,
SCOTLAND.

(EJ VO BG AND SOT   ————————————————
(VO BG 00-1:06
CRN: ABC SPORTS   HIGHLIGHTS
SOT 1:06-1:27
CRN: LEONARD   ————————————————
VO BG 1:27-1:37)

▲▲▲

Robin Roberts, featured throughout the book, is noteworthy here for tips
she offered in Chapter 1 that bear repeating about newscast anchor work: strive
for naturalness, calm yourself, and be so thoroughly prepared that confidence
never wavers. Tips include having a glass of water handy for use during breaks,
clasping your hands (speech instructors through the ages have taught the value
of touching fingers into the palms of the hands for "grounding" before public
speaking), or otherwise occupying your hands. Roberts holds a pen for effect
"as a little crutch," and she concludes, "Remember to breathe properly."

▲▲▲

Fran Charles is weekend sports anchor at WHDH-TV in Boston. Following are his tips for (a.) organizing a department, and (b.) preparation for sportscasts during the nightly news segment. All quotes in this section are attributable
to Charles.

ON STAFF ORGANIZATION:

1. Plan ahead. Compile a "day book." That is, organize news-release
    FAXes and letters by date to create a running file of possible material
    to use in shows throughout a given week.

Example: Thursday, January 29, 1998, the Boston Red Sox scheduled a news conference at 3 p.m. to announce the signing of infielder John Valentin to a long-term contract. The New England Patriots called a news conference the same day at 5 p.m. to reveal the hiring of Ernie Zampese away from the Dallas Cowboys as offensive coordinator. Additionally, we talked to Boston Celtics rookies Chauncey Billups and Ron Mercer for a taped segment to appear on the Sunday night Sports Xtra. "If we hadn't planned ahead using our day book, we would not have been in a position to get each story covered."

2. Make a habit of shooting packages every day. "This is a tough task. But it becomes very obvious to the viewer if you are always pulling highlights off the satellite feed." Enterprise feature stories are a must. "Remember, it's local news. Find as many local stories as possible. You are guaranteed to get a great response from viewers."

3. Build your Rolodex. Regardless of what story you work on, bring back a phone number to keep on file. The more subjects you have access to, the better your position to obtain comments when a big story breaks. "Strong sources will make a good reporter great."

Example: Chris Slade is an All-Pro linebacker for the Patriots. "We've developed a relationship through our station's coverage of the team. Slade called me right after he agreed to terms on a 5-year contract worth $13 million. We were first to report the story."

PLANNING SPORTSCASTS

1. When you hit the office, the first thing up is to scan the wires, check the daybook, read newspapers, and make some calls to get a feel for what's going on that day. From that, plan the content for the 6 and 11 p.m. sportscasts.
2. Meet with your staff to discuss all ideas about stories that should be included. Brainstorm, and prioritize the stories in order of importance.
3. Finalize which stories you will shoot locally or record yourself, and which you will take from the satellite feed. Avoid relying totally on the satellite, because it rolls so late in the day that you could short yourself on time to edit. In smaller markets this can become critical, because often you work by yourself and every minute is all the more precious.

4. Construct a "rundown" - the actual listing of stories - and assign times to each story. Make certain that everything fits into the time allotment, which usually runs 3-4 minutes during the week, and up to 7 minutes on weekend.

Example: A rundown for the WHDH 11 p.m. sportscast of 1-30-98:

Celtics / Hornets vo (voice over)	*1:10*
Celtics Reax w/sot (wipe to sound on tape)	*:25*
NBA Wrap vo	*:30*
NBA Scores w/ess	*:15*
Aussie Open vo	*:40*
Pebble Beach vo	*:30*
Bruins Tonight rdr (reader)	*:15*
Clinton / Red Wings top vo	*:20*

5. Constantly check the wires for breaking news.
6. Review scripts and edited material before you go on the air. Match every item to avoid mistakes. If you fall short of time to write in your highlights, jot down the information on a shot sheet before you hit air.
7. Include director's cues on your scripts. Chryon fonts, ESS (Electronic Still Store), over-the-shoulder graphics, in cues, out cues—note them all on your script. The director must know exactly where you are headed throughout your sportscast.
8. Double check that all tapes are properly cued and labeled. Take them to Master Control.
9. Check your appearance: hair and makeup. Men, straighten your tie. Avoid shine on your face, because studio lights can cause considerable glare.
10. Head out to the set and knock 'em dead! Take your time. The natural tendency is to speed up. Keep your energy level up—it's sports and should be exciting. Maintain a high concentration level. A well thought-out, planned show usually is a successful show.

Remember: "The only thing that matters is your sportscast."

CHAPTER 12
GETTING THE JOB/MAKING THE TAPE

"...Too many people aren't willing to pay the dues to get this far."
—Dan Patrick, ESPN

Okay, so now you have read all the sage advice, the tips, the philosophy, the formulas offered by the best in America on both radio and television air waves. You've studied what it takes to get where they are, in terms of work ethic, background, technique, and countless of hours of broadcasting news, views, and events. Now, you're chomping at the bit. You're ready to rock. You're primed to roll.

Gimme the mike. Turn on the red light. "Hello, everybody, it's a great night for . . . ."

But wait a sec. How *did* they get there. Literally, in the chair, on the air? What's the route? Is it smooth or bumpy, long or short? What do you have to do, who do you have to know, where do you have to go to get *there,* wherever that might be in your schemes and dreams?

As you head toward the wire, that's what these final two chapters are about. In this chapter you learn from numerous, multifaceted experiences of several prominent sportscasters, and specifically how they landed either their first job or their first major step up.

Three case studies in particular are enlightening:

• Charlie Jones illustrates spunk and persistence, having the gumption not only to seek the job, but also to go to great lengths for an interview with Lamar Hunt to land the Dallas Texans' play-by-play.

• Denny Matthews tells how he cut through the mass of applications with an imaginative application and got the Royals' attention when he was an inexperienced youth barely out of college.

• Brian Sexton is a textbook example of willingness to do anything and everything along the way, so that he was prepared when opportunity knocked.

Some familiar themes are repeated throughout these stories — "whatever it takes" and "go to Boise." Or, in a case like John Rooney, go everywhere. Their willingness to sacrifice, pay the price, and be nice served them well, along with fortuitous happenstance occurrences. And the guys with the "name" that helped—Buck, Caray, Harlan, McDonough—regardless of their well-known dads, couldn't have cut it big-time if they hadn't developed the talent, the drive, and prepared themselves for the opening. Each, indeed, stood at the ready; each had the right stuff (to borrow a term), and found a way to display it through differing means.

Advice from owners, managers, and talent scouts contains the essentials for making a demo tape to knowing when coming on strong will serve you in establishing this career. Finally, my final exam from the sportscasting course at Kansas is a real-world experience of presenting yourself for hire, replete with snappy appearance, appealing resume, and well-rounded demo tape. And you might be stunned at some of the blunt advice offered by two giants in different areas of the industry. Sound discouraging?

That's not the intent. We merely want each aspirant to the booth to look past the supposed glamour of the profession to the sweat and low pay and family separation and menial tasks and enormous commitment that is required to sustain this as a chosen career. You learn how to *make* things happen, instead of *waiting for* or *hoping for* something to happen.

With that commitment and some creative initiative, as demonstrated, the world is your doorstep. And a big door opens to a wondrous array of opportunities.

Go ahead...knock.

Charlie Jones

Charlie Jones knocked, and knocked, and knocked. Eventually, Lamar Hunt, who founded an upstart league known as the AFL and owned the Dallas Texans entry, simply couldn't ignore this persistent lad from Arkansas who was knocking down his door to work the airwaves.

Jones's journey to Dallas began over Thanksgiving dinner, 1959. *Sports Illustrated* had published a story about Hunt and the AFL that caught Charlie's attention in Fort Smith, Arkansas, where he worked on radio. "We were sitting around the Thanksgiving table," he says, unraveling the unusual story.

"My uncle, Burt Clendening, traveled the state of Texas. I asked him if he knew Lamar Hunt, figuring everybody did. He said he didn't, and asked why I wanted to know. I told him about this new American Football League and how I would like to broadcast the games. My Uncle Burt said, 'Well, it sounds like he needs somebody like you.' With that encouragement I put together a package—tapes, my background, a photo, all kinds of information—and sent it to Lamar. I didn't hear from him, so I figured the U.S. mail service wasn't cooperating at all."

Not to be discouraged easily, Jones decided that he had to make a bold attempt to catch Hunt's attention. "We figured that on a Saturday morning we would drive over to Dallas and see Lamar Hunt. But I couldn't just simply show up. I had to arrive with a little fanfare. My brother came up with the idea to get an old-fashioned, large alarm clock, set it for a specific time, and send it with a big, label-type card hanging from it that said, 'The voice of the Dallas Texans will arrive at your office at 11 o'clock Saturday morning.'"

Jones mailed the clock to arrive on Friday. Laughing, he says he was afraid it wouldn't arrive, and that he and his brother would be arrested when and if some postal worker heard a tick-tock-tick-tock in a mailed package. He also figured on Hunt being in his office on a Saturday morning.

Then, trying to look the part, Jones bought a huge, 10-gallon cowboy hat. "I'm in downtown Dallas at 8 o'clock in the morning on a Saturday," he said, "and I'm the only person in Dallas wearing a cowboy hat. So I put it in the trunk."

He showed up at Hunt's office at precisely 11 a.m. "I walked in on the ground floor of the Mercantile National Bank, and I saw Nancy Peterson. As soon as I walked in the door, she said, 'You're Charlie Jones.' I said yes, and she said, 'Lamar got the clock.'

"I said, 'Oh, that's great, will I get a chance to see him?' She said no. My face nearly dropped to the floor."

Peterson informed Jones that all the team owners had a meeting at the Hilton across the street, and that Hunt would be attending all day. She said, however, that he left word for Jones to stay overnight, and that they could meet at 4 p.m. on Sunday.

"I had $6 in my pocket," Jones said. "Enough to buy me gas back to Fort Smith. She told me not to worry, that they would pay for the hotel room. The next day I sat down with Lamar and we visited for four hours. He told me he would think everything over, and he would call me the next morning.

"Monday, I returned to work at a radio station and the phone rang at about 11 o'clock. It was Lamar, and he offered me the job.

"He asked me how soon I could come to work," Jones said. "I told him the owner of the station where I worked has been really nice to me, so I wanted to have lunch with him on Tuesday and give two weeks' notice. I told Lamar I would be down to Dallas in two weeks."

Jones made an appointment for lunch with his station owner. He explained the situation. "I told him how happy I was, and that I wanted to give my notice. The owner told me that if I was planning to leave, to just go ahead and make that my last day.

"I got back to the station and was packing, and the phone rang. It was Lamar. He asked how the lunch meeting went. There was a long pause, and he started laughing. He said, 'You got fired, didn't you?' I said, 'Yeah, I did.' He told me not to worry, that he would put me on the payroll that day and I would move to Dallas the next Monday and go to work."

Again, although this is a tale of considerable persistence, Jones wasn't just some stiff from the backwoods of the Ozarks who jumped off his truck and onto Lamar Hunt's payroll. At the University of Southern California, Jones had undergone heavy voice training. "I had tried out for a school play at age 15 and got turned down because my voice was too high," he said. "At USC I learned to think of my voice as an instrument, find the ranges I could work in."

As a student he also worked relentlessly at the campus radio and TV stations. "We [students] would hang around until 2 or 3 in the morning, reading copy and listening to each other. I learned breathing exercises, and some tricks of the trade."

Denny Matthews

The Denny Matthews story illustrates similar creative initiative but with a different twist as the career unfolded. While Jones moved from that early Texans' experience into a broad-based television career that landed him on national network, Matthews settled into a role with the Royals, and was satisfied with only that role. He started with day one of the Royals' existence, and never left, turning down several offers, including the Yankees.

How he got to Kansas City in the first place is a classic.

"I took a tape recorder and went to St. Louis," he says. "I was applying for a major-league job, so I thought it would behoove me to do a major-league game, so they could see how I handle it." Matthews was from a nearby Illinois town. He had played football and baseball at Illinois Wesleyan and had begun pounding the pavement in search of his first broadcasting job.

He didn't aim low, he shot for the moon—an opening with a major-league expansion team. He and more than 100 other guys.

"I broadcast a Cardinals game into the recorder," he said. "Then I took out two or three innings that I felt sounded representative of my work for a demo. A friend asked how many were applying for this job, and I told him they said about 130 or 140. He pointed out that a lot of tapes would be rolling through the Royals' office, and he suggested that I do something unique, something different. I dressed up [the tape], and it was a little bit corny, but it worked."

He wrapped the tape and resume into a package with a beer theme, on a tray like servers use in a bar, and sent it with a note that said, "I'm not a Busch-leaguer. I'm a Schlitz announcer." That was the Royals' major sponsor at the time.

But, Matthews is quick to point out, "The tape obviously was decent, or they wouldn't have considered me. Later, after I had my interview with Buddy Blattner, the Royals' original lead announcer, and was selected to be his assistant, he told me what impressed them.

"He said they could tell I had done my homework, knew about the players, gave some background. They could tell I had played the game, had a feel for it, the way I handled description and hitter reactions to different pitches. Blattner said those three things were crucial in them selecting me—making a tape, good description, and background work."

Blattner mentioned something else to Matthews, who got quite a chuckle out of it. "He told me I didn't have any bad habits," Matthews says. "I said, 'Hey, I don't have *any* habits!' Good or bad, I didn't have much experience at all. That was another thing that fell in my favor— it was a brand-new team, and they wanted a young guy with their young team, and thought it would be a good combination."

It became a marriage that was moving into its 30th year when he was interviewed for this book.

"I was so naïve when I started, I didn't know what was going on," he says.

"You pick things up and learn. All you can ever do is the best you're capable of. If people like it, then great. If they don't, you move on. I've been fortunate."

With a laugh, Matthews adds, "I think the key has been playing hockey in the winter time." (He is an avid hockey fan and player, participating still in amateur competition—his off-season pastime, rather than broadcasting other sports.)

Matthews offered one bit of solid of advice to aspiring sports broadcasters: "Life on the road can be a little tough. I work out and watch my personal habits. If you let yourself go, then your concentration won't be there for the games."

Brian Sexton

Brian Sexton also started with an expansion franchise, the Jacksonville Jaguars of the NFL, on radio, almost three decades after Matthews. But Sexton took an entirely different path, one that virtually all of our sources talked about: Chanute, Kansas, was Sexton's Boise.

"It took a lot of selling," he says, summing up the whole of the parts that landed him a major-league play-by-play position.

"You've got to get yourself out there in front of people and convince them. A combination of that and some talent, and a little bit of luck."

Sexton started making his luck happen on radio at Chanute after graduation from the University of Kansas, and from there he leap-frogged to Wichita. "I sold advertising, and on the side I put together an evening talk show for no pay, just because I wanted to keep working at those skills. I knew sales, though, would be my key to staying in radio.

"It was, and it wasn't. I got fired from one job [KNSS, Wichita], and I hung on with another job and I kept selling and getting sponsors involved. Those sponsors liked what I did, and so the radio company that owned our station transferred me down to Jacksonville [WOKV] with sales as the basis."

The strong lesson to be learned here, especially for anybody with stars in their eyes about stepping right out of school into a major-league job: Have the willingness to handle whatever duties are needed, especially selling. The networking with sponsors helped Sexton, and all the while he readied himself so that when the door swung open, he was ready to walk through it.

"I thought I might get a shot at doing the halftime show or the pregame show," he says. "When they didn't have a play-by-play guy and wanted to air a coach's show in the fall of 1994, before they had a team on the field, they asked if I might be interested.

"Preparation was the key to that."

Are you listening? Hear it again: preparation was the key...

"I out-worked a lot of people," Sexton says. "I paid an incredible amount of attention to the subject matter and worked at being conversational. The Jaguars liked what they heard from me. I was young, I didn't have a Southern accent, I was somebody who could develop. They also liked my relationship with the coach [Tom Coughlin], so it made a natural fit."

What is to be gleaned from Sexton's rapid rise—a major-league announcer in his mid-20s who was willing to start at a tiny burg in rural Kansas, who was willing to work for free to gain experience, who didn't get discouraged when he got fired? "I believe that hard work, being in the right place at the right time, having a plan for yourself, and then never, ever, ever resting on your laurels can take you a long way."

In these condensed versions of unusual success stories, you don't get the full picture on obtaining the first job and moving to your chosen destination. Jones, Matthews, and Sexton all were college-educated, and had taken training to develop their skills in the trade. At the end of the chapter, you will find suggestions and examples of how to compile a resume, make a tape, and especially how to prepare yourself for an interview.

Jim Nantz

Jim Nantz gets a kick out of telling his "accidental tourist" story of getting a big break in the business:

He was a non-scholarship, walk-on golfer at powerhouse University of Houston, working at the campus radio station on the side. Through the athletic department he earned a few bucks as public address announcer at home basketball games. That led to a host position on Coach Guy Lewis's television show.

"Eventually I was working for free at the CBS radio affiliate in Houston," Nantz said. "That opened the door for press passes. The news director at the CBS television affiliate saw me on the *Guy Lewis Show* and asked me to audition as third person on their sportscast at the end of my junior year. That meant I would anchor 21 weekends a year—40 percent of the time."

He got the position based solely on the coach's show and an audition. "The news director never asked or knew about my background," Nantz said. "I was really aghast that I could walk in as a college junior. The next thing I know, I'm anchoring on the air in the fourth largest city in the country, getting off the air and going to eat at the cafeteria on campus and living in the dormitory."

After college, Nantz worked for KSL as the No. 2 anchor in Salt Lake City. "We subscribed to a major consultant, and I learned some good things there. I loved to write...to put the right words together. I'd write all of my opens. I do a daily radio show for CBS radio now, and I write it all."

At age 26 he was working college football and bowl assignments for NBC-TV, followed by college basketball, and then studio host for March Madness. "Come Final Four time in Dallas I was opening up for the network, reading a tease that I had written, and I was still 2 months shy of my 27th birthday. The week after that I was in the tower at No. 16 at Augusta describing Jack Nicklaus's heroic back-nine charge on the way to his sixth green jacket. Now I'm on the golf tour full-time.

"All of these things happened without me picking up the phone and saying, 'You know, I'd love to work the Masters or the Final Four.' Some people campaign, and I'm proud that the only thing I've done is request not to be put on an assignment, because I don't think my knowledge is suited for it."

Herb Carneal

Some great announcers had no formal training. Hall of Famer Herb Carneal of the Twins is an example. "I lucked out," he says.

Well, you decide how much of his story is luck.

"As a kid in Richmond, Virginia, I listened to games on radio at night wherever I could find them, and I would hear people like Bob Elson, and I thought, gee whiz, what a job that would be. So I mimicked them, aloud, to myself. I read ads from the newspapers even, like they read commercials."

He tells how the kids in our neighborhood bought bubblegum cards and composed teams. They made up a game to play with dice, using the cards, and kept stats. "I was the broadcaster for those imaginary games," Carneal said. "I'd say what a guy was hitting, how many home runs he had, all the stats we kept, and that was my start."

After high school he "wandered in" to a small local station. "They needed somebody, and gave me an audition that must have been awful, but they assigned me to open the station in the morning and I didn't do anything except station breaks. But it was a foot in the door."

Eventually, he worked some sports for that tiny station. That eventually led to a job with the Springfield Cubs in the International League. After three years, a friend in Philadelphia at KYW called Carneal with news of their need for a football announcer who also would do four sports shows a day on radio and one on television. "There was no baseball, but when he talked money my eyes opened up, and I decided that if I had any brains I should take the offer."

He did, and the path opened up for major-league baseball. In fact, Carneal had a unique distinction of working both Phillies and A's games on one station, while handling sportscasts and football for the station that first hired him. Carneal worked the Baltimore Orioles alongside Hall of Famer Ernie Harwell before moving on to the Twins.

Fred White

Fred White's switch from the insurance industry into broadcasting makes a nice tale of how want-to and dogged determination can cut a wide swath.

He was working in Danville, Illinois, as an insurance man and wanted to change careers. "A friend asked me to be his color announcer on local broadcasts," White recalls. "I did, and he quit to go to work for the FBI, so they offered me his job.

"Eventually I read about a job in Hastings, Nebraska. I sent them a tape of football, but they told me I needed baseball, since they did American Legion games on radio. So one day I was on a sales call and I dropped by the local stadium, sat on the roof, and made up the names of all the players while I did a broadcast.

"I didn't know the nickname of the opposing team, so I called them the Berries. Everybody was hitting .350 or .400. I got the job off of that tape, and the next thing I had to do was find out where Nebraska was. I never was much of a geography person.

"About 2 1/2 years later I moved to WIBW in Topeka, Kansas, which turned out to be one of the best moves I ever made. I was smart enough to know that you have to get in a good station where people can hear you."

His advice to aspiring broadcasters: "I'm from the old school. I've never had an agent. Today you almost have to have one. Find people you can trust, and be a person that others can trust. I've met wonderful people and gotten some breaks through the years, but I spend a lot of time on the phone, keeping up contacts and staying in touch. Let people know you're interested in jobs they might have. Ask someone who's coming to town to lunch. Networking is probably the most important thing we do. Once you get the job, really bust your tail the first few times, and then relax and do your thing. Know that you're good enough to do it. They hire you because they like the things you do."

Jack Buck

Jack Buck landed his first job while he was pumping gas. "I worked at a gas station from 11 at night to 7 in the morning. A fella came in for gas, and he told my cohort about a job downtown. I was typing and wasn't even listening. But my partner made the comment, 'Mind your own business,' as though I were eavesdropping. It got under my skin. So I called the radio station. I got the name of the program director—Ed Sprague—and called him at home at 11 at night. I asked if I could audition for the job.

"He said yes, and asked what time he could see me. I said, 'What time do you go to work?' He said 8 o'clock, and I told him I'd be there waiting for him. I was there waiting for him, and I was on the air that night."

Buck told this story in the context of his strongest advice for the new sportscaster facing the big, bad world. "You have to figure out how to get a job. You can't get experience until you get a job. Hundreds of us have solved that problem. It's up to the individual to be creative enough to get the job."

Kevin Harlan

Lest you think that somebody can cruise into and through the business on name alone, take a closer look at Kevin Harlan's background. He's the first to admit that it didn't hurt that his father, Bob, is general manager of one of the most famous football teams in history: the Green Bay Packers. That might have opened some doors, or at least stood him in good stead as a reference point.

But Harlan didn't just strut into the Kansas City Kings out of college and say, "Here I am world, yours for the asking." He says, "I had an advantage, but I wanted to make it on my own." Here's what he did to get that first, major break:

He worked more than 100 football and basketball games as a junior and senior in high school at a local station in Wisconsin. As a freshman in college, he worked on the student station at Kansas, KJHK, handling news shows and play-by-play, as well as programs on the local Lawrence station, KLWN.

Harlan then held internships at Topeka's WIBW radio and TV, performing as a weekend anchor on Sunday nights and calling high-school football and basketball games, and at ESPN. "I saw what Ray Scott [Packers' TV announcer], Curt Gowdy and the network announcers did in preparation [for NFL games that he grew up around]," Harlan says. "I did not want to reinvent the wheel—I just copied what they did. I worked all week in college getting ready for a game."

Eventually, while still in college, he worked for KCMO radio in Kansas

City producing *Chiefs Sunday*. As graduation neared, he accepted a position to go to Hattiesburg, Mississippi, as voice of Southern Mississippi sports. But Neil Funk left the Kansas City Kings to do the Philadelphia 76ers, and Harlan applied. "They hired me for $25,000 a year to do the Kings," he said.

He stair-stepped to University of Missouri sports, and then into the chair for play-by-play of the Chiefs. He left that for Minnesota Timberwolves basketball and the FOX network telecasts of NFL football. Today he is the play-by-play voice of the NFL and NCAA Final Four on CBS and of the NBA on TNT.

▲▲▲

Tom Cheatham

Tom Cheatham has served as director of the radio network at Oklahoma State University, and for the NFL Chiefs and AL Royals in Kansas City, dealing with talent ranging from a greenhorn Kevin Harlan early in his career on football to veteran Denny Matthews on baseball. He is now general manager of the Kansas City Knights of the new ABA.

Regarding the "Boise" notion, Cheatham passes. "I'm not as much a fanatic on that as Keith Jackson."

"Denny Matthews worked with nobody else but the Royals for 28 years, and that's amazing. Sometimes, in a way, that might hurt him [because he's not been around much], that could be a disadvantage." Matthews never pursued other broadcast interests in the off-season, either, such as the football and basketball that many baseball play-by-play announcers indulge in, including his long-time partner, Fred White.

While Kevin Harlan burst onto the scene quite young as play-by-play for the Kansas City Kings in the NBA, he had performed a ton of grunt work several places on internships and, in the case of Lawrence and nearby markets while he attended the University of Kansas, on spunk.

"The biggest advantage that Kevin had," Cheatham says, "was that he started with bad teams—both the Kings and Chiefs. It's easier to announce a winner. You have to work really hard when the team is not that good, and that's what you learn primarily in the small market.

"You also learn the commercial side to it sometimes. The work ethic you establish in the small market helps you in the long run."

▲▲▲

To pursue your first broadcasting job and subsequent work after that, every broadcaster should create and continually update demonstration tapes, either audio or video. The tape should contain short segments that capture your essence of style, description, voice, and energy. In this section, we turn to a couple of people who work on Chiefs football, the owner of a TV-radio conglomerate, and the talent scout at powerhouse ESPN for insights into what to lay down on the tape.

Tom Cheatham—What radio talent scouts listen for on a demo tape

Cheatham gives a strong rundown on what radio talent scouts listen for on a tape. Included in this section is a step-by-step rundown on this veteran talent scout's pointers for putting together a tape.

You've heard it from many sources so far: It all starts with description. If you can't paint a visual image for the listener who isn't watching the tube, (a) you have done the listener an injustice, and (b) you will lose that listener.

Enthusiasm is great, but it is secondary to the ability to paint what is going on in interesting, concise, descriptive, rapid-fire terms. "I'm looking for use of adjectives," Cheatham says. "Different ways to describe a play and the game. Kevin [Harlan] and Denny [Matthews] both have excellent command of descriptive adjectives."

Cheatham says that good radio also features good interviewing technique. "You need that ability to interview. Many play-by-play announcers are not good interviewers," he pointed out. "They sometimes lack good imagination, too, because play-by-play is describing what you see."

Interviewing challenges the imagination. A pre- or post-game program can be a good source for honing both areas—interviewing and imagination. "Too many announcers think of pre- and post-game shows as a way to eat up commercials so you can make some revenue, and that's true," Cheatham points out. "But it's your lead into the broadcast and your conclusion. If you can make your pre-game and coach's shows hot and entertaining, you'll be good." Cheatham says he also listens for compatibility with a partner in the broadcast and variety. "Make the game more entertaining," he says, "but maintain the integrity of the game."

Enthusiasm obviously is a prerequisite to good broadcasting, but it comes wrapped in many different shapes and hues. Matthews' style on the Royals is understated, whereas Harlan is somewhat overstated. "Over-enthusiasm hurt

Kevin early," Cheatham recalls. "You must know the flow of your sport to know when to get up there and when not to."

He cited basketball as an example: "A lot of players can dunk, and that's not a big deal. You might be screaming what a great dunk it is, and your team is down by 10. Avoid that. Many over-sensationalize. You can't afford to. Maintain credibility. Show some objectivity, whether you're working for the home team or not."

If you work for Cheatham, you will wear out the tape machine. "You have to listen to yourself," he insists. "I made Len Dawson, a Hall of Fame, superstar quarterback, listen to himself after every game." (Dawson provides color commentary on Chiefs radio.)

When you listen to yourself relentlessly on tape, you must temper your self-judgment. Too often a broadcaster is terribly harsh on himself. The purpose is to hear both good and bad, hone the good, weed out the bad, and continually improve.

"Have somebody there to give direction," Cheatham says. "Most on-air talents give their own direction.

"Len was harder on the quarterbacks. He was so good at it, he knew exactly what he was looking for. We caught that by him listening to [his own] tapes. When somebody critiques you, remain open-minded. Be sympathetic to the needs of the team you work for—they can approve or disapprove of you—but have somebody outside of that mix give you direction, too."

Tom Cheatham on making a successful demo tape

"When auditioning for a radio play-by-play position in either football or baseball, prepare a tape of 8-12 minutes. Here is what I listen for:

"One. Play-by-play description. I want to hear the exciting, big plays, and the routine or normal plays.

"Two. Interviews. I want a pre-game show to get the feeling the announcer has in interviewing the coach or manager and some players.

"Three. Ad lib skill. Let me hear you being questioned.

"Four. A scoreboard report. Preferably a post-game show.

"Five. The qualities of (a) accuracy, (b) descriptive style, (c) pacing, (d) working with an analyst or other partner, (e) personality, (f) sense of humor, (g) reporting ability, and (h) conversational style.

"I want a painted picture of the game, good pacing in all aspects of the broadcast—not just the exciting plays, but also in carrying out a conversation—good teamwork in the booth, a 'real' personality that isn't manufactured (and without any, you have no chance), handling of the news aspects of the event, and someone talking to me, not at me, in a style that will wear well."

What were the key factors in Cheatham and KCFX, the flagship of the Chiefs, hiring Harlan as the team's play-by-play announcer?

First, his use of adjectives. "Possibly the best I've ever heard," Cheatham says. "When he described the action, you could 'see' the play in your mind." Second, voice quality. "He sounded really enthused, like he was enjoying it." Third, the way he included color commentator Len Dawson where he fit.

Bill Newman (Team Manager)—Natural enthusiasm is the secret to a great play-by-play

General manager Bill Newman hired Cheatham to oversee the Chiefs network when KCFX blazed new trails in the late '80s, taking on an NFL network on FM—daring at the time, but soon to become a frequent venture. Newman shares what he looked for in the hiring of Harlan and his successor, Mitch Holthus, for play-by-play:

Be a student of the game

"I wanted a student of the game, to know not only the Chiefs but their opponents inside-out. Also, I looked for a person with a great work ethic who would do whatever it takes to get the job done each week."

Newman says that voice quality was important, but not so much as the ability to converse with the everyday fan. "I was looking for an announcer who can relate to the common person," he says. "I wanted someone with a natural, enthusiastic style who would not use a lot of sports jargon. Enthusiastic, but not contrived.

"It was nice if he had a deep voice, but not as important as ability to relate."

Finally, like Cheatham, he emphasized the ability to follow and describe the play. "He could not be cheating on his call, or late with the call," he concluded.

Terry Shockley (Station Owner)—Know your station

On the television front, Terry Shockley has accumulated a group of six TV stations in Wisconsin. He said that familiarity with a particular station's market is one of the first qualities he must find in a job candidate for anchor and reporting positions.

"You must know what sports the station covers, how they cover it, whether they do sports news programs, broadcast a college or pro team's games, etc. It's very important that [persons applying for work] come in very prepared, and, of course, well-groomed to present themselves in a good physical presence." Put your best right up front.

The opening seconds of a demonstration tape turns Shockley on or off. "The person seeking the job in television news must have their best foot forward right at the beginning of the tape," he said. "Your best story, your best on-air delivery right up front."

Realize, he says, that a candidate probably will receive just 2-4 minutes of viewing of the tape from a general manager, program director, and/or news director. "Early impressions will be lasting impressions."

He also deals in radio. Of both media he says, "We don't need a lot of long play-by-play segments in sports tapes. We need to hear a couple of touchdown calls, some set-up plays, a couple of sequences, and finally some exciting plays to experience the repertoire of the applicant."

Al Jaffe (Super Scout)—You have to put in the time

Al Jaffe is the super scout for the super network, ESPN. "I'm like a basketball recruiter, trying to find people who can come in here as freshmen and contribute immediately," he says. And, like many freshmen he alludes to, many talents arrive at ESPN before they are primed and ready, yet they get a lot of playing time.

"Our freshman usually breaks in on the 2 a.m. *SportsCenter* and move on from there," Jaffe says. "After four years, when they are seniors, they know the system—ESPN—and they have developed a style, so they are ready and able to contribute. I'm the assistant coach who gets them here, they go to the head coach who brings them along."

How ESPN finds its on-air talent

Jaffe outlined where ESPN seeks its *SportsCenter* talent:
• Tapes, sent directly to him.
• Agents who send tapes. "I've gotten to the point of trusting a few. If one of them says, 'Al, you should really look at this tape, it's somebody special,' I'll look at it. Other agents I tell that we'll look at them, but they're going on the shelf for now."

262 The Art of Sportscasting

• Headhunting. "I go to smaller markets and watch local sports anchors. I take a lot of notes. In one trip I can sweep the country.

What he looks for
  • Writing.
  • Sense of style.
  • Smarts. "Like, they'll make a reference to a historical anecdote that fits a story, or it's clever or funny."

Jaffe says that a *SportsCenter* hopeful must have a good general knowledge of the four major sports—football, basketball, baseball, and hockey. "Once they get here, we'll look at weak areas and work on improvement. Most put in their time and do their homework and get up to speed on sports they weren't strong in."

Further, ESPN requires effective communication skills presented in a compelling manner that reveals that the broadcasters "really knows their stuff." Substance is more important than style, in Jaffe's world. "Their first responsibility," he says, "is to give the audience an informed sportscast. Our people have the freedom to make it entertaining as well."

Speaking directly to the student in college who is pursuing this career, Jaffe says, "Get a lot of hands-on training. As a teacher I would assign a lot of stories and packages. I'd also like to have a newsroom and have people switch jobs every couple of months. It's important that students have a strong journalistic and news background.

"It's very important to have internships while still in school at a local TV or radio station [for] hands-on experience. Certainly, work for the campus radio or TV station."

▲▲▲

For a wrap-up of getting a start in the business, brace yourself for these bits of advice from two heavyweights who, when asked what they would tell students about entering the field, said, in so many words, "Don't."

Dan Patrick

Dan Patrick, the renowned ESPN anchor (featured in Chapters 11) says, "I would not encourage them not to get into the business because too many people aren't willing to pay the dues to get this far."

He points directly to himself as exemplifying an attitude that he sees all too often in students today—call it the "starry-eyed" syndrome. "I was like everybody else, wanting to be the next Brent Musburger, Bryant Gumbel, Bob Costas," he says. "But I failed to see where they started, how long it took them to get where they are.

"It's so easy to say, 'I want to do that,' but do you want to go make $10,000 a year in Poughkeepsie, where you have to shoot your own video, and do a stand-up, and do your own interviews? Really sacrifice?"

This is what Patrick says to students who ask his advice: "If you are in this to be on TV, if you are in it for the money, then don't get in it at all. You will be unhappy. If you get in it because you love sports, love to read about it, love to go watch games, and then to talk about it all, okay. But too many people go into it for the wrong reasons.

"So I always preface anything I say about this business with, 'Don't get in it.' And then when they ask why, I tell them all of the downside. If they're hungry enough to say, 'I would do that,' then I encourage them to go for it."

He cites examples from the ESPN environment. "A lot of people come here for two years to serve as production assistants, and then they want to get into TV, on air. I say to them, 'What are you doing here, then? Get out—go get a job.'"

Patrick can think of half a dozen or so who left for jobs paying $12,000-$14,000 a year. "I tell them that if they don't get it out of their system quick, they never will. Get into any type of broadcasting facility, no matter what it is—radio, TV, public radio, public TV. Once you're in, you hear about jobs, or you can get promoted. You learn to understand things, get hands-on experience.

"But don't expect to just walk right in at ESPN and say, 'Okay, I'm ready, here I am.' It will not work that way. It's becoming tougher and tougher to get involved in this business, and to move up, to get into ESPN or FOX or NBC, because so many people want to do it. I find this to be the most competitive job field in America.

"Because, how many people have sat down and watched *SportsCenter* and said, 'I can do that, I want to do that.'"

Patrick suggested several factors to help further your success:
• Know your craft.
• Be willing to work very, very hard.
• Be willing to start in a market that might be ranked 150th or worse, and perhaps not until you're in your late 20s.

"I wasn't on the air until I was 27," he recalls. "I got started late, but I knew how badly I wanted to do it. I remember when I was doing headline sports at CNN, and I thought, I just gave up a job in Dayton doing weekends, and I thought, 'What am I doing here?'"

"But it turned out that I was at CNN at a great time, and six months later I was in New York taking Keith's job [Olbermann, later his on-air partner]. But if hadn't taken the chance, taken a $10,000 pay cut, then I wouldn't be where I am today."

On the matter of lucky breaks and all of the stars being aligned just so, Patrick says:

"A lot of it is luck. But when your time is called, and you know your craft, then you get your job. A lot of times people are called, and they're not ready for it, and they fall flat on their faces. And then they never get back up. So *know* what you're doing because you will get a chance one way or another, in some market."

Advice from John Rooney

John Rooney also spoke candidly in, at first, discouraging terms in his advice for students of the craft:

I asked Rooney, "What you would tell young broadcasters, two or three tips that would make them successful?"

Rooney's response: "Run...get out of the business [laughing]...you want no part of it."

His take on the negative side differs from Patrick's, geared more to industry trends.

"The way it's going right now I'm inclined to say that—run, stay away—because of all the acquisitions and takeovers [of stations]. You're probably going to make more money working on a garbage truck than you are starting out and trying to make a career in broadcasting."

Amplifying, Rooney says, "Right now the way groups of stations are clumped under two or three different umbrellas, the competition is out on the market and salaries have gone down well below three figures for big jobs now. Some guys are getting hired at the major level for three, four, five hundred dollars a game. It's really sickening.

"From a sportscaster's standpoint, unless you're a Bob Costas type, you're in trouble."

For those who refuse to buckle under the trends, or under the threat of long hours, low pay, Rooney says it simply: "You have to go out and work, go work. What do you mean by work? Go find somebody who knows what they're doing, ask them a lot of questions, and find out how to do it. That's how I did it. I didn't know you hook up this, hook up that, and call on the telephone to get the game on the air. I had to go to somebody and find out. If you need to do a term paper, you go to a library. So go to a radio or TV station and find out, it's that simple."

It's that simple. It's that complex. It's that easy—put your nose to the grindstone, and grind, and grind, and grind. It's that hard.

Advice from Bob Costas—Grabbing at an opportunity

Bob Costas relishes the story of how he manipulated his way into his first play-by-play position in professional sports, while he still was a student at Syracuse University.

During his senior year, when he was handling Syracuse basketball on the student station, the announcer of the Syracuse Blazers, minor-league hockey team, quit a week before the season started. A friend recommended Costas to the local station, and he met with the station manager.

"I told him that I didn't have any hockey tapes available at the moment," Costas said. "The reason I didn't, but I didn't tell him this, was that I had never done hockey. He listened to my basketball tapes and hired me.

"I had to cram to learn the game in a week. I hadn't done a game and hadn't even seen many. I listened to tapes of other announcers, asked a lot of questions, and learned the terms."

Now the story gets juicier. Costas memorized the rosters of the teams for the first game during a 7-hour bus ride to Johnstown, Pennsylvania. "Home of the great flood," he says. "We get there, and just before game time I learned that the Johnstown players had changed jerseys. So I improvised.

"I picked out two names. They were everywhere, and they did everything in the game. One was Galen Head. Once I think I even had him passing the puck to himself. We rode the bus back with a huge barrel of beer on ice, and there I am, on a bus full of drunk hockey players, bouncing along to arrive back in Syracuse at dawn, and I'm studying for a classical literature class at 8 a.m."

A post-script is that the Johnstown team played its games in the rickety old arena used in the Paul Newman movie, *Slap Shot*, and Galen Head wound up as an extra in the movie.

▲▲▲

TOM HEDRICK'S FINAL EXAM

The final exam for Journalism 685 (Sports Broadcasting) is a pragmatic exercise that helps students obtain jobs. The University of Kansas has an outstanding track record of having its sports broadcasters go to work, and rise to great heights in the profession—Gary Bender, Kevin Harlan, Roger Twibell, and others.

I have taught the Journalism course for over 30 years. Long ago I realized that most seniors in the class had not acquired the skills and know-how to interview effectively. This is especially important when you realize that most stations have 50 or more applicants for every opening and countless resumes on file at all times. Many times, 100-150 tapes will land on a news director's desk.

This final exam, which includes the assembling an audition tape, helps determine whether a student will land a position after graduation and be taken seriously in the industry.

For their final exam, the students must make an appointment to spend 30 minutes with me, their instructor. They must bring an audiotape and their resume to the meeting. In addition, they must be dressed for an interview—either in a business suit or blue blazer with a "power" tie (men), or a business dress or suit that is not too flashy (women).

I play the role of general manager of a radio or television station interviewing a new prospect. I ask whether the student desires to work in radio or television. I play the student's tape. The tape must contain a quick rundown of highlights, 3 minutes of play-by-play in basketball (or baseball), 3 minutes of play-by-play in football, a 3-minute sports newscast, and a 3-minute pre-game or post-game interview.

If the student wants to work in television, he or she produces a tape that contains a billboard (composed on computer) that tells his or her background, and then a montage of stand-up reporting with 4-5 different lead stories, 2 outstanding feature packages, an anchor shot, and an interview.

After review and critique of the tapes, I begin the job interview process. I lead with having the students tell about themselves, and why they want to work in the business (easy hours? high pay? fame and glory?).

The student must select a lead story for a specific market: e.g., what is the lead on a Topeka, Kansas, TV station if KU, Kansas State, and Washburn play games on the same night?

The student is required to analyze what is good and what is not acceptable among the work produced on the student radio station. This includes what they like or don't in voice quality, in story selection and priority, and so forth—a drill that gives an indication of whether they are doing their homework.

Next, I ask the student to discuss his or her own strength and weakness.

In 60 seconds, the student is required to formulate a statement that requests that I (as general manager) make a pitch to the station owner to hire him or her.

The student reveals all practical experience.

I discuss with them how to work on a weakness.

The student is asked what he or she can do besides sports. Can he or she sell? Produce general newscasts? Operate the board? Ad-lib well enough to be a disc jockey? (I ask this because the reality is that usually the GM cannot hire a student for sports only, especially in small markets.)

Finally, the hardest question of all: How much money would you need to make?

The student usually has one of two answers. The safe answer is: "What do you routinely pay your entry level employee in this market?" Or, the student can try some gamesmanship by inflating the salary request to see what limits can be stretched to: "I have some student loans to pay off, I want to dress professionally, and when I go to the market I want to eat three square meals a day. I want to feel good about myself like you feel good about yourself. I was thinking between $16,600 and $17,500 to start."

Here's where I turn hard-nosed. I tell them that 50 people are waiting in line for this position. I say that I can offer $15,000 to start, plus a medical package. They can expect an increase of $1,000 a year after I see how the new broadcaster works with others at the station and how the public responds to his or her work. After a year, a retirement package becomes part of the benefits, which is vested with interest if and when the employee leaves the company. I end with, "Take it or leave it."

The student must respond, perhaps inquiring about the entire benefits and incentive package (if courageous enough), and then either accept or decline the position.

END OF FINAL EXAM

My policy is that if a student messes up a couple of the questions or stops in the process, the student waits outside of my office 30 minutes and then is informed of receiving an 'F' for the course. After the cool down period, the student then receives specific feedback about where answers were weak. (Universally they are weak on the salary negotiation and on discussing personal strengths and weaknesses about their work.)

This interview process, the audition tape, and a recommendation from a professional will get a student a job. And when he or she lands that first job, he or she discovers that it was a far easier experience because he or she has already been through the wringer.

CHAPTER 13
POLITICALLY CORRECT

"I'm worried about offending someone every time I open my mouth . . . .
You have to be guarded."—Joe Buck

So, there you are, briefcase full of research, rack full of audition tapes, brain full of knowledge, adrenaline revved, all spit-and-polished and (as grandma used to say) full of vinegar, saying, "OK, World, here I am!"

One last thing. Something nobody else will tell you about in frank, up-front terms, one of the most brutal aspects of sportscasting, and the broadcasting business in general:

Office politics.

The skills to play the political game are as important as any you have developed this side of great work ethic and voice/personality development. In learning them, you acquire the people skills that set you apart from others applying for the same positions.

Mitch Holthus, one of our best sources, believes firmly that in today's broadcast world you get hired and move ahead on 35 percent talent vs. 65 percent people skills. That is startling, coming from a "new-era" talent. Old-school announcers like Bob Starr, Jack Buck, and Jon Miller say that when they got started, the balance was 70-80 percent talent vs. 20-30 percent politics.

Take this time, then, to brush up on such nuances as how to work a room, what to say, when to say it, and to whom. Absorb people skills that will facilitate getting the first job, or the next step up, and that will avoid the pitfalls that will hold you back. Learn to get along with the people you work with and around, the people whose games you broadcast, and the people in your listening and/or viewing audience.

You are about to indulge in some horror stories, involving great broadcasters like Ernie Harwell, one of the nicest guys in this or any other business, and Gary Bender, who twice was squeezed out of networks because of politicking. Bob Starr was blackballed, Nebraska announcer Kent Pavelka's brassiness left him in the cold, and I was pressured out of the KU Jayhawks booths because I refused to play the political game.

Nobody phrases it more succinctly than John Rooney when assessing that facet of the business:

"Make as many phone calls of thanks and write as many letters of thanks as possible to people along the way who help you. Everything from a guy spotting for you to an athletic director who put in a good word for you at a luncheon. They are crucial. The landscape is very level. There are very few mountains—guys who stand out. So what makes a guy stand out? Hard work, constantly bettering his craft, and the little political things.

"Avoid talking behind anyone's back. If you have something bad to say, say it to your wife when you know no one else will hear it. Never in a crowded room. If someone else hears it, it will get back to the person, and you will be in trouble. Nowadays there is very little difference between talents. It becomes a political game . . . and you have to play it."

So, let's play ball . . . .

First and foremost, understand fully that this is show business. Emphasize the word *business*. Listen to Terry Shockley, the Wisconsin television magnate: "We want to have fun, we want to entertain and inform our viewers. But we also must make a profit for our shareholders. We keep that in mind when we hire newscasters and sports announcers."

SONS LEARNING FROM FATHERS

This realization, that the business and entertainment side overrides the journalistic side, can lead to some cynicism, which can have a negative and destructive effect on your attitude. The late Bob Prince, longtime Pittsburgh Pirates announcer from the early school of sports voices, once told Joe Castiglione that in the '70s the surefire way to the booth was to be a 20-game winner, a .300 hitter, or an NFL quarterback. That changed, he says, to have a father established in the business.

It's easy to fall prey to that thinking when you tune into virtually any major sporting event and see or hear Thom Brennaman, Kevin Harlan, Joe Buck, Sean McDonough, or Chip Caray.

Yes, their fathers' positions undoubtedly helped them, at least by laying the footsteps into the industry for them to follow, if not the connections once they followed. But make no mistake—even while drawing those inferences—these are strong, well-prepared, excellent announcers who, whether the doors opened easier for them or not, have made it on their own merit.

Harlan, whose father, Bob, is C.E.O. and president of the Green Bay Packers, openly admits that his father's network of friends fit the old chicken-soup theory: It might not have helped, but it certainly didn't hurt.

Brennaman's dad, Marty, is the voice of the Cincinnati Reds. Buck's father is the legendary Jack Buck, covering Cardinals baseball more than 40 years and for 17 years the voice of CBS Radio Monday Night Football with Hank Stram. McDonough's father, Will, is a longtime newspaper columnist who transferred his talent to broadcasting. He is now retired from NBC.

Caray is third generation. His father, Skip, has for three decades handled the Braves and Hawks in Atlanta, and grandpa Harry—hadn't he been doing baseball since the Cro Magnon and Neanderthal Ages before his death at age 77 just before spring training 1998?

Watching these young lions in action immediately reveals that they learned their lessons about the basics: Preparation and personality, etc. But they also learned the ropes from masters on how to listen and be nice to persons who might be in a hiring mode.

Harlan addresses the matter frankly. "The most important thing I learned from my dad was to be nice to everybody. You never know when a person you have been nice to will be in a position to hire you. I also learned the importance of always doing my homework. I saw the announcers that my dad and the players respected, like Ray Scott, Pat Summerall, and they always were prepared."

Connecting the two theories—being personable and being prepared—Harlan says, "The good announcers were nice to everybody from the star quarterback and all-pro wide receiver to the backups, the water boy, and the trainers. Those announcers took time to listen to everybody, never knowing when they might pick up valuable information."

Harlan speaks most definitively on the art of mixing with a crowd. "You don't want to ignore anybody," he says. "When I go to a cocktail party, my wife, Ann, preps me on who is there and reminds me of their wives' names. You have to work the room. I know a very successful general manager—not my dad—who carries on conversations of 30 to 40 seconds with everybody in a room. When he leaves, everybody thinks he is a great guy. He's nice to everybody."

McDonough believes he didn't receive any special privileges or considerations as the son of a noted sports journalist. But he states firmly that he learned the ropes and how to prepare by hanging around his father. "Kevin [Harlan] and I are as opposite as night and day on the air, but we both have in common that we're nice to people. A nice person can still make it in this business."

That's away from the booth. What about at the game, on the air? Politics enters into that, too.

Joe Buck took lessons that he learned from his father and applied to minor league baseball.

The younger Buck handled the Louisville Cardinals for two seasons, both as announcer and traveling secretary. "I learned how to be prepared, and how to get along with the players," he says.

The lesson that Jack Buck taught him quickly was to avoid being overly-critical of the minor league players. "Dad reminded me that I had grown up watching major league baseball, and I was used to the highest caliber of play. He reminded me that I was going to Triple-A, and, even though it was good baseball, it wasn't major league quality. He always told me not to get on a player unless I felt I could have made the play myself.

"For the most part you have to respect these athletes and what they can do…which is far more than I was able to do, and you work [the broadcast] from that basis."

That attitude not only made him politically correct with the players at the time, but also stood him in good stead with players who later were with the parent St. Louis Cardinals when Joe moved up to do their games.

"When you listen to guys from the older era, like my dad, Harry Caray, the late Bob Prince, they can get away with a lot more on the air than I could," Joe Buck adds. "My dad can say stuff, and Harry pushes it to the limit, that I could never get away with—with either the public or the players. They ride players so hard sometimes that what they say makes the players mad at them.

"In this era, society is so politically correct that I almost put everything I say through a filter in my head. I'm worried about offending someone every time I open my mouth, even though I might not mean to. It's tough to develop a style or get a sense of humor on a broadcast. You have to be guarded. What comes out of that, unfortunately, is a watered-down version of my personality."

About handling the politics of his trade, Joe Buck concludes, "I had a head start with a guy like my dad. I benefited from it with those who hired me, and also with people who work the audio, the camera—all the people he's been nice to through the years. I had some extra good marks before they even met me.

"Fortunately, because it's a political world, I'm doing a little better than the normal guy starting out because of who my dad is. I try to be as humble as I can be. It starts with not thinking that a broadcaster is the most important person in the world. It's the most enjoyable work, and I'm lucky to be doing it. I don't want to get a big head about it. I don't think that what I'm doing is that important.

"So, if the execs from TBS are sitting around when I do a Braves game, I shake their hands. Who knows, someday I might be asking them for a job."

And no matter how rough the water might get, or who rankles whom in a given situation, Buck says you must keep the matches in your pocket. "Never burn bridges. People in this business get recycled. People who might be in a lower spot at one network later could wind up in a top spot at another network. If you have been nice to them, you could gain a few extra steps ahead of the next guy. So, be nice and shake as many hands and get to know as many people as you can."

"The politics, and the luck, can make your career, or break it."
—Bob Starr, California Angels

STAYING OUT OF THE TURMOIL

The industry has changed drastically in that regard. The veteran announcers, many of whom are in the sports broadcasting Hall of Fame, didn't play political games outside of being cordial. They concentrated on preparation, appropriate appearance, and consistent professionalism on the air.

Vin Scully, who places strong emphasis on being yourself, points out that he doesn't even go to the office. "Not unless they summon me," he says. "I don't ever want to get involved in office politics." On that platform, he has performed for the Dodgers and networks at the highest level of competence for more than 45 years, and he's in the Hall.

On the other hand, Scully and Jack Buck have been intricately involved with the clubs they announce for, compared to, say, Bob Starr, who described his apolitical approach with the Angels. Starr, you remember, is the announcer who advises two good reasons to keep your mouth shut: You might learn something, and you will not show the world how dumb you are.

"When I first came to California people wondered why I did not hobnob with Mr. Autry. [Gene Autry was the team owner.] I was the same with Mr. [August] Busch in St. Louis," Starr says. "They are at one level, and I am at another. If they ask to see me, fine, I'm happy to meet with them. There is not a thing in the world I have to do with how they run the ball club. When they put nine players out there, my job is to make them sound as good as possible and as honestly as I can, but I don't believe in getting involved in the politics of the club. A lot of people in our business do, and they revel in it, and get by with it.

"Basically, guys of our era show up at the park three hours early, dress appropriately, do the homework, be nice to people—and that should work out. Isn't that a pretty safe way to play it? I've never been very good at the politics in this business."

It might well have cost him, too, back during the '70s. "I was blackballed," Starr says, bluntly. "I got cross-ways with a fellow who was running a station in Boston where I worked. The situation was untenable, so when my option ran out I had offers for four play-by-play jobs—Kansas City Chiefs, Minnesota Vikings, Miami Dolphins, and Cincinnati Reds—all within a span of three weeks.

"A week after we made contact in each case, I called to see how things were going, and I couldn't get an answer from the people who had wanted to hire me. Suddenly, I am the person they want one week, and the person they least want to hear from a week later.

"A friend who had moved to San Francisco as executive producer of a [TV] news department had been asking me to leave Boston and come out there. I told him about the situation, and he said that we were going to track this down, and he had one of his staff call my station in Boston under the guise that he was considering hiring me.

"So my friend gets the party line. He's this; he's that, all of which was negative. I moved to San Francisco to work with my friend, and I got back on track. He put me on the main stream again. I was out there a year, and everything worked out well. But it was a terrible feeling."

Starr says he has the same sickening feeling for another announcer friend, whom he would not name, who "cannot get a job because of the same kind of situation…he has been dealt a reputation, therefore he can't get work. It is not right, and I know who is responsible, and there is not a thing I or anyone else can do about it."

(Editor's note: Starr passed away in July of 1998.)

Keep the ego in check…and never back management into a corner. Here's why….

Another from the old school who says he never played the politics well is Keith Jackson, Mr. College Football on ABC…and see what it might have cost him.

He says two realities of the business drive it. Write it down:
• It is driven by sales.
• If you are honest, it will cost you income.

Jackson says, "Sooner or later you'll be in a situation where you have to say, 'I won't do that.' You'll make some salesman mad, and generally salesmen are management. But, I still have to wake up every morning and look at the people I cover, and the salesmen don't."

You can hear the yearning in his voice for the good ol' days of just do your job well, and let the chips fall. "This era is not so golden," Jackson says. "You've got coaches running up scores to get votes in the polls. They recruit out-and-out bad people and try to rehab them on a college campus…like putting the fox in the henhouse. It's never going to work."

His view of the way politics should work in the industry boils down to his simple formula, referred to many times in this text: Go to Boise, and do it all. Work hard, 16 hours a day, however many days it takes; open the doors, sweep the floors, handle all broadcasting chores.

While old-fashioned work ethic and values served Jackson well, he also personifies an excellent example of how to handle the nasty side of the business. He faced what seems so inevitable for anyone who goes into this business—getting fired—and had the good sense to keep his mouth closed and his ego in check.

Some might not recall that Jackson is the answer to a trivia question: Who was the first play-by-play announcer on ABC's *Monday Night Football?* Yes,

Keith Jackson sat right there alongside color commentator Dandy Don Meredith, and the halftime-highlight commentator, the late and inimitable Howard Cosell.

Chris Schenkel, another longtime network staple (he voiced the weekly pro bowling tour from its inception to the close of its long, long run on TV) told the story behind the Jackson firing with more candor than Jackson, who declines to poor-mouth anybody. "Keith did really well that first year of *Monday Night Football*," Schenkel says. "The show went over well.

"Roone decided he needed [Frank] Gifford's name and Madison Avenue appeal, but Roone didn't tell Keith directly. I begged him to. 'Tell Keith. Please tell him, because it's going to get out.' And it did." (Keith learned of his firing in a newspaper radio-TV column.) "That newspaper column came out, and Keith was devastated. To his credit, he bit his tongue. He didn't like it, but because he was a professional and he kept his cool, ABC assigned him to college football and he's been there ever since. The moral here is to keep your ego in check."

As a result, Jackson became a college TV sports icon.

Another giant got the axe—right at the zenith, just as he was cruising toward the finish line with the considerable accomplishments of his sterling career. Ernie Harwell hardly flinched at what seemed such an abrupt and thoughtless decision.

He had been the revered Voice of the Detroit Tigers for more than three decades, for generations of Tiger fans. If you ask around the industry, nobody receives higher marks for humility, kindness, and genuine friendliness than Harwell.

He was a pioneer (little-known fact: on TV he called the famous 1951 Bobby Thomson home run for the Giants that beat the Dodgers in the playoffs), and he was popular.

When Bo Schembechler, heretofore a college football coach and administrator, became president of the Tigers, he was charged with the daunting task of revitalizing them financially. He decided to get rid of the old, including Harwell. It was announced during the season that Rick Rizzs would replace him in the booth.

It created a ruckus in Detroit. The groundswell to get Harwell back was enormous. "Overwhelming," he called it. Yet he never uttered a negative word about it.

"It was a business decision," Harwell says, "and I did not take it personally. I was hurt and disappointed," he says. "But I didn't let it get me down. It hurt my wife more than me. She was sick at the time. When they made the announcement, I made myself accessible to reporters. Many of my friends thought that was too kind. But I figured that since I always let the press talk to me in good times, they should be able to in bad times, too."

By playing the politics strait-laced—understanding that the decision was a business strategy, being nice, and never swaying from his personal credo—Harwell was rewarded. "I have never been more warmed than when people wrote and called the club and the radio station," he says. "But I never took it personally and I completed the season as best I could."

As a result of not whining, complaining, blaming, or badmouthing, he picked up assignments with CBS Radio. Later, to appease fans, the Tigers rehired him to do the middle innings on radio. And in 1997, at age 77, they signed him to a three-year contract to handle commentary on PASS-TV with former player Jim Price for 70 to 80 games. Now, at age 80, he is calling Tiger games on WJR radio.

"During the bad times, I had my family and my Christian faith that pulled me through," Harwell says. Typically, he did not mention his talent. He held his ego in check, and enjoyed the fruits of his popularity.

Some announcers never have to play such politics. Jim Nantz stands as a perfect example. He was the right guy in the right spot at CBS Sports, and now he's their most fair of fair-haired announcers. "You'd be amazed at how little input I get about my work," he says. "It's not that I'm untouchable, or that I don't need help."

He doesn't even have an office or a phone. If you didn't know he worked at CBS Sports, you'd never find out by walking through their New York headquarters. "It's surprising how removed I am from all that," he says. "I do a daily radio show for CBS, and all my TV assignments…I've never had anyone come in and look at a tape with me. I've heard things like, 'Well, Jim, what were you guys thinking?' Everybody out there makes mistakes, but most of the analysis you do on your own."

Nantz keeps an office in his home, and an assistant runs it. "My office is wherever I'm broadcasting," he says. "I never have to be [at CBS] in New York. We live a vagabond existence…on the go so much that we're never around the home office enough to get involved with the politics. I'm glad I don't have to be exposed to all that."

An interesting and appropriate source for the topic of playing politics is Jay Randolph, whose longevity spans the Cardinals, Reds, and Marlins on TV; Big Eight basketball for 25 years; NFL and PGA for 30 years on NBC.

His father was governor of West Virginia and a senator for more than 30 years.

Randolph's starting point for remaining politically correct in the business: Look in the mirror. If you can live with the person staring back, you can live with anyone. That's the one person you can always count on.

"There's not much loyalty anymore, probably not since the '50s," he says. "It's gone. So it's essential that you see yourself with confidence, believe in your ability, and get to like the person you see in the mirror.

"If you like the way that person looks, sounds, behaves—that will be a big help. Read aloud into the mirror. Try to see yourself as others see you. We have a lot of insecure people in the business, because it's a tough go. It's important to look in that mirror each and every day and gain some confidence."

POLITICKING TO GET THE JOB

Randolph threw a new slant on analyzing the audience, too, applying it to the subject of this chapter. You have studied earlier how vital it is to know your listening/viewing audience inside-out so you can deliver what they want. The same holds true of another audience, too, the people you are working for. Randolph says, "The sponsors, the athletic directors, the presidents of teams, the athletes...all of those people you will interact with. Constantly keep analyzing that audience so you can please them."

Applying that to the pursuit of a first or higher job, he says, "Be persistent in wanting to see the general manager or the program director of a station in person. Knock on their door and keep knocking until you see them face-to-face. Tell them you may not have a job at the moment, but you have a tape for them to listen to, and that if they have a job you'd like them to call so you can go in and audition.

"Tell them, 'I'd like a shot at the job because I can do the job for you. I want to do the job.' You've got to constantly keep plugging."

Politicking becomes vital in this situation because news directors and program directors have two stacks of tapes on their desk, typically. One stack belongs to individuals who look and sound good but never have been to see them. The other, shorter stack, belongs to individuals who have the professional sound and look and also have established a personal contact and relationship. One of them will get the job.

DON'T BACK MANAGEMENT INTO A CORNER

An important tip to learn from the outset is never to back management into a corner. No ultimatums. No this-or-else threats. That constitutes a losing proposition. You lose the inside track, or, in the case of a prime example, the job.

The example is Kent Pavelka. He broadcast Nebraska Cornhuskers football for 12 years at KFAB in Omaha after several other seasons as color commentator—considered a prime position, because Nebraska is a national powerhouse every year. Nebraska won the national championship in 1995, and, coincidentally, the broadcasts rights changed hands to Pinnacle Sports.

Pavelka gave the new rights holder his contract demands based on his attorney's advice to ask for more than he was likely to receive. Then the political game began.

Pinnacle all but laughed at him, rejected his proposal summarily, and declined to hire the man whose bombastic style Nebraska fans had grown accustomed to for many, many years.

Pavelka screamed to high heaven in the local media, blasting the injustice of it all. That prompted Pinnacle to go public with his proposal, shedding new light on how they could be so disinterested, especially in the face of such overwhelming approval. Pavelka asked for a $150,000 salary, $5,000 talent fee for each game, a private plane in which to travel to away games, a suite at all home games, a country club membership, 25 tickets for each home game, and a new car.

That left Pavelka out of the Nebraska booth and back in the role of sports programming director at KFAB. Warren Swain took his seat alongside former Husker linebacker Adrian Fiala in the play-by-play booth.

Pavelka told us, "During the new bidding process for the rights I received every indication from [Nebraska] administration and athletic department officials that if KFAB lost the bid, they hoped I would work for the new rights holder. Of course, I was interested. When Pinnacle got the rights, they contacted me about doing the games.

"My attorney and I put together a proposal that was very ambitious. I asked for a lot—$150,000, new car, permission to market my highlight tapes, and various other prerequisites—expecting we could negotiate downward. In the Omaha market, several morning disc jockeys make more than $100,000 a year. Truth is, I figured after 22 years of service, and after building a pretty strong following, that I could expect to do as well as people in the same market who spin records in the morning.

"I figured wrong."

He says Pinnacle labeled his proposal as "ludicrous" and declined to negotiate. "They hired a journeyman broadcaster from some other part of the country, and I've been told they are paying him very modestly," Pavelka says.

He had carried the political game another step before the changeover took place, but struck out there, too, as he learned another harsh lesson about who carries the weight in this business. "I attempted to get the athletic department to help me by urging Pinnacle to negotiate with me," Pavelka remembers. "My feeling was that I had made a proposal, and if it wasn't acceptable, Pinnacle should make a counter offer. They never did. And the folks at the University, who had told me they very much wanted me, would not get involved on my behalf.

"Pinnacle thought I was out of line, and they wanted to put me in my place. I continue to believe that the real losers are the fans. It's pretty clear that our broadcast was something special to many of them."

Pavelka is wrong in one assessment. The fans are still there, especially in Nebraska. The broadcast is a monopoly, in that sense. The fans will listen, regardless of who is calling the game.

Pavelka backed management into a corner, and he paid dearly.

In another way, Bob Carpenter had a similar experience. His example also demonstrates what Keith Jackson says, that at some time or another you probably will be asked to do something that cuts against your grain. What are you prepared to do at that point—back management into a corner? Stand your ground? That, of course, will be up to you. But be advised on what can happen, such as in Carpenter's case.

He was a television sports anchor at the time in Tulsa, Oklahoma, and doubling on play-by-play of minor-league baseball. The owner of his station lived in Fort Smith, Arkansas. He strongly suggested that Bob cut back on football, baseball, basketball, and golf coverage and hit stronger on hunting and fishing—activities that were the GM's favorite and are of high interest in his lake-and-forest locale.

"Every time that discussion came up, I simply said that I believed the Tulsa market had more interest in the major sports than hunting and fishing," Carpenter says, adding that he continued to emphasize Tulsa and Oklahoma college football, Oral Roberts, Oklahoma and Oklahoma State basketball, the Tulsa Drillers, etc.

One Sunday night before Bob was to go on the air, shortly after another dead-end discussion about coverage of the great outdoors, another sports announcer showed up at the station. "Here I was, the sports director, being replaced, and nobody even had the courtesy to tell me," Carpenter says. "Taking a stand for something I believed in cost me my job."

He deemed that he could live with that at the time. All's well that ends well: Carpenter moved on to handle college basketball and major-league baseball for ESPN, and TV for the St. Louis Cardinals.

In some cases, you bend. Jack Harry has worked television in the Kansas City market since the early '70s as an anchor and sports director (currently with KCTV-5). Once he stated on a weekend sportscast that Chiefs general manager Carl Peterson was "a bean-counter who was trying to put people in the stands, and trying to save some money when he let Neal Smith go to the Denver Broncos."

The station general manager, John Rose, summoned Harry to his office and told Harry that the Chiefs no longer welcomed him at the stadium. Harry says that he couldn't believe it, although he should know better after all these years. He continued in his job, but his example points out how if you are going to speak in politically incorrect terms and insensitive to your colleagues, expect to hear about it. Remember what was said about sales driving the business? KCTV carries the ultra-popular (and profitable) Marcus Allen Show. Don't forget that without sales and profits, there is no viable platform—no booth for sportscasters.

Sometimes, as in Harry's case, you are prudent to remain silent, keeping in mind that management might seem "wrong" but holds the trump cards and the responsibility for the team, and are well within their rights, too.

To illustrate, check out a tale from veteran Marty Brennaman. Several years ago he was on the air with a Cincinnati Reds game, and the general manager of the Reds had another announcer auditioning in the booth next to where Brennaman and Joe Nuxhall called the game at Riverfront Stadium. When

Brennaman learned about the presence of Dick Carlson (former voice of the Kansas City Chiefs, now with KIRO in Seattle), Marty spoke up in front of newspaper reporters.

"I can't believe they actually had someone in there auditioning for my job when I was on the air calling the game," Brennaman told reporters who covered the team. "If Dick Wagner doesn't like my work, then he can get someone else."

Writers jumped all over his comments, and the public reacted in favor of Brennaman. Vin Scully was in town with the Dodgers and he sat down with Brennaman and offered some advice, which basically was to do the job, keep quiet, and let nature take its course "because you are more popular than the Reds general manager."

Scully was correct. Brennaman held his tongue and has remained a constant in the Reds booth since 1973. In 2000, he was voted to the Broadcasters Wing of the Baseball Hall of Fame, along with his manager, Sparky Anderson, and Tony Perez.

HANDLING THE CRITICS

A hurdle that sportscasters must clear today that was scarcely heard of before the '80s is the newspaper critic. Following the lead of *USA Today,* most markets have a columnist who lets it rip in the local press…and rip they do, pointing out mistakes and foibles, often with cutting remarks. Anybody on the air is fair game.

Some big-name announcers believe that the trendsetter, Rudy Martzke in *USA Today,* actually cost them work, namely Gary Bender and Jack Buck.

Martzke liked to refer to Buck as Jack "65" Buck, insinuating that Buck had grown too old and the games had passed him by. Buck, in his usual droll manner, says, "I read that so often that I thought for a while '65' was my middle name."

Bender begrudges both Martzke and another well-known network announcer, Brent Musburger, for nailing him twice. During his 14th year at CBS-TV, Bender found himself in a power struggle in which Musburger garnered more air time on play-by-play assignments. Bender was released from his contract.

After he went to ABC-TV, the situation repeated itself after six years. He was released from his contract again, and he surfaced at TNT. "We are victims of our background," Bender says, putting a spin on the circumstances so that students can understand how the game is played.

"Some say that I was never critical enough. [Martzke pounded Bender for that trait.] Well, that's my nature. I'm not a critical person. My dad was a coach, so naturally I am not going after a coach on the air. I like players and respect their ability, so I'm not going to be very critical of their play.

"However, many of the young Turks today who have great jobs are not bothered a bit by being critical of a coach or players. That has never been my style. You have to be you, and be the best of what you are when you are on the air. I can't be somebody I'm not."

On the other hand, we need feedback. We need to know from some sources how we are faring. But we need it in constructive ways. Not the way Martzke & Friends deliver it, and sometimes not even the way we deliver it to ourselves. Listening to your tapes in self-critique sessions can be very helpful, but it can cut both ways. An individual striving for excellence tends to be his or her own worst critic. The tendency is to hammer yourself too hard, or to be too nit-picking. Also, token pat-on-the-back, way-to-go encouragement and patronizing from friends or loved ones helps *not at all*.

The ultimate is a mentor or coach who will listen objectively and feed back what you are doing well, and ways to improve.

(For example, for two years I was hired to listen and give feedback to the broadcast team of the Jacksonville Jaguars, including my former student who handles play-by-play, Brian Sexton.)

Given this necessity—honest, constructive feedback—the amazing thing is how little of it takes place. Here we are in the communications business, and much of the time nobody is communicating in the work place. For examples, listen to two young television anchors in the Topeka, Kansas, market.

Taylor Wilson, formerly of KSNT, the NBC affiliate in Topeka, Kansas, tells a story of his first job in Roswell, New Mexico. "We really had problems [with staff communication]," he says. "We took video from the network and tried to get it ready for the sportscast. We never communicated, though. So there was a lot of screaming and yelling.

"It was very uncomfortable. We had an affiliated station in Albuquerque, and we really had difficulty getting video from them. Many times we counted on it, and got it late or didn't get it."

Wilson recalled a state high-school all-star football game for which his station counted on receiving highlights from the affiliate. "Their sports was on before ours, so I could tape it off the air. But 20 seconds into highlights, we got their anchor instead of me suddenly showing up on our air. Because they had the same set, it was confusing to our viewers."

He says that in five years he never received a critique from the news director. "We didn't communicate, and we'd lose stuff. It happens every day—one person assumes something, and it doesn't happen. I concentrate on communicating very specifically on how I want things. If you are not specific, you either won't get it, or you won't get it right."

Jason Lamb at WIBW, the CBS affiliate in Topeka, moved on to weekend anchor at KTKA. He made this severe career move for two reasons. One was that he married and wanted more regular hours and the other was lack of communications on the job. "I also left because of the trend in local TV that local sports is not important and doesn't matter in the scheme of things," he says, pointing out that his station went from 41/2 minutes a night when he started there to 3 minutes by the time he left. Further, Lamb notes that in his 11/2 years at the station, he never received a communiqué from the news director "…and there was very little communication between anybody in news and sports.

"Greg Sharpe [the sports director] evaluated my work and communicated with me every month or so. But the news director never did. I received general observations, but never a specific do-this or don't-do-this. The freedom was nice, but I wanted input and never got it. In fact, [the news director] left the studio during the 10 o'clock newscast after the weather and never even saw the sports."

"You don't want to be overbearing in asking for favors in networking, so that you become obnoxious."—Bob Costas

"Stay out of office politics . . . Your energies should be directed into your work, so that you can advance. Office politics are a waste of time."—Joe Castiglione

SOME FINAL THOUGHTS ON BEING A PRO FROM THE PROS

• Terry Shockley: "You must get along with the bosses and the people in your community. Constantly sell yourself. Take care of your personal life, or eventually it will take over your professional life."
• Robin Roberts: "I have been extremely blessed by the people I've worked with. When I did my first prime-time *SportsCenter* with Chris Berman, he treated me with great respect. I thought, 'If people saw Chris treating me with

respect, then they would think I'm OK.' We all argue sometimes, because we are like a family here, but we argue respectfully."

• Chris Berman: "This business is so much fun. Trust your own instincts. Anyone who gets into this to make big money or to become a big star will do neither. But, anyone who understands that those things are possible, files it away, and does all the other things necessary to the job might just attain that."

• Pat Summerall: "I still do my homework. I enjoy going to practice, getting on planes, talking to athletes and coaches, and working with John Madden. Nobody can ever accuse me of letting the game pass me by."

• Linda Cohn: "For women, competition is stiffer because a lot more women want to be sportscasters, and maybe now a woman can be accepted for what she is saying and not for her gender."

• Steve Physioc: "I tell all students four essential ingredients to succeed at this. First is to be on time. If the producer says to be there at 4 o'clock, I'm there at 3:55. Second, be prepared. Do the research, talk to the players and coaches, take a lot of stories up to the broadcast booth. Three, be enthusiastic. And number four is to be easy to work with. They sound rather simple, and maybe don't sound like much. You will be surprised at how much work you can get if you follow those four steps."

• Curt Gowdy: "You can either be bigger than the game itself, like Howard Cosell or Harry Caray, or you can let the game, coaches, and players be the stars. I prefer to let the game and the players take center stage. I would feel uncomfortable being bigger than the game."

Bob Costas brings to a head all the inner workings of plying the trade in a politically correct manner by being remindful of how it begins, how it goes, and how it ends. "What the young men and women interested in this business must understand is that you don't start out where Dick Enberg is, or Brent Musburger, or Al Michaels, or Bob Costas," he says.

"There is a route to follow. And often it is a zigzag route. In the beginning you have to be willing to take almost any job. That gives you a reasonable chance to gain hands-on experience and make contacts. There is nothing wrong with a young announcer whose objective is to somebody be on network TV taking a job broadcasting Class A baseball in Walla Walla . . . . nothing wrong with that at all.

"In fact, in many ways that might be the best possible experience in which he or she learns from experience—from mistakes—and makes good contacts. You hope to be appropriately aggressive...not obnoxious."

Costas says that he loves the eagerness and zest of aspiring students and young broadcasters, but he cautions, "If you think you're going to make the jump from the classroom to ESPN, huh-uh. That happens maybe once out of a thousand times. For most of us, it's through the minor leagues and some small markets. It isn't just how good you are, it's making those contacts, maintaining them, being willing to take a job that isn't an ultimate objective, and work hard at it—just to get better and to further your confidence . . . . If you can impress people as an ambitious person who has a nose to the grindstone, well, people remember that."

Joe Castiglione highlights the "hidden enemy" aspect of the business, which often can become a cutthroat environment with everyone protecting their own best interests.

"As you work your way up the ladder do not expect everybody to be rooting for you, especially where you work," Castiglione says. "There are jealousies at all levels. Some big-league broadcasters will help with leads and contacts, but there are those, particularly on the management side, who will attempt to hold you back."

As an example he recalled the time that, while working in Youngstown, Ohio, as a TV anchor, a Pittsburgh station called to offer him a couple of weekends of fill-in work. The Youngstown general manager nixed it, saying that Pittsburgh might try to hire him away. "It hardened my resolve to leave, and when I was hired in Cleveland six months later, did I ever enjoy announcing my resignation to that GM."

On the whole, Castiglione advises, "Stay out of office politics. The term in office usually is short, and the rewards are not worth the effort. Your energies should be directed into the work, so that you can advance. Office politics are a waste of time, especially in the transient world of broadcasting.

"By the same token, if management changes, have some concerns. Management loyalties, if they have any, usually are ego-driven or financially-driven—that is, by the size of your contract—and management will tend to be more loyal to someone they hired than someone they inherited.

"The quality of work sometimes is not the major consideration. So if management changes, have a tape and resume ready. Trust is found only in the small print of your contract, or the size of your paycheck. Broadcasting sports is a job where you always have to answer to somebody or something, and often times it's a ratings book."

THE PROFESSOR AND THE POLITICS

Students at KU relish my climactic lecture at the end of a semester called, "Egos…and Watergate," which covers the content of this chapter. Among many examples, some of which you have read here, I cite some from my own career path:

One important bit of advice: Be careful about sticking up for a coach when you know that the coach might be in trouble. I speak from two experiences on this. Years ago, Curt Gowdy recommended that I not be so strong in favor of Kansas football coach Jack Mitchell after he had a losing season. My family had taught me to always be loyal to my friends and coaches. I did not listen to Gowdy.

The reason I no longer do KU football and basketball is that I was a strong backer, on and off the air, for football coach Don Fambrough and basketball coach Ted Owens. Combine that with the fact that the Jayhawks had three, one-victory seasons in a nine-year stretch, and the basketball team won one Big Eight title and went to one NCAA tournament only to lose that game to UCLA. All of these hurt me. I'll explain that part in a minute.

Here's a real-world scenario. Kansas was facing archrival Missouri in a bad season after having won eight games the year before. The local newspaper called for Fambrough to resign. Riding to the game on the team bus I thought about that.

Joe McGuff of the *Kansas City Star* and a friend, Dick Purdy, asked me how I was going to handle the situation. I said that if KU was getting beat badly, I would just do the call. But if KU played over their heads, I would indicate that the Jayhawks were playing for their coach. Well, that's what happened. KU was a 21-point underdog, and finally lost 14-10.

Several times during the broadcast, I stated that the players were playing for their coach, whose job was in jeopardy. David Lawrence, my color man that day, who had played for KU, agreed. After KU lost, I had a gut feeling something bad was going to happen. Many alumni wanted Don fired. The next night a prominent alumnus who was a close friend called me and said that he admired my loyalty, but not to say another word…that I may have said too much already.

I got the message. Fambrough was dismissed a few days later. A month later, I ran a check on how the wind was blowing for me to continue as the Voice of the Jayhawks. I discovered that I would not be asked back; so I started searching for another job.

At age 49 I found that not many jobs available, especially for a guy who had been with teams in a losing down cycle and whose supervisor was not willing to recommend him. So I assessed the situation and called the chancellor of the university and made an appointment to talk about it.

On that call he encouraged me to continue to run the network and call the games. However, I was burned out from calling the games, producing both coaches' shows, running the network, teaching two classes at KU, and picking up high school games on the side. I wanted to freelance and teach.

When I met with Chancellor Gene Budig, he asked me what I wanted to do and said he would support me. I asked for a two-thirds appointment on the faculty so that I could handle ESPN Sunday night college baseball and Wisconsin Badger football.

He asked if I wouldn't rather have a three-quarters appointment. I told him I was not a great mathematician but that sounded like a better deal to me, and I took it. I was able to take on the ESPN, and I did Wisconsin football two years and later UMKC basketball for nine seasons.

But the message was clear at KU. I had been very vocal in my support of the coaches which put the administration in a bad position since they had a different agenda. I did what I thought I should do. The politics were just not in my favor. But the lesson to be taken here is that the chancellor was able to see beyond the conflicting opinions. The head of the university can make wonderful things happen in a matter of seconds, and that came about because I always was honest with the CEO of my school.

Recalling this reminds me of something that Dan Rather told a group of young journalists in a workshop at Southwest Texas State University. He told them to write down two lists. One is a short list of what you won't do under any circumstance—absolutely will not and cannot do. The other is a long list of what you *will* do. "You need this," he says, "because when the time comes you might have just 15 seconds to make the most important decision of your life, and the lists give you guidelines to refer to immediately."

The situation also reminds me of the old saying, "It's not what you know, but who you know." I have two good examples in my professional career. When I was in Cincinnati doing the Reds, Paul Brown—the late coach and owner of the Cincinnati Bengals—asked me if I missed doing football. I answered in the affirmative.

He asked if it would help if he called Pete. I paused and said, "As in Rozelle—that Pete? That would be like St. Peter calling the Almighty." He laughed, and the next day he called NBC and ABC. I had tried for seven years to meet formally with NBC about working some NFL games. It took one phone call from a great NFL coach, and I was working the next Sunday at a Denver Broncos-Kansas City Chiefs game.

Before that I could not even get my foot in the door.

Another illustration of right-time, right-place came when the Chiefs took on the Green Bay Packers in the first of what became known later as the Super Bowl. Two weeks before the game, Chiefs coach Hank Stram picked up the phone and called Bill MacPhail, the head of CBS Sports.

He said that he was arriving at the game with his coaches and players, and that he had a great young announcer who had never been heard before, and he wanted him there in some capacity, too. Later I received a call from CBS Radio and I was asked to handle color with Jack Drees on the coast-to-coast broadcast because I was the voice of one of the participating teams.

I did nothing different, but my team won. Remember what I said earlier about KU's losing trends factoring in? In 1978, I still had KU sports when the leader of Jayhawks basketball was Darnell Valentine. They won the Big Eight with a 13-1 conference record. That winter I was asked to call either the Kansas City Royals on TV, or the Kansas City Chiefs on radio.

Again, I had done nothing different, but I sounded better because my team won.

I'll never forget Skip Caray saying, when asked his opinion on who was the most popular broadcaster around, "I don't know, but I'll bet he has a winning team."

Amen.

I've learned to trust two things implicitly: The guy I see in the mirror, and a two-page legal document. I didn't enter this noble profession with that attitude, but I've become a selective optimist. In another era I could shake hands with Dick Evans and Lamar Hunt of the Chiefs and know that I would be their voice the next year, and that Bill Grigsby, a fellow broadcaster, would get us a $25-a-game raise. You could count on it.

According to Dr. Del Brinkman, the former dean of the KU journalism school and now at the Knight Foundation in Miami, Florida., I have become "a cynic with hope."

Don't get me wrong. I love this profession.

My wife, Lee, says that I have more bounce in my step and more lilt in my voice when I'm going off to call a game or do a newscast. I've never considered doing anything else in my life. And there are definitely some trustworthy people in management.

I've dealt with four general managers and several team and university administrators and coaches whose word is a bond, as good as gold: Hank Booth at KLWN in Lawrence, Kansas; Brad Howard of KOFO in Ottawa, Kansas; Terry Shockley of KCOW in Madison, Wisconsin; Nick Marchi of KCWJ in Kansas City; Dan Connell, senior vice-president for marketing with the Jacksonville Jaguars; Bob Frederick, the athletic director, and baseball coach Bobby Randall at KU; and athletic director Dan Harris and football coach John Frangoulis at Baker University.

But I want you to understand fully: This is a business. The second thing I trust is the two-page legal document. The document spells out what I do, what they do, who is responsible for phone lines and travel, and how much I'm paid. Some people accuse me of getting paid by the word. If I did, I'd be the richest guy in the world. But even though you have been given, in the last two chapters, some good, strong reasons to consider the consequences of this career choice, the final words, coming directly from my heart after broadcasting more than 900 football games, 2,500 basketball games, 2,000 baseball games, and writing countless scripts for sportscasts, ring loud and clear:

If you love it, and you have the ability, go for it.

SUMMARY

This is the essence of what marks the differences that sets apart the best in this business, as derived from the cumulative experiences of myself and all the professionals who contributed to this book:

• *Dedication to homework.* Those who prepare stick around many, many years. Remember Costas: "No matter how grand your style, if you do not do your homework, it will not be enough."

- *Willingness to go to the small market.* Kilgore, Texas, or Hutchinson, Kansas, and forget the money. Work as many shows and games as possible. Keith Jackson: "Go to Boise."
- *Network.* Make phone calls to other sportscasters in larger markets, and program directors and general managers who might help you. John Rooney says he makes 10-15 calls a day to network. Fred White: "I don't play politics, but I do pick up the phone and ask how I can get a job, or for help getting it. Attending practices and networking gets a lot of work."
- *Listen instead of talking.* It speaks (or doesn't!) for itself.
- *Look the part.* Always dress for the next job. There is only one first impression. Women must be more cosmetically appealing than men.
- *Know players' names and give the score.* You can't say it enough, or incorrectly.
- *Be yourself.* You are no Scully, there's only one Costas, stay who you are.
- *Arrive on time* (better yet, early). Some coaches will leave you in the dust if you're late to a bus. Four o'clock doesn't mean 4:01.
- *Talk to one person on the air.* Assume a conversational style. Gowdy: "I'm talking to my friend in the living room."
- *Look and act like you're having a good time.* Listeners/viewers don't care about your rough day at the office, that your car broke down, that your spouse is angry at you, or you have a touch of fever. Put on a happy face.
- *Have an ego, but don't "be" an ego.* Gary Bender: "We all have egos, and this is an ego business. But keep it in check. A nice person will go a long way."
- *Have a plan.* Draw a road map for your future. Detour when it is called for, but light the path ahead. Harlan: "Get a road map, and follow the men and women before you who have been successful. No need to reinvent the wheel."
- *Do the little things.* Go to practice, write to a coach or another sportscaster who has been nice to you.
- *Abide by the Golden Rule.* This common-sense credo pays big dividends. Brace yourself for times when it will not be applied in return.
- *Mentor others trying to make it.* Many of the big names—Michael, Carpenter, McDonough, Twibell, Bender, Harlan—never turn down budding sportscasters who ask them to listen to their tapes. Always help someone else. George Michael: "Because Jack Buck took time to listen to my tape, I will listen to every kid who sends me a tape."
- *Prepare for other avenues besides sportscasting.* Be willing to sell advertising, to pull a shift playing records, to report the news, to produce and line up guests.

Jack Buck was a cabby and waited tables. Brian Sexton was working as a bartender when he caught a break. Terry Shockley: "We can't afford to hire somebody at an entry level to do just sports. That can be the emphasis, but we encourage people to go into news or sales, too. We are selling ourselves and a product every day."

• *Have other interests outside of sports and work.* Bender is neck-deep in the Fellowship of Christian Athletes. Harlan and Linda Cohn spend much time parenting. Bill King visits museums in every city he visits. Avoid one-dimensional living.

• *Retain a sense of humor.* Costas is a good model (in virtually everything). He laughs at himself, heartily. Most of the great ones do.

Remember that this is the best of two worlds—getting paid to talk to the best athletes and coaches, and to watch (and translate) games as somebody else's eyes and ears. It is not brain surgery. I have worked this profession for 43 years, and never once felt that I have worked for a living. My strongest hope and desire is that you can enjoy the same. I know you will benefit from the advice and real-world situations throughout this book, and in this concluding chapter.

So, let the games…and careers…begin.

About the Author: Tom Hedrick

For the past 43 years, Tom Hedrick has been a play-by-play announcer. His credits include the Kansas City Chiefs for seven years with the KCMO radio, and during the same period, he called three Super Bowls for CBS Radio. Other CBS Radio broadcasts by Hedrick include play-by-play for the Cotton Bowl for nine years.

For 16 years, Tom was the announcer for the KU Jayhawks (1960-66 and 1974-84). He did the play-by-play for both football and basketball while running the network distribution for the games. During his stay with Kansas, he was voted top sportscaster in the state of Kansas a total of six times. He called other Big Eight football and basketball when he joined CBS affiliate KOLN-TV in Omaha where he announced for KU rivals the Nebraska Cornhuskers from 1967-69. He later returned to Kansas to once again be the Voice of the Jayhawks.

Hedrick continues to be the Voice of the KU Baseball Jayhawks and has held that assignment for 31 years. During this term he has had co-hosts such as Paul Splittorff, Brian McRae, Gary Bender, Kevin Harlan, and John Wathan. Other baseball assignments include the Cincinnati Reds (1971-72) and the Texas Rangers (1973). During the '72 campaign with the Reds, he was accompanied by Yankees Hall of Famer Waite Hoyt. While in Dallas with the Rangers, he also did preseason games for the Dallas Cowboys.

Hedrick was voted Sportscaster of the Year in 1970, one of his busiest years. At that time, he was doing early morning sports with KCMO radio, the Kansas City Chiefs' Radio, and weekend sports with KCTV-5.

Currently, Tom teaches courses in sportscasting and news performance at the University of Kansas. He is a member of the Broadcasting Sequence in the School of Journalism, and his students in sportscasting have all gone on to wonderful jobs in the business. Several have national network careers, including Kevin Harlan (ESPN/Minnesota Timberwolves), Gary Bender (WMAQ/Chicago Bears), and Brian Sexton (Jacksonville Jaguars). In addition to teaching, Tom has also been the Voice of the Baker University Wildcat for the past 11 years. Recently, Tom worked with the University of Missouri-Kansas City basketball team as their play-by-play announcer and was in charge of advertising for the games for nine years.

Hedrick lives in Lawrence, Kansas, with his wife Lee. He has one child, Nancy, who also resides in Lawrence.

More broadcasting titles from Diamond Communications....

HEART STOPPERS AND HAIL MARYS:
100 of the Greatest College Football Finishes (1979-1999)
by Ted Mandell

IRISH ON THE AIR:
The History of Notre Dame Football Broadcasting
by Dr. Paul Gullifor (Available 2001)

THE BABE SIGNED MY SHOE
by Ernie Harwell

IT'S NOT WHO WON OR LOST THE GAME,
IT'S HOW YOU SOLD THE BEER
by Bob Wolff

THANKS FOR LISTENING!
by Jack Brickhouse with Jack Rosenberg and Ned Colletti

AIN'T THE BEER COLD!
by Chuck Thompson with Gordon Beard

TRAVELS WITH CHARLIE:
DAYS IN THE BROADCAST LIFE OF WSBT'S CHARLIE ADAMS
by Charlie Adams

"I DIDN'T KNOW YOU WERE SO TALL..."
by Charlie Adams (Available 2001)

THE MIGHTY 'MOX: THE 75TH ANNIVERSARY
HISTORY OF THE PEOPLE, STORIES, AND EVENTS
THAT MADE KMOX A RADIO GIANT
by Sally and Rob Rains

Notes

Notes

Notes

Notes